ROAD GAMES

ROAD GAMES

A YEAR IN THE LIFE OF THE NHL

ROY MACGREGOR

MACFARLANE WALTER & ROSS
TORONTO

Macfarlane Walter & Ross
37A Hazelton Avenue
Toronto, Canada M5R 2E3

CANADIAN CATALOGUING IN PUBLICATION DATA
MacGregor, Roy, 1948–
    Road games : a year in the life of the NHL

Includes index.
ISBN 0–921912–58–7

1. National Hockey League.   2. Ottawa Senators
(Hockey team).   I. Title.

GV847.8.N3M3 1993   796.962'64   C93–095184–0

Printed in the United States

CONTENTS

ACKNOWLEDGMENTS

The author is grateful to Jim Travers, editor of *The Ottawa Citizen*, for catching a political writer completely off guard with the suggestion that he switch for a while to hockey. Thanks also must go to the *Citizen* and to publisher Russ Mills for support, to sports editors Graham Parley and Tom Casey for advice and corrections, and to David Staines for his sage advice on structure and writing. Colleagues in the Ottawa press were always generous with information and advice. The idea for this book came from Gary Ross of Macfarlane Walter & Ross, and his continuing interest and advice had much to do with the final shaping. Jan Walter kept the schedules and managed the production with skill and good humor – even when no one else was able to laugh. Matthew Kudelka corrected the grammar and spelling at warp speed. The Ottawa Senators Hockey Club was always good for facts and help and travel organization. Patricia Loewen mailed off clippings, as did Mike Peluso and Brad Marsh. E.J. McGuire provided endless help with the chapter on hockey violence. Colleagues across the continent were helpful both in person and in print. Russ Conway of the *Lawrence Eagle-Tribune* was particularly helpful and inspirational. Tom Hill at the *Citizen* helped me overcome various computer foul-ups with skill and patience. Emmylou Harris and Van Morrison helped with the typing. To the hundreds I interviewed – many of whom, as promised, will never see their names in this book – a heartfelt thank you. To the family that, during one stretch, put up with 32 straight weekends alone – Ellen, Kerry, Christine, Jocelyn, and Gordon – you're owed.

xi

CHAPTER ONE

THE DRAFT

Montreal, Quebec

MEL BRIDGMAN WAS UNDERSTANDABLY NERVOUS. THE GENERAL manager of the Ottawa Senators had always considered himself "a notorious slow starter" during his 14 years as an NHL player. In Switzerland, where he played a final season, it had taken him three months to discover that bacon did not come prepackaged but was sliced on the spot at the local butcher's. Bridgman did not like surprises. His packed hair, heavy moustache, and thick glasses left very little face to read, but it was clear that he was nervous. And with good reason: at 37, he was about to get off to another slow start, in the first job he'd ever held that didn't require protective equipment.

The NHL had come to Montreal to hold its 1992 expansion draft. In the Hotel Radisson, the two newest franchises, the Senators and the Tampa Bay Lightning, were about to choose 21 players each out of a Blue Box of discarded athletes from the other 22 teams in the league. For their respective $50 million expansion fees, the Senators and the Lightning would be offered "snow in winter," in the words of John Ferguson, Ottawa's director of player personnel, who sat beside Bridgman.

At the other table sat Tampa Bay president and general manager Phil Esposito. His tan was oaken, and with his gaudy jewelry he seemed the height of flamboyance beside the Senators' decision makers in their dark suits and business suspenders. Esposito had already scanned the list of available talent and declared that the players on it would make "a hell of a golf team." The names, when familiar, were of aging veterans with hefty contracts.

Bridgman had a plan. To the extent that any draft could be prepackaged, his was. His scouts – like him, inexperienced – had gone over the list of available players until they knew it inside out. Unfortunately, one of the choices they most wanted to make was no longer possible – the Senators had been working for days on a conditional list supplied by NHL headquarters. The final list had been placed in a sealed envelope and handed to Ferguson as he and Bridgman entered the room. No one had thought to open it.

All the players and possible scenarios had been computerized by Bridgman, who believed firmly in systems. The Senators' entire draft data base was on the hard disk of an Apple laptop at the opposite end of the table. Unfortunately, when the group's computer wizard bent down to plug in the machine he discovered that the power line was dead. And no one had thought to bring a charged battery.

If there was one small comfort for a panicking Bridgman, it was that he had been making side deals before sitting down. The established teams were keen to protect players that they had been forced to place on the available list. (Each team could protect only 16 of its players, two of them goaltenders.) Under the rules of the draft, established teams could lose only one player per position, and two players in total. The New York Rangers wanted to see their surplus goaltender, Mark LaForest, go early, which would halve the threat to their remaining roster. Bridgman had agreed to take LaForest, whom the Senators had no intention of using; in return, one quiet day later in the summer, the Rangers would magically deliver two young minor-league players to the Senators for what hockey euphemistically calls "future considerations."

The draft had rules that forbade such side deals, but Ottawa was not taking them seriously, and neither was Tampa Bay. The Senators had struck a second "future considerations" agreement, this one with with the New Jersey Devils, who were anxious to keep Viacheslav Fetisov. Detroit was rumored to covet the veteran Russian defenseman. If Ottawa selected instead another Devils defenseman, Brad Shaw, high in the draft, New Jersey would return the favor later by delivering a promising young minor-leaguer to the Senators.

At 6:08 p.m. a tiny man with an overblown yellow tie approached the microphone. John Ziegler, president of the NHL for the past 15 years, was about to complete his final official act before retiring with a $2 million golden handshake and a pension of $250,000 a year. "Phil, Mel," Ziegler announced. "Start your engines. The sixth National Hockey League expansion draft is about to begin."

Bridgman's best-laid plans collapsed as quickly as Esposito could turn toward the Florida media contingent and roll his eyes. With NHL owners, managers, and coaches watching from seats at the back of the room, and hockey fans across the country watching on The Sports Network, Bridgman fell apart. He had only learned of the computer failure when, on Ottawa's second pick, the action came to a sudden and embarrassing halt. After a flurry of cellular calls and hand-delivered messages, the deal with New York was suddenly off. The Rangers were now insisting on an entry-draft pick from Ottawa to complete the deal. The 17 computerless hockey minds at the Senators' table huddled frantically while Ziegler and NHL vice-president Brian O'Neill fumed on the stage and the seconds turned into minutes. While the cameras ran, Bridgman began to twitch as the Rangers rearranged the deal: in return for taking LaForest, Ottawa would get only one of the two agreed-upon players, along with New York's final draft pick in Saturday's entry draft. Bridgman moved to the microphone and announced nervously that the Senators were selecting Mark LaForest.

In the next round Ottawa did New Jersey the favor by taking Shaw. Then Bridgman stumbled again when he selected Canadiens enforcer Todd Ewan, only to be informed by a sarcastic O'Neill that Montreal had already lost its quota of two players – one of them, Sylvain Turgeon, to Ottawa. "Ottawa apologizes," Bridgman said when he returned to the stage to select, instead, a fringe player from the Philadelphia Flyers.

Without the computer, nobody at the Senators table even seemed capable of running a pencil through a name on a list – but then, they had the wrong list anyway. At pick No. 40, Bridgman tried to pick forward Todd Hawkins of the Maple Leafs, only to be told – again with heavy sarcasm – that Toronto could lose no more players. Flustered, Bridgman returned to the podium and selected C.J. Young from Calgary, only to have O'Neill inform him that Young was not on the official list, which was still stuck in its unopened envelope on the table between Bridgman and Ferguson. A furious Ziegler sent a scribbled note to the Ottawa table telling them to get their act together and reminding them that there were to be no side deals. Phil Esposito rolled his eyes again. On his third try, Bridgman selected Darcy Loewen from Buffalo – and finally got it right.

When the draft finally ended, Bridgman had a list of 21 players. Goaltender Peter Sidorkiewicz, considered expendable by the Hartford Whalers, one of the league's weakest franchises, was the gem of the lot. Turgeon was a former first-round draft choice – second overall in the 1983 entry draft – who had fallen in seven years from a 45-goal season with Hartford to a nine-goal season the previous year with Montreal. Ottawa's list included the league's leader in penalty minutes, Chicago's Mike Peluso, as well as Edmonton centre Mark Lamb and New Jersey veteran Laurie Boschman – the remainder, as Ferguson had put it, "snow in winter."

Still rattled, Bridgman returned to the Bonaventure Hotel to nurse his wounds and prepare for Saturday's entry draft. On the night desk of his hotel room, a few feet from the portable compact-disk players and a stack of CDs topped by the Crash Test Dummies, sat the Master Plan. A yellow binder with green and yellow tabs, it held the computer printouts of every entry-draft prospect and every possible permutation. On Saturday they would precheck the power line and carry extra batteries for the laptop. Bridgman would not be able to sleep this night for thinking about the upcoming training camp and the potential line combinations.

THE SECOND PHASE OF THE TEAM'S DRAFT SCHEME HAD BEEN SO CARE-fully thought out that it even had a marketing plan to go with it. The team had been named the Senators after the team that won ten Stanley Cups between 1903 and 1927 before fleeing town for St. Louis in 1934. The modern Senators would bask in the ageless glory of the "Silver Seven," which had featured such legends as one-eyed Frank McGee, who once scored 14 goals in a Stanley Cup game and later died in action during the Great War. The new logo would be of a Roman Centurion – so what if Don Cherry had ridiculed it on *Hockey Night In Canada* as looking like a condom package? – and their star player, their future, would be an 18-year-old whose first name was "Roman." A marketer's dream.

Bridgman and Ottawa's chief executive officer, Randy Sexton, had decided months earlier that their first pick in the entry draft was going to be Roman Hamrlik, a young Czech playing in Prague. They had traveled together the previous winter to Vierumaki, Finland, to watch the Four Nations Cup and had been overwhelmed by Hamrlik's poise and abilities. Big, strong, and able to score, the (then) 17-year-old had been the star of the tournament. But it was not his play that had persuaded them – it was Hamrlik's character.

Toward the end of his team's match against Russia, Hamrlik had blocked a shot. He finished his shift in pain, and when they visited him in the dressing room he was still hurting, and limping visibly. They had intended to walk with him back to their hotel and talk to him there, and Bridgman now offered to arrange a ride so that the young man could rest his leg. Hamrlik refused. Twice on the mile walk Hamrlik slipped on the ice, and twice more he refused a ride. At the hotel he sat, smiling but with sweat pouring down his face, while Sexton and Bridgman asked him tedious questions about what sort of person he was and what he would think of Ottawa. At the end of the interview he took himself to the hospital to have his broken leg set. "He's our guy," Sexton decided. Bridgman agreed.

By the flip of a coin, first pick in the entry draft had gone to Tampa Bay. But the Senators were certain that Hamrlik could never be sold in a Florida market where, during the first season, they would be handing out brochures to the fans explaining such matters as the icing rule and "What is a puck made of?" Esposito had already tipped his hand on how desperate he was for marketing tricks when he announced that Tampa Bay would be inviting Manon Rheaume to attend the Lightning's training camp. She had played less than a period of Major Junior hockey, but she was extremely photogenic and, of course, a woman in a very chauvinistic sport.

Esposito couldn't possibly go with an unmarketable commodity such as Hamrlik. Who, then? This was not one of those rare years when a franchise player was available to the team selecting first overall. A franchise player is someone around whom an entire team can be built, a player who can carry a team to years of packed arenas and Stanley Cup championships. Guy Lafleur had been selected first in 1971 and five Stanley Cups had followed for Montreal. Denis Potvin had been first pick of the Islanders in 1973 and four Stanley Cups had followed. Mario Lemieux had gone first to the Penguins in 1984 and Pittsburgh had just won its second straight Stanley Cup. Eric Lindros, drafted the previous year by Quebec, might ultimately be worth a Stanley Cup to two teams – first the Nordiques, because of the established players they would receive for the rights to him, and then, once he had matured, to the team that was able to sign him. (It would be Philadelphia, after the biggest trade in NHL history.) But there was no Lafleur available in 1992, no Potvin, no Lemieux, no Lindros. Some of the scouts were talking about 1993 as another year for a franchise player – perhaps two or three of them, including a kid named Alexandre Daigle in Victoriaville.

But in 1992, none of the top choices was going to ensure the eventual success of the team selecting first. With season-ticket sales going poorly in Florida, Esposito could hardly afford to choose as his centerpiece a teenager who could not even speak English. He had to go for Todd Warriner, the flashy blond star of the Windsor Spitfires. The Ottawa front office was so certain of this that they'd laughed when Esposito called to suggest they give him a draft pick from farther down in exchange for letting them know what Tampa Bay's first pick would be.

Esposito rose from the Tampa Bay table at the Montreal Forum on Saturday morning with Warriner in mind. The Windsor left winger had been his personal choice from the start. Esposito's scouts, however, had been arguing vehemently all week long in favor of Hamrlik, and Esposito – to even his own amazement – told the huge gathering of draft hopefuls, and their parents, agents, and girlfriends, "Tampa Bay selects Roman Hamrlik."

Ottawa's computer was working fine. This time it was Bridgman who became unplugged. But having heard rumors for the past two days that Esposito might yet bend to the advice of his scouts, Ottawa's general manager had another name ready: Alexei Yashin, a gangly center with Moscow Dynamo. Bridgman had only seen him play once – extraordinary, considering he would be their most significant property – but scout Tim Higgins spoke well of him. Besides, they had liked him enormously when they spoke to him the evening before. He believed in working toward "a cleaner environment" for the world, and this strongly impressed the Senators group, who placed great importance on character. They would pass up 19-year-old Darius Kasparaitis of Lithuania, another talented young European, and one they had seen play, because he'd been arrogant during his meetings with Senators staff, disdainful of the translator, conceited about his abilities. He had failed the Senators' "character test."

When Bridgman selected Yashin – no Russian had ever been drafted so early by an NHL club – he set off a race to grab European players, who by the end of the day would account for 11 first-round selections, and 88 in total. The rush to claim foreign players caught everyone off guard. Toward the end of the draft, the North American hopefuls still in the stands were in tears, their parents booing.

When it came to the European talent, however, the Senators were out of their element. "There's no denying it," Randy Sexton said, "we don't have as good a handle on Europe as we should." Even so, they had Phase II of their Master Plan to fall back on. According to Bridgman's scheme, they would select Hamrlik and then – to create a comforting "culture" in which he'd prosper in Ottawa – two other Czechs. One of them, Hamrlik's 18-year-old friend, Radek Hamr, was considered by many to be too small to play in the NHL; the other, 30-year-old Tomas Jelinek, thought by all to be too old to adapt to the North American game, was originally intended to be Hamrlik's "uncle."

Even after Esposito had rasped "Roman Hamrlik" into the microphone, Bridgman selected both Hamr and Jelinek, who would now have no one to befriend or advise.

"We have a hockey team," Mel Bridgman announced.

FIVE YEARS EARLIER, A BROWN OLDSMOBILE SIERRA HAD BEEN MOVING through the night along Highway 417 – the Queensway – which cuts across Ottawa from east to west. Some nights it would travel back and forth from midnight until dawn. "I knew I was missing something," Bruce Firestone would say of those long months in 1987 when he went off driving after his family had gone to bed. "But I didn't know what it was."

Firestone is the son of O.J. Firestone, a noted economist, academic, senior bureaucrat, minister's adviser, and collector of Group of Seven art. The senior Firestone's place in Canadian culture, if not in heaven, is guaranteed by dint of his having bequeathed the 1,200-painting Firestone Collection to the Ontario Heritage Foundation. O.J. Firestone was adored by those he worked with and served but feared as a hard taskmaster by those he raised. For Firestone the shadow was about as long as it gets for an ambitious young man determined to be known as something other than his father's son.

The Firestones were one of the first Jewish families to move into the upper-class neighborhood of Rockcliffe, where the Protestant and Catholic elite of Ottawa lived. Bruce was the third of four children and the one to go up against the domineering father, which he did with the blessing of his mother, O.J. Firestone's first wife. A strong-willed woman who now lives on her own, Isobel Firestone once described her husband as the "headmaster." There was no room for discussion, not even when they divorced.

Though socially awkward, young Bruce was bright – some would say brilliant – and he flew through Ashbury College, an Ottawa private school, and on to the Massachusetts Institute of Technology to study engineering. At 22 he was working in New South Wales, Australia, as far from Ottawa as it's possible to get. He married and became a father while completing a Ph.D. in civil engineering at Australian National University. Then his marriage disintegrated. In the middle of a custody battle, he fled with his young son to Canada. The ugly and drawn-out custody fight went through two courts before an out-of-court settlement was reached. The boy would remain in Canada, Firestone said, to be close to his grandparents and, of course, his heritage.

O.J. Firestone had dabbled in real estate as well as Canadian art, and his small family holding company, Terrace Investments, had grown during the 1960s and 1970s into a promising enterprise. Bruce Firestone had returned home to discover that his mother and one of his sisters were seeking to have the company dissolved and the money divided up. Bruce decided the time had come to make his own mark. By this time O.J. was of retirement age, weary of managing a real estate company and glad to have his son back in the operation. Bruce's mother still took the dispute over Terrace Investments to court, at one point stating for the official record what Bruce Firestone was telling himself each night when he could not sleep: "He is 26 years of age and he still has to prove himself."

This court battle, which split the family, was finally resolved three years later through a financial settlement with those who did not wish to see Terrace survive. Bruce had an organization, however fledgling, and deep pockets to finance his dreams. Some of these merely raised eyebrows: the battery-powered Frisbee that would not lift, political buttons, a casino in downtown Ottawa ("They laughed him out of City Hall on that one," his mother says). But some of them – an equipment-rental firm, a business newspaper – raised expectations and at times more capital. People in Ottawa began to talk about the shy young man with the calf eyes and the odd manner of speaking that at times makes it seem as if he is leaving messages on answering machines rather than engaging in conversation. Some declared him a "nut," others said he was "brilliant." They spoke of the temper that caused him to break bones hitting walls, and they spoke, with uncertainty, of his potential. If he had a tendency to fly into rages, he also had a knack for seeing an opportunity where others could not. O.J.'s son had become Bruce Firestone. He intended to become much more.

Firestone had his epiphany not on the Queensway, which is where he had expected it, but on the Ottawa River Parkway while jogging one bright day. It was, in retrospect, amazingly simple: the National Hockey League was talking about expanding, so why not to Ottawa? If there were going to be new teams, one would have to be in Canada – hockey was Canada's game, after all. And Ottawa was Canada's capital, so the only possible site was Ottawa. He never questioned his own logic, though others would. In a new blue Saab, he took the idea back onto the Queensway. For a full year he continued driving long into the night, thinking, refining. He gathered numbers, and he looked for a site, and on a cold Saturday in March 1988, he finally told someone what he was thinking.

WHEN THE POET EARLE BIRNEY CALLED CANADA "A HIGH SCHOOL land, frozen in its adolescence," he might have been thinking of the

Lions Arena just off the Queensway, where the young Terrace hot-shots gathered for their weekly game of shinny and a few cold ones in the dressing room. On this particular day Firestone waited until there were only two others left in the room. One was Cyril Leeder, a young accountant who had once played Junior hockey in Brockville; the other was Randy Sexton, who had been Leeder's teammate before going on to a hockey scholarship at St. Lawrence University in upstate New York. Both were 28 and as ambitious, if not as visionary, as Firestone. Cold beers were opened and Firestone laid out the idea. Sexton, then a stocky 28-year-old with an MBA and a striking resemblance to the young James Cagney, leapt at it. He had coached and managed at St. Lawrence; his lifelong dream had been to make it to the NHL; if he couldn't as a player, why not as an owner, perhaps even a manager? Leeder was more cautious, with good reason: he had once worked on a group thesis on how to put together a professional hockey team. He knew how ridiculous the whole notion was.

Firestone was adamant: "They will expand in the next three or four years and when they do, Ottawa is going to bid for a team, and we're going to be the ones bidding." Such naïveté may have been a blessing. They adopted Tom Petty's "I Won't Back Down" as their theme song and began to prepare for the impossible. They started assembling the land they would need by knocking on farmers' doors at the far end of the Queensway.

On April 6, 1989, John Ziegler announced that a report on expansion would be presented to the NHL Board of Governors during the December winter meetings. Speculation was that the league would expand by as many as three teams. Some 30 North American cities, including Hamilton, Saskatoon, Kitchener-Waterloo, and Halifax, were said to be interested. The Hartford Whalers had been sold only the year before for $38 million, so it was anticipated that the price would be less than that, given that the Hartford sale involved a complete package: organization, players, minor-league operation.

On June 12, Terrace Investments Ltd. sent a letter to Ziegler informing him of its interest. Ten days later, Bruce Firestone called a press conference and announced his plans: "We have 100 million dollars in assets and we're putting them on the line." Two years earlier Dun & Bradstreet had listed the value of Terrace's assets at $7.8 million. It was a time of tightening real estate prospects in Ottawa. No one asked to see the money.

Firestone proposed to build a $55 million, 20,000-seat arena as well as a $30 million luxury hotel and office complex, all on a 600-acre site already assembled, once Terrace was granted the franchise. He added that he was asking hockey fans in Ottawa to send in $25 commitments to get on a list for season tickets. The money would be nonrefundable, but if Ottawa won a franchise, it could go toward the purchase price of the tickets. He wanted to attract 15,000 such commitments to demonstrate to the NHL that Ottawa fans were serious about wanting big-league hockey. Alan Eagleson, then executive director of the NHL Players' Association, ridiculed the idea: "He's either dreaming or doesn't know what he's talking about. Anybody in his right mind would be crazy to send him 25 dollars they won't get back if he doesn't get a team." Even Ottawa's mayor, Jim Durrell, panned the idea. "It's not that the area isn't a big enough market to support a professional hockey team," he said, "it's just that we're not going to get it." He spoke for all who were afraid to hope. Firestone responded coolly that "the NHL will take us seriously because we have a bunch of money to wave in their faces."

In the end, that would be the deciding factor. But getting to the end was hardly as simple as Firestone made it sound. Backed by the slogan "Bring Back the Senators" and by the expertise of the public-relations firm Burson-Marsteller, Firestone, Sexton, and Leeder began working furiously, in part to prove the pessimists wrong and in part to show that youth and enthusiasm will win out. So thorough were they in their lobbying that by the time it was over, Cyril Leeder had filled one drawer of his desk with black-bound exercise books, each filled with the essential small-talk for breaking the ice with the NHL owners of the day: favorite restaurants and vacation spots, preferred wines, names of wives and children, children's universities and careers.

The three had, however, little in common with the established owners. Randy Sexton's own father, Al, came from a humble background in the Gaspé region of Quebec. He had never played hockey because his family could not afford a pair of skates. Firestone came from money, but even he could not relate to wealth of this magnitude. Most NHL owners were fabulously rich and inhabited a clubbish world. Many had links back to the days of the Original Six, when one owner, James Norris Sr., was referred to in the Chicago press as the "robber baron." NHL owners included drunks like Bruce Norris of the Red Wings, criminals like Harold Ballard of the Maple Leafs, beer barons like the Molsons of Montreal, and extremely wealthy families like the Jacobs of Boston. And many of the newer owners were also multimillionaires – Mike Ilitch of the Red Wings made his money in pizza, Bruce McNall of the Kings in coin dealing.

These established owners had in common not only money but, almost without exception, ego. "When you're a shipbuilder," George Steinbrenner once said, "nobody pays attention to you. But when you own the New York Yankees, they do, and I love it." Peter Pocklington, who went from selling used cars to owning the Edmonton Oilers, admitted, "I got into hockey because I wanted to be recognized in the streets." No one should underestimate the impact of megalo-mania in the business of professional sports. In 1983 Pocklington entered the race for the leadership of Canada's Progressive Conserv-ative Party, convinced that he was not only the best owner – his team was about to embark on a successful campaign for the Stanley Cup – but also the clear best choice as Canada's next prime minister. (The party preferred Brian Mulroney.)

In dealing with egomaniacs, the three young men from Ter-race put flattery to work. When dealing with the wealthy, they spoke the language of money. No matter what a franchise cost, they said, Ottawa would be good for it. In claiming in the official application that it had assets of $105 million, the young men had used some cre-ative mathematics. They merely guessed what the land they had assembled at $10,000 an acre might be worth if everything came true. Suspicion was quick to rise that the franchise quest was merely a ploy to gain the necessary rezoning for development.

In the eyes of the other owners, Terrace clearly had some-thing. "I must admit," Pocklington said at the time, "it's a smart way to do a business deal. Normally, sports franchises are purchased by wealthy individuals who have already made it. They normally write a cheque for one, but in this case, it was a creative way of creating a lot of wealth and doing the job."

The Terrace group eventually produced a leather-bound, 600-page application detailing its plans. There is, wrote Firestone, a "nat-ural relationship between hockey and real estate." It is the land-development scheme, he told them, "that will allow us to pay the National Hockey League's asking price for an expansion franchise." He was not just talking about filling a nonexistent rink with 22,500 fans, he was talking about filling new homes with 9,000 people. No rezoning, no rink; no rink, no team. If it all came together, Firestone told the owners, the value of the enterprise would increase from its current $105 million to $400 million by 1997. He had them spinning with greed. NHL rinks had been filled to roughly 90 percent capacity since the first expansion back in 1967 – when franchises had gone for a mere $2 million. More recently, hockey's owners had been trying to reach into other pockets besides those of the fans coming in the front door. Already there were parking lots, concessions, souvenirs and other merchandise sales, corporate boxes – why not houses for fans and potential fans?

When the NHL Board of Governors announced that the expansion fee would be $50 million, Terrace did not even flinch. Others did. The enormously wealthy Pettit family in Milwaukee, which had a good existing rink and a terrific potential market, canceled its application after consultants determined that the true value of an NHL franchise was not much more than half of $50 million. This opinion gained support in 1991 when the Stanley Cup champion Pittsburgh Penguins were sold by the DeBartolo family for $34 million – a figure that included a lease in a large downtown arena, an organization, a team and – most important of all – Mario Lemieux.

Still, other groups remained in the hunt. When franchises work, as they do in cities like Detroit and Boston, the owners can expect roughly a 30 percent profit on gross revenues. Besides – as Ziegler would discover when he produced charts showing that NHL teams were doomed to lose $52 million during the 1992–93 season and $102 million during 1993–94 – few people believe the owners' claims of losses in hockey, any more than they do in baseball.

Bruce Firestone was stating the obvious in his application when he said, "The most promising scenario occurs when the owner of the franchise also owns the arena and has full participation in stadium revenues – concessions, souvenir and merchandise sales and the rest." He was speaking the language of the other owners, and it pleased them that Terrace, unlike other groups making bids, never questioned the value of a franchise.

A fact-finding mission of NHL governors flew into Ottawa to check out the credentials of Terrace. During that trip they stood on an overpass and stared out over the fields while Firestone painted his dream for them. Then the Terrace gang took them to lunch on Parliament Hill, where the NHL officials spent an hour or two meeting the political elite of Canada.

The Senators – as Terrace was slowly becoming known – produced brochures and booklets that felt substantial and made the dream look possible. They hooked up with 88-year-old "Fearless Frank" Finnigan – his jaw still challenging, his white hair still thick – who had starred for the Senators when they last won the Stanley Cup, in 1927. While he looked on, they promised to retire his sweater on the night the franchise was reborn. They brought in Scotty Bowman, the coach with the best winning record in NHL history, to sweep the Ottawa media hounds off their feet. They began working through the local levels of government to get their land rezoned. They got the premier of the province, David Peterson, to offer support. Most impressive of all, the $25 pledge for tickets that Firestone had launched to general ridicule was a stunning success. And throughout this time they lobbied the NHL owners – sending birthday cards, and dropping off their formal application books by limousine service. "If you're assessing how these guys have handled expansion," said Brian Burke, who was then the Vancouver Canucks' director of hockey operations, "they should publish a textbook on it."

There were still ten cities with formal applications – Ottawa, Hamilton, Phoenix, Miami, Houston, Seattle, San Diego, Anaheim, Tampa, and St. Petersburg. Although the two Canadian bids were considered small-market – Ottawa is even smaller than Hamilton, which is in Ontario's densely populated Golden Horseshoe – there was a growing sense that Canadian owners would be pushing for one of the expansion franchises to go to Canada. Not because they wished to share the television revenue, but because the Canadian clubs were beginning to feel swamped by the American ones. Of the 22 existing teams, only seven were Canadian; two more American teams and Canadian bloc votes would be even less effective. A Canadian franchise was increasingly believed to be in the works. Hamilton, which had both a big market and a good arena, had one great hurdle to leap: its proximity to Buffalo and Toronto. Either the Sabres or the Maple Leafs could block the bid on the grounds of territorial invasion. Hamilton was willing to indemnify both teams, but Buffalo, at least, did not seem willing to listen.

In December 1990 the Board of Governors gathered again at The Breakers in Palm Beach, Florida. Terrace arrived with 150 supporters, including Jim Durrell, who had shed his doubts and was now the group's most eager supporter. Also on hand was a firemen's band that led loud, chanting parades up and down in front of the hotel: "Bring Back the Senators!... Bring Back the Senators!..." The Terrace group made a 45-minute presentation to the board, highlighted by Durrell's assurances that the necessary rezoning of the agricultural land would go off without a hitch. Then Firestone made an emotional appeal that seemed to go over well. The day ended, however, with a collapse of confidence. At a private dinner, one owner took the Ottawa people aside and informed them there was no way they were going to win. The message, says Leeder, was "devastating."

The city of Hamilton, meanwhile, appeared to be making headway on the issue of indemnification; also, Hamilton now had access to the deep, deep pockets of Ron Joyce, the king of Tim Horton Donuts. On top of that, Hamilton had sold 16,000 season-ticket applications in a matter of days. The other sure winner seemed to be St. Petersburg, whose bid included a 20-year lease on the 55,000-seat Florida Suncoast Dome. The key figure in the St. Petersburg bid was Peter Karmanos of the Detroit-based Compuware Corporation. It would turn out that Karmanos had even enlisted the backing of Alan Eagleson, who was closely connected to John Ziegler. Karmanos had paid Eagleson $40,000 for his support and promised him a $1 million brokerage fee if St. Petersburg won the franchise.

So confident was Karmanos that he tried, at the last moment, to strike a small financial favor with the NHL owners. He did not care for the $5 million nonrefundable first payment they were demanding. He was not going to default, so why not drop the condition? It was a terrible miscalculation on Karmanos's part, for he did not understand what drives the NHL and every other professional sports league. Ottawa and Tampa Bay – called by *The Globe and Mail* "the two most unlikely candidates" – were the only bidders to accept the conditions without reservation.

The board convened at 9 a.m. on December 6 and decided quickly. The Senators, waiting back in the Seagull Room of The Breakers, were sure they had lost. Firestone, having tallied the votes and come up short, told his people to prepare for the worst. When a league official arrived at 1 p.m. to escort them back and led them down a freight elevator and then an outside fire escape to a dripping basement room filled with sacks of potatoes, they were convinced they were being assembled to applaud the victors. They were led to another room, where they joined what they believed was another losing group, from Tampa Bay. From there, all were led into the meeting room. As they entered, the governors stood and began shaking their hands and congratulating them. It took Firestone several seconds to realize what was happening. When he saw the press release with Ottawa's name on it as a winning bid, he burst into tears.

THE NHL HAD DECIDED TO GO WITH THE FULL $100 MILLION IN FRANchise fees and let the two winners sort out how they would make the payments. The franchises were conditional only on the new clubs meeting their payments – the $5 million immediate bill, the first $22.5 million due in June, and the second $22.5 million due in December. Phil Esposito's bid was so shaky that at one point his Japanese investors put a stop payment on the June installment. He made the payment, but three months late and only after a frantic restructuring of the partnership. Several of the American governors had faith in Esposito simply because he was of proven "hockey" stock, having both played and managed in the NHL. Few had such confidence in the Senators, all of whom were strangers to the inner circle. What the Ottawa people did offer was cash on the barrel – even if they had no idea how they might find it. As well, other Canadian owners had not wanted to see two new American teams and had backed Firestone when it seemed likely that Buffalo would block Hamilton's bid.

Peter Karmanos was furious. Not only did he have Eagleson on his side, but he had one of the best sites, a rink, and known financial capabilities. He vented his frustration in an interview with Bob McKenzie of the *Toronto Star*. The league, Karmanos claimed, did not even follow its own rules. "They asked for a net worth of 100 million dollars," he said, "and neither bid has that. They said no partnerships and both are partnerships. The owner in Tampa isn't even the same owner who applied for the franchise in the first place. They said they didn't want anything to do with real estate deals and that's what they've got. They wanted the money paid in a specific time frame and with specific terms and conditions and neither lived up to that. They said you needed a signed lease with an arena with revenues from parking, concessions … I could go on all day. They asked for all this and more and then they ended up waiving most of it anyway. It makes me sick. It's a shame they're ruining a great game like hockey with such poor mismanagement." The NHL, Karmanos concluded, is "as poorly run a professional league as there is."

Firestone, Sexton, and Leeder now had to put together an organization. Then they had to ice a hockey team. No problem. Their cockiness grew over the next two weeks as Terrace launched a ticket drive that completely sold out the Ottawa Civic Centre's first year and put $14 million in their bank account. "People told us we'd never get a franchise," Sexton told *Saturday Night*. "And we did. Then they said we'd never sell our season's tickets. We sold out in ten days. Next they said we'd never make our payments, or win the OMB hearing, or make the second payment – and we did them all. There are only two things left: we'll never build the Palladium or win the Stanley Cup. We'll prove them wrong."

Bruce Firestone had what he wanted: a title. He was now Governor Bruce Firestone, to be known from now on, in the obsequious hockey world, as "Mr. Firestone." He had reached the pinnacle of acceptance and respect in the one country on earth where parents would rather their child grow up to be a journeyman hockey player than a neurosurgeon. His job was ideas, and he was now content, for the most part, to hand over to Sexton and Leeder the task of assembling the franchise.

Terrace made a number of botches in the early task of finding someone to run its hockey operations. They wooed and then dumped Denis Potvin, the former Islanders superstar. They insulted

Scotty Bowman by offering to make him "assistant to the president" – an office later held by Jim Durrell, who was eventually forced to resign from the mayor's chair under charges of potential conflict of interest. Another old NHL hand, John Muckler, then of Edmonton, had been invited to apply; when he learned he would not have control over further hiring – the Senators had already selected an assistant GM for him – he elected to go to the Sabres instead. Bowman said aloud what Muckler had feared: "I don't think [the general manager] will have the same duties as every general manager."

"We're not going to give the general manager the keys to the house and say, see you in five years," Sexton, the emerging hockey spokesman, said at the time. "We are an active, collegial group here. But on the other hand I've never seen the Stanley Cup won by committee. On a trade, the final decision is his. If you don't have the authority to put a team together, you're not a GM. Five years ago, the GM ran the whole show. The game is more complex today, with the salary structure, and the international talent pool – the GM's role is more complicated."

"My biggest concern," said Bowman, "was how I'd fit in. You have a manager and you have a president. You don't want to be starting a job wondering if you are stepping on anybody's toes."

Word was getting out in hockey circles that the Senators were less than professional, and the organization scrambled quickly to establish an aura of competence. Mel Bridgman, with his Wharton MBA barely framed, had been approached by Durrell about the job of assistant general manager. The top job hadn't been on the table – he had, after all, not one day's experience running a team. Durrell brought Bridgman to Ottawa to meet the three principals, who thought he would make a promising assistant. Bridgman had NHL credentials, including stints with Philadelphia, Calgary, New Jersey,

Detroit, and Vancouver – twice he had been a team captain – and he had unbridled enthusiasm. The idea was to have him learn under Muckler, but when Muckler turned them down and it began to look like the Senators would never attract a *real* NHL personality, they panicked. They offered the eager Bridgman a job he had never anticipated in his wildest imaginings – general manager in charge of hockey operations, with a $225,000-a-year contract over five years. It was a rash decision, soon regretted.

Bridgman set out to assemble a scouting staff. Almost exclusively he hired ex-teammates who, like himself, had no experience. Bridgman, with his scouts, began scouring North America for available talent, but the team had no one on the ground in Europe, where many of the game's future stars were now developing. A few months before the draft Bridgman tried to overcome this organizational weakness by bringing in John Ferguson as director of player personnel. Ferguson had been out of hockey for three years. When the Senators called him he was a partner in a standardbred racetrack in Windsor, Ontario. Long before that, however, he had played with Montreal on five Stanley Cup championship teams. Later he had been a general manager for both the Winnipeg Jets and the New York Rangers. As a GM, he had been one of the first people in the NHL to seek out European talent.

The more immediate concerns of the new club were how to come up with $45 million and how to get the rezoning proposal past the Ontario Municipal Board. David Peterson's Liberals were out of power. Bob Rae's New Democratic Party now formed the government, and had decided to challenge the rezoning on the grounds that good agricultural land must be preserved. A hearing was scheduled for late spring.

The first priority, however, was money. Though the Terrace

group had claimed to have numerous limited partners lined up, it could produce only one: Brian McGarry, a local funeral-home owner, who put up $200,000. The Ottawa Jewish community did not come through as expected. Terrace claimed to have leased more than 50 of the 176 luxury boxes in the yet-to-be-built Palladium, but in fact only a handful were booked.

Terrace's financial credibility was in tatters. The league had insisted that the $14 million in advance ticket sales be held in trust; Terrace claimed that it was, but it turned out not to be. Only a public outcry forced the group to put the cash in trust. With the June payment deadline bearing down, there was talk of collapse. But in May, Durrell produced a miracle for the team in Las Vegas singer Paul Anka, an Ottawa native who had not performed in his home town for a decade after a nasty review in the local press. Now Anka was sounding as if he wanted to come home. "It's something that will draw me closer to Ottawa," he said of his possible investment. He spoke of the joy of getting involved with "people you're going to have fun with."

Durrell and Firestone met with Anka in Atlantic City. According to claims later revealed in court, the Terrace group believed that Anka was telling them he could raise $9 million in a weekend using only a telephone. Anka represented the financial credibility they so desperately needed; as the deadline moved closer, they grew increasingly certain that his pulling out would destroy the franchise. He could therefore ask whatever he wanted in return for his blessings.

The deal he struck with the group was remarkable. Terrace would give Anka $547,000 worth of units in the Senators team. He would have an option to buy half the Palladium project for a mere $4 million. He would receive a $450,000 performance contract for three concerts. He would be named an alternate NHL governor and be paid an additional $50,000 salary. He would serve on a team advisory board, at $2,000 per diem plus expenses. The team would institute the Paul Anka Award, to be given annually to the player who shows community involvement, leadership, and good sportsmanship. All Anka had to do was bring in other investors with $10 million. He would be good for another $1 million himself.

It didn't happen. The team made its June payment thanks in large part to loans arranged on the ticket money held in trust. Meanwhile, the OMB hearing went badly until Firestone – against the wishes of his partners – promised to freeze all further development except the Palladium itself for 25 years. The OMB voted in favor of the rezoning but demanded that the stadium be scaled down from 22,500 seats to 18,500, that the number of luxury boxes be reduced to 104 from 176, and that Terrace pay for the Queensway overpass that would be required at the arena site. In return, no freeze would be applied to the remaining land. The Terrace group had won, but the $155 million scheme was now going to cost $190 million because of the overpass. Worse, the Canadian economy was shrinking around them.

On October 3, 1990, with Terrace begging for help, Anka finally produced his list of potential investors. It contained only the names and office phone numbers of, among others, actors Clint Eastwood, Tom Hanks, and Sylvester Stallone, singers Frank Sinatra and Anne Murray, casino owner Donald Trump, basketball star Magic Johnson, boxing promoter Don King, businessman Essam Kashoggi, television news anchor Peter Jennings, director Norman Jewison, composer Burt Bacharach, and comedian Rich Little, another Ottawa native. A worried Firestone wrote Anka, "I sincerely hope you will be able to make those introductions for us."

There seemed no way possible that Terrace could make the

final payment by December 16. Even the three dreamers were becoming resigned to defeat. In desperation, Firestone had approached Ottawa entrepreneur Rod Bryden in July to see if he could help them arrange the financing. Bryden, 49, was no jock, but he had founded Systemhouse and built it into the largest computer integration company in the world. Three years earlier his companies had produced more than $1 billion in revenues on assets of $1.6 billion. But with the recession came disaster. In 1990 his holding company, Kinburn Corporation, went under with a debt of $831 million. A year later the Systemhouse board had forced him out. Still personally wealthy, Bryden had set up a small operation, Stormont Corporation, which specialized in "the management of complex corporate transactions." He was just what the Senators needed.

The business of hockey piqued Bryden's imagination. Working from the nineteenth floor of the World Exchange Plaza in downtown Ottawa, he engaged the investment firm of Wood Gundy and raised more than $20 million, but Terrace was still short. On December 16 – payment day – Bryden put in $3 million of his own money to close the deal. For his efforts he acquired 50 percent of Terrace. He also took on the job of running the company that owned the team.

The deadline had passed and Anka had shown no interest in exercising his option on the Palladium. Nor had he, as expected, shown up in Florida for the NHL winter meetings. Firestone and friends presumed he was out.

Bryden and Firestone squeaked the final payment through on deadline. The franchise was no longer conditional. Anka, however, was threatening to sue now that the franchise was confirmed. The Senators ignored the threat; it was his fault, they said, not theirs. The singer flew to Ottawa on January 20, 1992 – a bitterly cold winter's day – and called a press conference at the Westin Hotel. Smiling through a tan even Phil Esposito would have admired, he announced, "I'm here to de-escalate."

Anka spoke again of how much he wished to "put something back into my hometown." He told the cameras, "I love hockey. I want to be there when the Canadiens come in and we beat them." But when he met with Bryden at a lawyer's office on Elgin Street, he sat with sunglasses on and mouth closed while his advisers spelled out a new deal. Anka might consider dropping the suit, they told Bryden, if the Senators compensated him with $7 million and a 10 percent interest in the new rink. Bryden told him to forget it.

In May, Anka launched a $41.6 million lawsuit claiming that in the weeks leading up to his option deadline, the Senators had denied him significant information relating to the team's financial strength. Among the punitive damages Anka claimed was damage to his reputation as a performer.

Bryden petitioned the court: "We need to know what reputation was injured and how we caused the alleged injury, because I cannot understand how owning a piece of land in Kanata would change public opinion whether or not Anka can sing." Terrace countersued, claiming damages of more than $28 million for everything from breach of contract to fraudulent or negligent representation. (The squabble is expected to be settled out of court in the late summer of 1993.)

Such huge numbers only served to underline the potential value of a successful sports franchise. Bryden projected that, in its first year in a tiny, makeshift facility, the Ottawa Senators Hockey Club would bring in revenues totaling more than $27 million through ticket sales, concessions, parking, corporate boxes, souvenirs, and merchandising. With a payroll of approximately $6 million and fixed costs figured in, the Senators would show a gross profit of nearly $13 million, before servicing the debt load. Net profit would still exceed $2 million. "What had begun as a carrot to lead people to tract houses and office buildings," said *The Globe and Mail*'s *Report on Business*, "became a profit centre in its own right. Hockey fever had replaced developer's delirium."

ON THE NIGHT OF OCTOBER 8, 1992, HOCKEY FEVER WAS RAGING IN Ottawa. The 10,449 paying customers crammed into the refurbished Civic Centre to see the Senators play the Montreal Canadiens. Top tickets were going for $100 at the box office, $200 on the street. This would be the Senators' first NHL match in Canada's capital city since their last home game of the 1933–34 season, when the New York Americans beat the last-place Ottawa team 3–2 and disgusted fans littered the ice with carrots and parsnips. The Senators finished last that year. Having borrowed and lost $60,000 in the previous two years, the owners of the original Senators could no longer afford to operate.

On this Thursday evening 58 years later, more money passed through the beer stands than was lost in 1933 and 1934. While Roman columns descended from the rafters, and trumpets sounded, each new player skated out past explosives and fountains of sparks and smoke and dancing spotlights and the cheers rising ever higher for names that only short months ago would not have inspired a return phone call from another club. Mila Mulroney and her boys were there. Don Cherry was there. Gil Stein, the NHL's acting president, was there to drop the puck. "With every fibre in my body," Stein said, "I believe this will be the greatest season ever."

The Zamboni driver wore a Spartacus costume and sunglasses and high-fived the fans. A lion with orange hair was lowered onto the ice driving an all-terrain vehicle. Olympic silver medalist Brian Orser did a backflip. *Hockey Night In Canada* went live, as Foster Hewitt used to say, coast to coast. As Bruce Firestone, Randy Sexton, and Cyril Leeder walked out onto the ice surface to chants of "Bruce! Bruce! Bruce!" a voice intoned over the loudspeaker, "The Roman Empire was built by men of courage ..."

The players were introduced one by one. The new coach, Rick Bowness, had come to the Senators in June after being fired by the Boston Bruins. Like Bridgman, Bowness had not been the first choice. The players picked up in the June draft were on hand. Laurie Boschman, who had blanched when he heard he had been chosen by Ottawa, was captain. Sylvain Turgeon and Brad Shaw were his assistants. The third assistant, 34-year-old Brad Marsh – who had been given to Ottawa by the Maple Leafs during the summer – was not dressed. The fans cheered Doug Smail, at 35 still able to outskate anyone else on the team, and Norm Maciver, a small, slick defenseman who had been picked up only four days earlier from Edmonton in the fall waiver draft. Goaltender Peter Sidorkiewicz, the immediate fan favorite, was cheered wildly, as was Mike Peluso, who would be expected to stand up for the Senators when others dared to laugh.

Jody Hull and Neil Brady were dressed, unaware that they had come to the team to complete the secret deals struck in June. The fans cheered Darren Rumble, a rookie who had become so acclimatized to the minors that during the exhibition season he had carried his own pillow and wrapped his own sandwiches for the flights. And they cheered Darcy Loewen, who would land Ottawa's first bodycheck when he slammed into Montreal's Stephan Lebeau. Three provinces away, in Sylvan Lake, Alberta, Gerry Loewen, the local Shell dealer, shook his head in front of the television and repeated what they had been saying ever since his son left home for Junior hockey: "If the circus was in town, Darcy'd be the one they'd shoot outta the cannon."

The circus *was* in town. The NHL was back in Ottawa. And the Senators looked like a real hockey team. Twenty-six seconds into the second period, on a clean sweep from the left side of the crease, 24-year-old Brady, the grandson of a Montreal Forum ticket-seller, scored the first goal of the game and of the new franchise. The Civic Centre exploded. When Doug Smail put his second goal of the game into the empty net, at 19:45 of the third period, Ottawa, miraculously, had won its first game, 5–3. The next day's *Ottawa Citizen* featured a full-color photograph of Senator defenseman Ken Hammond with both arms raised, under the headline MAYBE ROME *WAS* BUILT IN A DAY.

THE RESULT MADE NO SENSE. BUT THEN, THE FRANCHISE MADE NO sense. Even so, there it was: the Ottawa Senators had defeated the venerable Montreal Canadiens, a team with Patrick Roy and Kirk Muller and Mathieu Schneider and Vincent Damphousse and Brian Bellows and Eric Desjardins and Denis Savard. Bruce Firestone bragged that the team had already proved it was "competitive."

In one night, the Senators had dismissed the concerns raised by the media that this team of discards would struggle as the Washington Capitals had struggled 18 years earlier, when they set the benchmark for horrible expansion teams. The Capitals had managed only eight wins and 21 points in 1974–75. The Senators already had a win and two points. They were technically in first place!

After the game, in the club room at the Civic Centre, where team executives wined the corporate sponsors, people cheered every time a new Senator walked in from the dressing room.

"Peluso!" John Ferguson boomed as the towering enforcer entered to general applause. "If you can't get laid tonight, you'll never get laid!"

Grown men laughed so hard they had to wipe their eyes.

CHAPTER TWO

THE EUROPEANS

Vancouver, B.C.

AT MIDNIGHT, UNDER A WARM NOVEMBER RAIN, THE LINEUP FOR DICK'S
on Dick stretched half a city block. The queue to get into the popular
Vancouver bar was for ordinary people, not hockey players. The
Ottawa Senators sprinted through the light rain from their bus, the
way opened by enthusiastic young doormen twice their size yet
cowed by the Senators' air of team, their sense of mattering. No one
protested, for being bumped made a place in line all the more valuable. These were NHLers entering the bar. No matter that half an
hour earlier in the Pacific Coliseum the Senators had lost 4–1 to the
Vancouver Canucks; no matter that, after the heady opening-night
victory over the Canadiens, they had lost a dozen games and tied
one, their 1–12–1 record by far the worst in the league. They were
pro athletes and as such had free admission to just about anywhere
in North America that youth and sports and sex and beer come
together under one roof.

Inside, laser lights played over two throbbing floors. Bars that
once smelled of smoke now gave off the spoor of the chase: sweat,
Obsession, White Musk. The Senators, some with gelled hair, a couple in silk Hugo Boss suits and Nicole Martin ties, others in mild
variations of the Guess and Gap standardwear of such bars, fit in
perfectly. Several had gathered on the upper floor, the better to view

the dancer in the tank top too small to carry a designer label.

Back of them, nursing a beer, was goaltender Darrin Madeley, *The Hockey News* college player of the year in 1991–92 with Lake Superior State. Madeley had signed as a free agent with the Senators and had recently been brought up from the minors so that Mel Bridgman and Rick Bowness could get a look at him. Two nights earlier he had debuted in Calgary and been yanked after six goals in the 8–4 loss. It had been a tough introduction to the big leagues for the skinny 24-year-old. "I knew I was in the NHL when Al MacInnis took his first shot," he said. "I thought it was stuck in my shin."

But nothing had prepared him for this night and Pavel Bure. Madeley had played hockey at the highest college levels, in the minor leagues, and now in the NHL, and never had he imagined he could be frozen by sheer speed. Bure had scored twice in Vancouver's effortless victory, and on one of those goals the 21-year-old Russian had flown up the right side and fired the puck so lightning-quick past the skate of a retreating Senators defenseman that Madeley did not even realize he had been scored on until the crowd roared and the linesman arrived in a spray of ice to fish out the puck.

Madeley had found the experience "hypnotic," almost as if there were two games going on at once – the one that the 15,332 fans were watching, and another, entirely different match, that began every time Bure came over the boards and ended only when he left the ice. On one mesmerizing shift the young Russian had swept three times through the Senators to create heart-stopping chances. Men who had spent their entire lives in hockey turned to one another in awe. For Madeley the game had become a series of one-on-fives every time Bure touched the puck. The Russian's ability to accelerate was a quantum leap greater than the NHL standard – to watch him was to know how manned flight was revolutionized when the first jet engine roared. No wonder they called Bure "the Russian Rocket." Pulling on his beer, Madeley spoke for all NHL goaltenders when he said, "They should get rid of him. Kick him out of hockey – make him illegal."

"Nobody plays like Pavel," Anatoli Semenov, Bure's older linemate with the Canucks, had said after the game. "Nobody. In Russia you say the name alone – Bure!"

Bure was NHL Rookie of the Year in 1991–92, despite a late start. He scored 22 goals in his final 23 games, 34 in total, and in the 1992–93 season he would score 60. Teemu Selanne, Alexander Mogilny, Mario Lemieux, and Luc Robitaille would all score more, but Bure's goals are as much conversation pieces as they are statistics. What Darrin Madeley saw from the Ottawa net is something Vancouver fans see almost every game. Bure's sense of the dramatic is as close as the modern game has come to reinventing Maurice Richard in his explosive prime. It is no coincidence the nickname "Rocket" is in use again after half a century.

In the dressing room Bure seems almost childlike, a pale young man with the body of a late teenager and the face of an adolescent. Physically he is the strongest of all the Canucks, and his toughness on the ice has become as well known around the league as his unpredictability with the puck.

His athletic grace he came by naturally; he's the son of a former Olympic swimming medalist. He chose hockey as his sport when he was five and chose, as his idol, the great Valeri Kharlamov, who showed the same explosive speed in the 1972 Canada–Russia series and who was killed in a car accident when Bure was ten. By the time Bure was 18 he had been tagged to play on a line with two other rising stars, Alexander Mogilny and Sergei Fedorov. It was expected that the trio would rise to the standards set a generation earlier by the renowned KLM line, which featured Vladimir Krutov, Igor Larionov, and Sergei Makarov. Mogilny, however, defected at the 1989 World Championships in Stockholm, and a year later, Fedorov walked out on the Soviets at another tournament. The line broke up before the country did.

Vancouver had taken Bure in the sixth round of the 1989 entry draft, which made him the 113th player chosen in the first draft to feature a European, Sweden's Mats Sundin, as the number-one pick. Gaining Bure's release proved far more difficult than the Canucks had imagined. The Soviets prized him so highly, and were so afraid of losing him as they'd lost Mogilny and Fedorov, that they refused to send him to the 1991 Canada Cup. A month later, with his father and younger brother – his mother would soon follow – Bure flew to Los Angeles to make his name in a more promising country.

Bure then discovered that he was still forbidden to play in the NHL. The league was so worried his defection would spoil future negotiations between NHL clubs and Russian clubs that it forced Vancouver to negotiate Bure's release as if he were still in Moscow. Finally, 14 games into the 1991–92 season, Vancouver had his signature on a contract that would pay him $2.7 million over four seasons. Two thousand fans came out to watch his first practice and ended up fighting over stacks of Bure photographs the Canucks were giving away. In Bure's first year the Canucks won their division for the first time in 17 years. Those promotional photographs now command $30 apiece.

FOR 30 YEARS EUROPEANS HAVE BEEN COMING TO NORTH AMERICA TO try the NHL. Ulf Sterner played four games for the New York Rangers in 1964–65 and went virtually unnoticed. Ever since, European players have been the target of attack, some of it verbal, much of it physical. North American players have always been quick to intimidate opponents who were not taught when young how to punch back. Because of this, Europeans in the NHL have found their durability more difficult to prove than their ability. One night, when Bure was caught on camera kicking a Winnipeg player's skates out from under him, Don Cherry called him a "little weasel" and added, "You'd never catch a Canadian kid doing that!"

In fact, the Europeans have usually been the victims. When Bobby Hull played for the Winnipeg Jets of the old World Hockey Association in the late 1970s, he called a press conference to demand, without success, stricter rules enforcement when he saw what other teams were doing to his Swedish linemates, Ulf Nilsson and Anders Hedberg. "If something isn't done soon," he said, "it will ruin the game for all of us."

Inge Hammerstrom of the Maple Leafs eventually packed it in when he could no longer abide the physical punishment on the ice or the mental abuse from his employer, Harold Ballard. Borje Salming, who came to the Leafs with Hammerstrom in 1973, stuck it out in North America for 16 seasons and was, in many ways, the first European to be accepted as tough enough for the NHL. Peter Stastny, a Czech star who joined Quebec in 1980 and plays now for New Jersey, was the second. There were other early Europeans – Vaclav Nedomansky, Stastny's brothers Anton and Marian, the Merlinesque Kent Nilsson – but none found similar acceptance. When Europeans did fight back, they were often dismissed as "dirty" and "cheap-shot artists" – especially by Cherry, who has led long campaigns against the Europeans in general and two players in particular, Ulf Samuelsson of the Penguins and Tomas Sandstrom of the Kings. This, in a league in which hooking, slashing, interference, and checking from behind go all but unnoticed.

By 1992–93, however, the durability of the Europeans was less of an issue. Too many of them were playing; too many were thriving. The game's youngest fans—those who wait with cards and pens – had found new idols. Gretzky is Gretzky and Lemieux is Lemieux; though none doubt their genius, both are now frayed by age and mortality. The new heroes have names like Jagr and Selanne, Federov and Mogilny, Kamensky and Sundin. The youngest North American superstar, Eric Lindros, is almost the only new home-grown hockey face with which children identify. The kids relate to those who play as they themselves dream of playing, and it's now the Europeans who are recreating the NHL game, just as youth reinvents the game on driveways and outdoor rinks. The Europeans even *look* more like their fans than their North American teammates do. Lindros, at 19, could pass for the much older brother of Jaromir Jagr, 21, or Bure, now 22.

By the end of the season, two Europeans – Winnipeg's Teemu Selanne and Buffalo's Alexander Mogilny – would lead the league in goals, each with 76. Selanne would easily win the Calder Trophy, awarded to the league's best rookie, over North Americans Felix Potvin of Toronto and Joe Juneau of Boston. (Lindros, in his first season, would not even be a finalist). Yet the final proof of the Europeans' emergence would be found not in the league awards but in the card shops. As children learned the difference between "listed" value and real value, they discovered that the trading cards easiest to cash in were those featuring the Europeans. When Beckett, the card-collector's bible, ran its spring list of "Hot" and "Cold" cards, Selanne, Bure, and Mogilny led the hot list; the rapidly cooling, unsought top five on the other list were (1) Brett Hull, (2) Eric Lindros, (3) Mark Messier, (4) Ed Belfour, and (5) Wayne Gretzky.

Some commentators argue that the European stars emerged in

the 1992–93 season because of rule changes, introduced during the exhibition schedule, that opened up the game. Referees had been instructed to call largely ignored infractions such as holding and hooking; as a result, the playing surface seemed suddenly larger, and the quick, sly players – many of them European – were able to search out and bolt through the wider defensive seams with a degree of success no one had anticipated. That didn't stop Cherry from sniping at them. The argument that the rules had been bent to accommodate them offended the Europeans, many of whom had come to the NHL driven by a need to be measured against the best.

But the rules being applied were not new; they were old rules that had been ignored for so long they had been forgotten by all but longtime fans. That they were being remembered now was an admission by the NHL Board of Governors that one way to widen the game's fan base – that is, to make more money – might be to make the game more appealing to American television audiences. One survey ranked NHL hockey 40th in popularity among American viewers, behind tractor pulls and bowling.

The key to increased revenue would be, some felt, a more attractive product that would bring the league a national network-television contract in the United States. The NHL's current American outlet, ESPN, would bring in $80 million over five years, a pittance when set against the almost $2 billion ($390 million from ESPN, $1.4 billion from CBS) that major-league baseball was supposed to get over a similar period. To get television acceptance, the argument went, hockey needed to become less violent, and that meant fewer fights and more opportunities to shine for the game's brightest lights. Hockey, many believed, was in danger of destroying itself by restricting the gifted and rewarding the restricted.

New owners such as Bruce McNall of the Kings and Howard

Baldwin of the Penguins had convinced the league that American television acceptance was hockey's door to the next century. McNall was particularly good at convincing other owners that there was a till other than concessions and parking – beyond, even, the millions that would flow from a national television contract. He projected all the way to the living room of the potential fan who was not even coming out to see the games, but who *would* pay almost the cost of a seat at the Gardens or the Coliseum for the chance to slouch on his chesterfield and dial up the night's game on pay-per-view.

"Imagine," McNall had said, "having three million subscribers to a cable system and your team reaches the Stanley Cup finals and you know that you can't get a ticket. So you pay ten dollars to sit and watch at home with your family or friends. It would be a great bargain. And if we penetrated only, say, 20 percent of that audience of three million people, that's 600,000 homes at ten dollars a home – six million. If you go through, say, 20-odd games in the playoffs, it's well over 100 million dollars. That's just for television cable rights to the playoffs."

For spinning such dreams, McNall was rewarded with the chairmanship of the Board of Governors, replacing Blackhawks owner Bill Wirtz. The old guard was rapidly disappearing – NHL president John Ziegler gone, Wirtz gone. To McNall would now fall the task of finding hockey's first commissioner. No one doubted that the new commissioner would understand that television was a priority and that hockey had much to learn from the National Basketball Association.

In the 1980s the increasing success of the NBA had rankled the NHL. When Ziegler succeeded Clarence Campbell as president in 1977, pro basketball was in much worse condition than hockey. In 1980–81, 16 of the NBA's 23 teams lost money. Franchises were collapsing and disappearing. The league did not even keep a tally of how much money was coming in from licensed products. Ticket revenues and television fees were worth a mere $110 million. In 1982, interest in the NBA was so low that the final championship game between the Philadelphia 76ers and the Los Angeles Lakers was not even televised live.

Under NBA commissioner David Stern, however, basketball had taken off. Revenues rose 400 percent. By 1991, retail revenues had reached more than $1 billion a year, making basketball the first sport where sales of licensed merchandise exceeded ticket sales. There are now 27 teams, and most of them turn a healthy profit thanks to revenue sharing and to salary caps that please both players and owners. In 1989 the NBA struck a television deal with NBC for $600 million over four years. In April the deal was renewed for four more years at $750 million.

The first priority of Stern and the NBA owners had been to bring back old fans and attract new ones. The key was the game itself: they would redesign basketball. The game was speeded up with a shot clock and also opened up, with an extra foul added to ensure that stars stayed in the game to the often-decisive end. The "extra step" in going to the net was overlooked to encourage players to try for more dramatic scoring plays. The superstars now had more room to play and more incentive to display their talents; and they now understood that the entire league was interested in promoting them. The league deliberately created a culture of celebrity. Michael Jordan and Magic Johnson and Larry Bird became household names, and attendance at NBA games rose from 58 percent to 91 percent of capacity. Stern's success was so spectacular that in 1990 the league's owners rewarded him with a five-year contract paying $3.5 million a year, then threw in a $10 million bonus.

Basketball's extraordinary penetration in both the United States and Canada went directly against the old saw about hockey: that its main problem was that most fans could not identify with the game. In the United States, where only 12 percent of the population is black, 80 percent of the players are black; yet basketball is replacing baseball as the game of the imagination, and not just at the professional level. Eight months before the 1994 U.S. college Final Four tournament in Charlotte, North Carolina, there were 533,000 applications for tickets to an arena that holds 20,000.

The American television fan has found it easy to embrace basketball and ignore hockey. Thanks to the mania around college basketball in the United States, NBA rookies like Shaquille O'Neal arrive as fully developed superstars, which makes their entry into the celebrity culture effortless. In hockey, young superstars arrive unknown and without warning from prairie towns and Russian villages. Also, the boom time for the NBA coincided with the emergence of championship teams in media centers like Los Angeles and Chicago. Basketball took off during the same period the Oilers in unknown Edmonton, Alberta, were winning five Stanley Cups in seven years (1984, 1985, 1987, 1988 and 1990).

The two games are played in similar venues, with five players on the attack. Both feature defense and offense, transition and speed, the search for advantage and the scoring play. There was, however, a critical difference between the two sports: basketball had seats to sell, hockey did not. Over the past quarter-century, attendance at NHL arenas has never dipped below 88 percent. In the end, the difference between actively seeking fans and taking them for granted accounts for all the other differences between the two sports. Marketing, Bill Wirtz has always insisted, is nothing more than "filling seats." If the seats are full, what else is there to do? As John Ziegler said, so often that it became his mantra, "If it ain't broke, why fix it?"

Then Bruce McNall came along with new ideas. Backed by owners who were interested in capturing the fans outside the rink – the fans he assured them were sitting there waiting for the game to begin – McNall spearheaded a powerful movement to do for hockey what had been done for basketball. When Ziegler's temporary replacement, Gil Stein, came to Ottawa in July 1992, he hinted at what was to come. "We need to blow away the clouds to see the stars," he said – and he was not alone in his thinking.

The NHL had just come off a troubled 1991–92 season highlighted by a players' strike, delayed playoffs, and collapsing television viewership in Canada. When Hartford and Montreal met in the opening round of the 1992 playoffs, the television audience was a disastrous 815,000 – 22,000 fewer than "The Tommy Hunter Show" was bringing in before being canceled earlier that spring. The strike was to blame, certainly, but more and more hockey executives – among them Edmonton's Glen Sather, Montreal's Jacques Lemaire, Chicago's Bob Pulford, Philadelphia's Bob Clarke, and even Boston's Harry Sinden – were openly questioning the fan appeal of grinder hockey, the style of play celebrated in North America and worshipped by the likes of Don Cherry.

At the end of the 1991–92 season, many teams that had finished the regular schedule high in the standings fell early in the playoffs. As soon as the playoff rounds started, the style of play changed dramatically; games played in May seemed unrelated to games played in December. Playoff officiating was so lax it barely existed. As well, some of the game's top stars – Gretzky, Lemieux, Mark Messier, Raymond Bourque – were injured at one time or another, often deliberately. A vicious slash by the Rangers' Adam Graves put Lemieux temporarily out of the playoffs with a broken hand.

Lemieux himself said that the time had come to change the rules "for the safety of the players – it's too dangerous to go out there now with the rules the way they are." The alarm was sounded to crack down on infractions, to open up the game for those who could really play it – to blow away the clouds to see the stars.

The NHL considered an array of solutions, including a larger net – six by eight feet instead of the present four by six – to create more goals. In the end, the NHL governors settled on a zero tolerance policy for the existing rules. At the same time, hoping to increase fan identification with the players, they voted to make helmets optional instead of mandatory. The helmet decision was an immediate failure; the players knew how important it was to protect the head from what the game had been allowed to become.

Some rules were new. There would be a two-minute penalty for "diving" – pretending to have been tripped or hooked – and the instigator in a fight would receive an automatic game misconduct. Other rules were merely refined: high-sticking would be called from the waist up instead of the shoulder up, and holding an opponent's stick would be a penalty. One rule was a return to the past: the coincidental-minor rule – instituted in 1984–85 because other teams could not cope with the speed of the Edmonton Oilers or the creativity of Gretzky – was dropped, which meant a return to the excitement of four-on-four play. Gil Stein even issued a video that each team was required to watch so that everyone would understand the NHL's new message: skill will be rewarded.

Throughout the 1992–93 exhibition season the officials called the games as instructed. Some nights there were as many as 40 penalties, and teams scrambled to rethink strategies. Specialty teams were suddenly more important than ever. Quick, mobile defensemen were now more effective than large, slow ones, whose main weapons had been interference and holding. As the players adapted, the game speeded up considerably, with the more skilled players – many of them European – rocketing through the newly created seams on the ice, to the delight of the crowds and (alas) the dismay of teams, such as the Senators, without highly skilled players. Coach Bill Dineen of the Flyers – the team once known as the Broad Street Bullies – pronounced the changes "ridiculous." Washington Capitals forward Dale Hunter, an aggressive grinder, complained, "They're three-hour games now. Special teams are the most important part of the whole game. I don't know if you want that."

Not everyone agreed with Dineen and Hunter. The Nordiques – a team built on speed and featuring a blend of young, skilled North American and European players – found that the changes improved their game. Fans began to pay attention to them; reporters began calling them "the team of the future." Not far into the regular schedule, however, the on-ice officials became less rigorous in calling infractions. "Everyone wants to get rid of the hooking and holding," said Pierre Pagé, the Nordiques' general manager and coach. "The media, the fans, the general managers, the coaches, the Board of Governors and the players. But it's gradually coming back."

Dave King echoed the sentiment in Calgary. "I'm worried," he said in early November. "You go to all that trouble to train the players and then it all changes back. It seems kind of silly." By December the new rules were a distant memory. "It's a joke," declared St. Louis Blues scorer Brett Hull, whose thoughts on hooking and holding echoed his father's a generation before. "They put in all these new rules and now there are no rules."

Soon it was business as usual, with most referees "letting the players decide the game." What happened? Comforted by its full arenas, the NHL left control to the individual owners rather than (as basketball had done) to the league; and hockey, as always, sought out the lowest common denominator. The Nordiques may have wished the game played one way, but the Senators and the Hartford Whalers could only compete as grinders, and two votes will defeat one every time. No instructions had to be sent out to the on-ice officials; what happened next happened by a kind of trickle-down effect, as almost everything does in a small community controlled at the top by a few. Most owners merely wanted their teams to keep up the only way they knew how. Most referees merely wanted to get along with most players. Most players merely needed the edge illegal tactics could give them.

"The majority are the ones who are calling the shots," said an angry John Muckler, Buffalo's coach, when he realized that the new rules were being abandoned and that his two best players, Pat LaFontaine and Alexander Mogilny, were once again being subjected to uncalled infractions. "The top ten teams would like to play hockey. That's where your Stanley Cup champion is going to come from – but if it comes to a vote, good teams are going to lose."

Fans were going to lose, too. By the time the 1993 Stanley Cup playoffs came around, grinder hockey would be as dominant as in the previous year. The Boston Bruins, who had made a dramatic shift from grinder hockey to a highly polished game featuring Adam Oates and two quick, inventive rookies – Joe Juneau and Dmitri Kvartalnov – would be beaten four straight by Muckler's Sabres, now grinding by necessity. The Nordiques would also go out in the first round. The sometimes magical Detroit Red Wings would fall in the first round to the Maple Leafs in a series that could have been mistaken for Australian Rules football on ice.

In Vancouver, after his brilliant performance against the Senators, Pavel Bure talked about the game he believes hockey can become: a perfect blend of the two schools, North American and European, with skills and speed ever increasing and the intensity of the North American game making such skills and speed all the more enthralling. "The best is half-Canadian and half-European," he said. "It's not important whether a player is a Russian or a Finnish player or a Czech. It only matters how we play."

In Bure's mind, the game's two greatest players at that moment were Mario Lemieux and Detroit's Steve Yzerman – "and they play like Europeans, I think." Such a coming together of the two styles could be, for Bure and others, the salvation of a league that must take control of its game. "For fans it's more interesting," he said. "We play this game for the fans."

ONE EVENING IN DECEMBER, WHEN DETROIT WAS IN OTTAWA PLAYING the Senators, Sergei Fedorov picked up the puck in his own end in overtime and sped down the right side toward the Ottawa net. When he reached the blue line there was only one defenseman between him and the net – Ottawa's Norm Maciver, himself snake-quick. Fedorov tried a play rarely attempted at this level and even more rarely completed: he flipped the puck past Maciver's right and scooted around Maciver's left. While the puck went one way, Fedorov went the other, cutting back in time to accept his own pass and fire it past Peter Sidorkiewicz to win the game. It was a breathtaking goal.

For the Senators, the same story unfolded with a dozen variations throughout the season. Winnipeg's Teemu Selanne moved up the left side of the ice, also in overtime, and somehow danced the puck back into his skates, back and forth between his skate blades, then ahead to his stick, which was now behind the Ottawa defender. He hit the post, but the move was dazzling. In another game, Buffalo's Mogilny flew up the ice with his tight, effortless stride and fired a shot so hard to the upper corner that the Ottawa goaltender might as well have been a cardboard silhouette. Boston's Dmitri Kvartalnov swept in from the right side and, perfectly timing his swing to the pass, scored so quickly that reporters had to race to the replay screens to find out what had happened. Nikolai Borschevsky executed a similar play for Toronto a few weeks later. And against Vancouver, Bure left the Senators in shock with a single third-period shift in which were compressed more chances, and at higher speed, than the entire Ottawa team could muster in three periods. It was the Canadian poet Al Purdy who first noted that splendid hockey is like good jazz: improvisational, imaginative, an experiment in tempo and range, creation on the fly.

Selanne and Mogilny turned out to be the great European surprises of the season. They scored the same number of goals, 76, and had the same effortless skating ability, but there the similarities end. Mogilny came from Khabarovsk, a city on Russia's border with China. When he was 15 he showed up at a practice for the Moscow Red Army and talked them into giving him a look. At 18 he was the talk of the Soviet Union. In his book on Soviet hockey, *The Red Machine*, Lawrence Martin noted that Mogilny had the ability to "shift like an X-ray" – a simile that would make perfect sense to those defensemen who have tried to cut him off along the boards.

The questionable part of his makeup was not his body, but his mind. Mogilny was, and is, a confirmed individualist whom hockey people find difficult to deal with, given their love of routines and his inclination to challenge them. No one found him more exasperating than Victor Tikhonov, the Soviet Red Army and national team coach, who could not comprehend why his young star wasn't interested in being made an enlisted officer in the army. In 1989 Mogilny beat up another Soviet player who had struck him first; for that, he was suspended for ten games and stripped of the great honor – "Merited Master of Sport for the Soviet Union" – that he had won the year before when the Soviets took the gold medal at the Calgary Olympics. Always the iconoclast, Mogilny made contact himself with the Sabres and then defected, leaving behind everything he had – and everyone he knew – in the Soviet Union.

"My decision," Mogilny said when he defected, "can show other people how to think." It sounded cocky at the time, but now that it is no longer necessary for a Russian player to defect, it's clear that other European players are indeed thinking along the same lines.

In North America he showed an instant taste for the rich life – for a new black Corvette and $400 shirts; soon, however, he also showed a crippling condition that might have kept him out of the NHL: he was petrified of flying. It was only after long sessions in psychotherapy, and months of driving all day and night to games, that he gained control, once again, of his own destiny.

Mogilny's adaptation was difficult partly because he was the first young Russian star to reach the NHL. In 1989 several aging Russians had been released and given permission to try their hand at the North American game. Of the five best-known – Sergei Makarov with Calgary, Igor Larionov and Vladimir Krutov with Vancouver, and Slava Fetisov and Alexei Kasatonov with New Jersey – only Makarov lived up to expectations. The arrival of the five and their conceded failure made it all the more difficult for Mogilny, and the other young Russians, to win acceptance.

By 1992–93, however, there could be no dismissing the Europeans as a fad. In all, 88 Europeans had been drafted the previous June, with the most dramatic exodus coming from Russia. By the time the season ended, 49 Russians had skated with NHL teams and another 48 had played in the minor leagues or in Junior. Just one

Russian team – the famous Red Army – had 22 former players in NHL ranks. The New Jersey Devils were nicknamed "Team United Nations." The Winnipeg Jets, with four Russians, two Finns, two Swedes, and three Americans in uniform, became the first NHL team on which Canadian players did not dominate the starting lineup. When NHL expansion began in 1967, Canadians held 96 percent of the available slots. By the time the 1993 playoffs opened, that figure had fallen to 66.2 percent – slightly below two-thirds. Don Cherry's response: "There should be quotas."

There won't be. When John Ferguson, who drafted Selanne for Winnipeg, returned from a European scouting trip in February 1992, he remembered best of all a popsicle-cold rink in Uddevalla, Sweden. The game he saw there was watched by only 75 legitimate fans – and 100 scouts. By the end of the 1992–93 season the Penguins had arranged a deal with Red Army that gave them greater opportunity to scout Russian players, as well as a program for sending North American players in the Penguins system to Moscow for training. Four other NHL teams – Hartford, Winnipeg, Philadelphia, and Dallas (formerly Minnesota) – had set up a joint company that would do nothing but scout full-time in Europe.

Despite Mogilny's cockiness, even he was caught off guard by the ease with which he began scoring in 1992–93. "I felt I would have a big season," he said one night in Buffalo after a game against the Senators. "But I didn't think I would have *this* big a season. I'm scoring a little too much." It seemed a strange concern. His contract, which had a base of $650,000, kicked in a bonus of $140,000 at 60 goals, with every goal thereafter putting another $4,000 in his pocket.

But he had his reasons: "Next year if not 70 goals, they will say, 'What's wrong with Mogilny?' It's like Brett Hull this year. He gets 50 goals and everybody says he's having a bad season."

48

After four years in the NHL, Mogilny was well aware of the knocks against him and other Europeans. The old guard in the rinks and the young guard in the bars still consider the Europeans suspect because – so it's said – the Stanley Cup must mean nothing to them. Not having grown up under its mystical allure, they can't share the same passion for it that a young player from, say, Kirkland Lake feels from birth. Mogilny's detractors liked to point out that his team was becoming an annual playoff tragedy, with no player contributing less than Mogilny, who had never scored a postseason goal. "I don't pay attention to those kinds of idiots who say that," he said. "After a while they will realize you're good. This year I am going to carry over into the playoffs. You got to shut them up with your performance." Mogilny was good on his prediction.

Such difficulty with adaption is not particular to Mogilny. Three weeks after Pavel Bure arrived in North America, he married a mysterious fashion model whose last name remains unknown and about whom he will not speak. They never did live together and are now divorced. Darius Kasparaitis, a young Lithuanian defenseman with the Islanders, had his new black BMW towed when he parked illegally while in search of Manhattan action. When paying his $200 fine, he jumped the queue by convincing the violators ahead of him that he had a plane to catch for a game in Chicago. Instead he returned to the party only to have the BMW again towed away on him. Back he went to the pound with a fresh explanation. "Late my plane – somebody steal my car," Kasparaitis told the head-shaking clerk. "Big joke." In July he was arrested for drunk driving and for leading police on a chase that, at times, reached 100 miles an hour.

Jaromir Jagr – the best hair in hockey if not the best at working the corners – arrived in Pittsburgh when he was 18 and is finally, now, as comfortable with the media and with fame as most North

American players. During one morning skate at Pittsburgh's Civic Arena – "the Igloo" – he was seen in animated, laughing conversation with the usually dour Tomas Jelinek of the Senators, who had been drafted to keep Roman Hamrlik company and ended up the only Senator who could not speak to any of his teammates. The Ottawa journalists asked what they had been talking about, for none had ever seen Jelinek so much as smile. The question made no sense to Jagr: "You guys just not as funny as me."

Jelinek's problem, according to the much younger Jagr, was age. At 30 he was just "too old" to adjust. "He played 15 years in Czechoslovakia," Jagr said. "It takes a long time to change for the NHL. He doesn't have time." If Jagr had to select the single most important thing to adjust *to*, he would not pick the intensity or the physical abuse or the length of the season, but the language. Jagr studied English with a tutor eight hours a day for four weeks before his first training camp, but still found it extremely difficult. The Pittsburgh coaching staff once tried to explain to him that European-style curved blades were not allowed in the NHL; Jagr, in his confusion, believed they were angry with him for not shooting enough. It was not until Pittsburgh traded to get a Czech "friend" for Jagr – Jiri Hrdina – that the young star came out of his depression. He now lives contentedly in the English world and has even brought his mother over from Kladno to be with him in Pittsburgh. He is, in many ways, the most interesting of the European players to talk to, for his interests extend far beyond hockey: he chose his number, 68, in honor of the Prague Spring, which took place four years before he was born.

TEEMU SELANNE CHOSE TO STAY IN FINLAND UNTIL HE FELT HIMSELF mature as a person as well as an athlete. It paid off handsomely, for

Selanne was as instantly at ease with the media and the public as the accommodating young Gretzky had been. Selanne grew up in Espoo, outside Helsinki, and his past rings as much of Canadian as of Scandinavian cliché: a supportive family, strong promise in minor hockey, hours of street hockey with his twin brother in goal and young Teemu endlessly practicing those plays that come only from the imagination. He waited in Finland until he was 22 and felt himself ready for the NHL. He came to Winnipeg at the start of the 1992–93 season and quietly began scoring goals faster than any rookie in history. In a year that was supposed to belong to Eric Lindros, Selanne was the new star, the overwhelming choice for Rookie of the Year. He was also the instant darling of the card-collecting set – a charming, green-eyed, handsome young man who was as accommodating as Lindros could be brusque.

Selanne had been drafted in 1988 by the Jets – tenth overall – but elected to stay with his Jokerit team in Helsinki. By 1992 he was able to claim Type IV free-agent status, which meant that any team could offer him a contract but Winnipeg could still claim him by matching the offer. (In doing what he did, Selanne set a precedent that would be followed in 1993 by Swedish stars Peter Forsberg, whose rights were "owned" by the Nordiques, and Markus Naslund, who had been drafted by the Penguins in 1991.) The Calgary Flames tried to get Selanne, but Winnipeg matched the Calgary offer: three years for $2.7 million. Winnipeg would quickly brag that he was worth every penny.

Selanne, on the other hand, would say nothing about the price he himself was paying on the ice. In Ottawa one afternoon he sat at the end of practice gently touching a bruise the color of a prairie sunset on his right arm. He had become such a prime target that at one point his frustrated coach John Paddock had asked, "Do we have to put number 66 or 99 on his back to get any attention on this?"

The subtext was obvious: there was one set of rules for North American stars, another for foreigners. During the European–North American matches of the 1970s, the Europeans had earned the contempt of referees for taking "dives." In the 1980s and 1990s they carried a reputation that was all but impossible to shake. North American players generally considered the Europeans phonies who would do anything – act, lie, cheat – to draw a penalty, and North American referees largely shared that opinion. A European, to be accepted, had to show not only great ability but also toughness and on-ice integrity. Any fall, no matter what the cause, was suspect. It's probably no coincidence that the NHL player considered hardest to knock off his skates is Fedorov of Detroit, with Selanne, Mogilny, and Bure all contenders. But still the stigma haunts them.

After watching Selanne day in and day out, Paddock came to believe that there were aspects to the Finn's game that no one noticed. "Considering all the crap he takes," Paddock said, "he could be the toughest player in the NHL." But being tough was not enough. Eventually, to protect Selanne and their other Europeans, the Jets arranged a trade with the Rangers for two enforcers, Tie Domi and Kris King, the ungainly Domi moving to skate periodically on Selanne's line. Thus, one of Europe's most skillful players was now teamed with one of North America's least skillful in the weird world of the NHL.

For a team like the Senators to stop a player like Selanne, it had to construct a jungle barrier of sticks and clutches and slashes and holds. Nothing else would work. The game against Winnipeg had gone into overtime, yet it felt about as dramatic as a chemistry lecture. "It sort of kills the game," Selanne said of the Ottawa tactics. He had liked the new rules and regretted their passing. Perfect hockey for him would be "skill hockey with harder hits – then hockey would be the greatest." What he was seeing, from the Senators and the other unskilled teams, was a style of hockey deliberately aimed at killing what he called "the stylish play."

There may be other reasons why "the stylish play" is in short supply in the NHL. Dave King of the Calgary Flames has more international hockey experience than any other North American coach, having coached some 750 games for the Canadian Olympic team. For King, the greatest shock in shifting from international hockey to the NHL last season was the lack of practice time. NHL teams have game-day skates, which the players call "no brainers," but no team has time to do any real teaching. "My previous experience was to play nine or ten games in 12 to 15 days," King said. "Then we'd have maybe ten days of training. You don't have that luxury in the NHL."

When Bob Gainey went to Minnesota to coach the North Stars in 1990 after a year of coaching in Europe, he turned the North Stars into a quicker, more skilled team simply by stressing a fundamental skill North American players take for granted – passing and receiving passes. Once the North Stars learned not only how to lead a teammate but how to place the pass so the teammate could immediately pass again or shoot without having to reassemble his stance, the speed and effectiveness of the whole team picked up. It *felt* European.

Such skills make a tremendous difference. To watch the Nordiques skate laps is to be astonished by the *hum* that rises from the ice. To watch the Penguins skate and pass during practice is to be struck by the silence that fills the arena, the strides so smooth, the passes so surely given and so softly taken. A blind man could have sat in one of these arenas and known when the Senators were on the ice for their practice, merely by the clatter.

THE EUROPEAN INVASION AND THE NEW RULES HAD AN EFFECT ON THE NHL that will likely persist, even though rules enforcement soon dropped out of the mix. Those two factors had the effect, Dave King said, of "making our game so much more interesting."

More than that, the Europeans and the rule changes were revolutionizing hockey. Owners, managers, coaches, and players all saw dramatic proof that there are other ways to move a puck down the ice and into the opposition's net and that it's possible to move side to side as well as up and down. It is now a given in the NHL that a power play has to feature a "wheel" – that is, someone, often a European, to captain the work in the most efficient manner. The accepted style of running a power play had been to pass the puck around and wait for the open man. The European style, King pointed out, operates "by design, not freelance. There's a plan and usually two options. The power play always has a pattern to it."

This different approach to controlling the puck rippled through every facet of the game. The penalty killers – of whom few are as skilled as Detroit's Fedorov – became aggressive rather than passive, individuals on attack rather than a foursome dropping back into the "box" to set up an "impenetrable" barrier. This new approach all but killed the dump-and-chase tactics of grinder hockey, which was the only style available to a team as deficient in skills as the Senators. Especially with special teams, coaches began to think more in terms of units rather than forward lines and defensive pairings. Instead of making headlong rushes, skaters now circled, dropped back, regrouped, then moved up through emerging weaknesses in the defense. For the first time, some teams began to exploit the diagonal patterns of the game, with players crisscrossing and relying – so it seemed – as much on telepathy and skill as on chalked X's and O's.

No matter what happened to the rules, North American-style

hockey was passé. One typical international tactic, "cycling," in which players turn and twist free in the corners while teammates interfere for them by setting picks, has become the style of the moment among the better players in the game. The best practitioners include, as well as Jagr and Fedorov, Detroit's Yzerman and Quebec's Joe Sakic. All these changes delighted King: "Any time in any sport you can enhance some skill players, you should do it. It makes no sense to take the game down to mediocrity. Imagine what life would be like if we operated that way."

It's ironic that in a year in which the NHL spoke often of the need to break into the American television market, many of the league's sensations would be Europeans displaying the game at its best in markets the new NHL was not chasing. But have the Europeans really begun to dominate the NHL? The ultimate test, many hockey people argue, is the Stanley Cup playoffs, when the game suddenly shifts in both style and intensity. It's as if the regular season is actually the exhibition season. (By the end of the 1992–93 season players were referring to the new rules as the "exhibition rules.") That the rules, old and new, die an annual death each spring is no accident. The arenas are full, and the playoff fans can be taken for granted. The playoff system is structured to permit not only the half-dozen top teams to go on, but another ten as well, many of them mediocre. It is not good for the fans, but it is wonderful for the owners. Since the hockey playoffs are professional sports' greatest financial windfall, owners are desperate to go on, and most owners have teams that can only go on if the truly talented teams can be literally held back.

One of the many upsets of the 1993 playoff season was the first-round fall of Dave King's Flames, a skill-based team. Selanne's Jets also went out in the first round. Bure's Canucks went out in the second. Buffalo did not make it through the second round, though Mogilny scored seven goals in nine games before breaking his ankle.

The spring of 1993 handed Jaromir Jagr his first Stanley Cup disappointment. In 1991, as a rookie, he had scored the overtime series winner against New Jersey that sent Pittsburgh on. In 1992 he had scored four game-winning goals and one spectacular goal in which he snaked in from the boards through three separate checkers before connecting with a backhand shot that Mario Lemieux called "the greatest goal I've ever seen." But in the spring of 1993 nothing Jagr or any of his brilliant teammates could do would take them past the surprisingly gritty, grinding New York Islanders.

The playoffs have not been kind to European stars. When the flashy Nordiques fell to Montreal in the first round of 1993, a national television audience watched a long, ugly chewing out of Mats Sundin by Quebec coach Pierre Pagé. Pagé, eyes bulging, seemed to be blaming the loss on Sundin and the two Russians sitting beside him on the bench, Valeri Kamensky and Andrei Kovalenko. For Sundin, who at 20 had led his country to the world championship, the moment had to be devastating. He had not played particularly well. Nor had Kamensky. Yet Pagé wasn't screaming at his captain, Joe Sakic, who had a terrible series. And in Chicago, no one was screaming at Jeremy Roenick for his dismal playoff and the Blackhawks' early ouster. Nor were they screaming at Adam Oates in Boston.

Two of the most impressive 1993 playoff performers had been rookie Europeans – the Islanders' Darius Kasparaitis and the Kings' Alexei Zhitnik – but Don Cherry could still gloat. The 1993 Stanley Cup champions, the Canadiens, did not have a single European in their final lineup. The team's one Russian, Oleg Petrov, had been unimpressive; the stars were all North American. "You can put me down as a bigot or a racist," Cherry had said back in December, "but

I'm going to give you a fact you can't argue with. They don't bring them over here to hit, to block shots, or to back-check. And God forbid they ever fight. They're over here for one thing. Points. And there wasn't one in the top 20 scoring last year. Case closed."

That was in 1991–92. Four of the top 20 scorers in 1992–93 were Europeans – Selanne, Mogilny, Sundin, and Bure. Three of the five top goal-scorers were European – Selanne, Mogilny, and Bure. Three of the five top rookie scorers were European – Selanne, Winnipeg's Alexei Zhamnov, and Quebec's Andrei Kovalenko. A European won the Calder Trophy for Rookie of the Year for the second year running. More indicatively, the players on the top "wanted" cards in children's trading circles were, without exception, Europeans. Case closed, indeed.

By the spring of 1993 the new rules had been forgotten. The ratings were coming in from the NHL's playoff-television deal with ABC. Hockey was the lowest-rated sports event the first two Sunday afternoons of the playoffs. At the same time, NBC had a runaway success with its NBA playoff coverage. The ratings for basketball broadcasts were up 16 percent from a year earlier.

The NHL's failed experiment "to blow away the clouds to see the stars" had its most lasting impact not on television or even in North America. By the 1992–93 season the exodus of players to the NHL had brought Russian hockey to the verge of collapse. The beautiful style of which Teemu Selanne spoke was still being played in Sweden and Finland, but less and less in Russia. Russian league games, now poorly attended, featured dump-and-chase, hooking and holding, uninvolved officiating, and power plays that ignored the "wheel" and relied instead on defensemen standing on the blue line and blasting away. Such is the natural outcome of the dissolution of talent.

In an interview in *Sports Illustrated*, the great Russian goaltender Vladislav Tretiak said, "The young players are all preparing to go to the NHL, so they play the Canadian style." Moscow Dynamo had even taken on a tutor to teach English to the players so they would be better prepared for professional careers. With 14 players on Dynamo drafted by NHL clubs, the Moscow "farm team" stood to make more than $3 million in transfer fees.

Ironically, the prize the NHL was chasing – American television – was changing the Russian game more profoundly than it was changing the game on this continent. "Young players watch the NHL once a week on television," Alexander Yakushev, the scoring star of the 1972 series, told journalist E.M. Swift. "It affects them. And Dynamo teaches the Canadian game, so it's not surprising the children's coaches demand that sort of play from the kids. They'll absolutely be less talented players than kids of ten years ago."

In Canada, children were playing like Pavel Bure and Teemu Selanne and Alexander Mogilny in the streets and on the few remaining open-air rinks. On Moscow rinks, children of nine and ten were embracing goon tactics. Of today's Soviet children, Yakushev said sadly, "They play like the Philadelphia Flyers of the 1970s."

CHAPTER THREE

THE VETERAN
AND THE ROOKIE

St. Louis, Missouri

Darcy Loewen did not know whether to laugh or cry. He was sitting, mouth agape, in Dierdorf & Harts, the best restaurant in St. Louis's refurbished Union Station, as a waitress made her way down the table with an entire tray of strange glasses that had barely been splashed with some dark liquid. Loewen had never seen anything like it: back in Sylvan Lake, fancy drinking was a frosted glass for your beer. But here was the waitress stopping and, with a flourish, setting one, two, three ... ten of the tiny glasses in front of a grinning Brad Marsh.

This was the first annual Ottawa Senators Rookie Dinner. The dinner had replaced, finally, the hazing of rookies, which used to involve the rest of the team holding the young player down in the shower while veterans shaved away his pubic hair with all the care of hydro workers clearing undergrowth. It was humiliating, painful if they applied after-shave, excruciating if they sprinkled liniment. More than one rookie had sat out games in more pain from his underwear than from the check that had supposedly shelved him. The Rookie Dinner was expensive, but modern rookies considered it a bargain by comparison. The veterans got to pick the restaurant, all the players got to drink and eat whatever they wanted, and the rookies got stiffed for the bill.

But this, surely to God, was going too far. Marsh had called for the wine list a second time, when everyone else had thought the meal was finally over, and run a big forefinger down the liqueur page until he came to the most expensive drink Loewen had ever heard of – a rare cognac worth $130 a glass. Marsh had ordered ten and handed them around to the other veterans. And now here he was, with a big, dopey grin on his face, wrapping his big hand around one of the glasses and throwing it back, then reaching for a second ...

Ten glasses at $130 each. Ninety seconds of drinking for $1,300! With all ten glasses empty without a rookie being offered so much as a sniff, Marsh was calling for the tab. And the head waiter, wearing a big smile, was setting the check down in front of Loewen, the total circled near the bottom: $6,000.

Loewen swallowed hard. For a moment he looked as if he, not Marsh, was about to pass out. The three rookies at the table huddled together and added their cash. Together, they could not even cover the cost of the ten cognacs. Sighing, Loewen reached for his wallet, pulled out his Visa card, and placed it on the tray. On ice or off, he would take the hits.

Now they were laughing at him, the veterans shaking their heads and howling. "It was tea," said Marsh. There had been no $130 drinks. And the bill was not $6,000 – Marsh had talked the waiter into delivering a phony bill after the phony drinks. Loewen let out his breath and reached for his credit card. The real bill was now in Brad Marsh's hand, and he was suddenly looking flabbergasted. The actual bill, the one that was supposed to make the $6,000 look like an absurdity, was for $4,300. Loewen threw his credit card back down.

The rookie Loewen and the 15-year veteran Marsh had quickly become the Senators' most beloved players, the ones the hometown fans taped up signs for on the end glass. They were also two players who were not even supposed to have made the team. Loewen had been an afterthought, yet he had survived both training camp and the exhibition season and was still a Senator when the snow began to fall. He had become the heart and soul of the worst team in hockey, just as he had been the heart and soul of every team he had been too small for – and yet had stuck with – since Squirt.

As for Marsh, he had been told every year for the past half-dozen that he was finished. The 35-year-old had not dressed for the Senators' first game. Nor had he dressed for the third, fourth, fifth, sixth, or seventh. It had been said during the exhibition season that he was finished, and by the time the regular season began some were saying that he should do the proper thing and retire – that the game had simply moved beyond him. But for the eighth game, against the New York Rangers, he had dressed, and played with ferocity in a hard loss. Since then he had rarely sat out. By the time the brutal realities of the first season were sinking in – on owners, managers, coaches, players, media, and fans – the veteran and the rookie had come to exemplify the one positive quality this wretched team could claim: hard work.

The two were emphatically determined to help in whatever manner they could – finishing checks, blocking shots, dumping players, hustling, clutching, grabbing, holding, knocking opponents off the puck, hindering, hampering, hounding. Each had also played some of the Senators' most effective shifts without a hockey stick. It had turned into that kind of season.

THE NIGHT AFTER THE ROOKIE DINNER, COACH RICK BOWNESS PUT Loewen out on the Senators' power play. Loewen was neither a scorer nor a playmaker, but Bowness was sending a message to the rest of the players: hard workers will get ice time. Loewen himself was surprised. Even his mother would have been surprised to see him out there. "Poor Darcy," Patricia Loewen would say from Sylvan Lake, "he has cement hands, you know." Never would this be more apparent than in a game against Buffalo, when Loewen broke his stick in the Sabres' end and raced past the Ottawa bench on his way to help stop the Buffalo attack. No fewer than six left-shooting Senators held out their sticks for him. He grabbed for each in turn, the shafts flying by like guardrails in a highway accident, the young winger continuing empty-handed down the ice and straight into his own crease, where he threw his body over the puck as if it was a live grenade.

A simple country kid whose ambition beyond hockey is to ride rodeo bulls, the 23-year-old Loewen had always left the bench as if he was coming out of a chute. He did not seem to understand the unwritten rules in hockey – for example, that a forechecking forward is expected to peel away from the defenseman once the puck has been thrown up the ice. At the Civic Centre his signature play was to hammer a huge defenseman so hard behind his own net that onlookers expected the Zamboni doors to burst open and the two players to fly into the Rideau Canal.

He had arrived in Ottawa with zero career points and six career nicknames – "Tasmanian Devil," "Taz," "Roadrunner," "Buzzsaw," "Chainsaw," and "Pinball" – but none quite did justice to his style of play. His father said, "If you blew up a balloon and let it go – that'd be Darcy.'" On a team lacking in skill, size, and speed, Loewen had spirit, and the Ottawa fans took to him the way, 30 years earlier, Toronto fans had taken to Eddie Shack.

Loewen had no idea what made him so popular. He was always surprised when kids recognized him, that someone might wait, shaking, while he scribbled the autograph he had practiced a hundred times back home on the kitchen table, never thinking that anyone but himself would ever study it. He had no idea what he was doing that was working, especially since it had never worked before in the NHL. Like so many athletes, he could only say, "I just play my game." Asked how much of the ice surface he saw when he was in the middle of the play, he said he didn't even know which rink he was in once the puck dropped. "I get into my zone," he said. That zone measured one inch thick and three inches in diameter: the size of the puck.

It was his zone – his inability to know even where he was once the game was underway – that endeared Loewen to Bowness. As the opening week became the opening month, as Christmas drew near and the new year arrived, Bowness was concluding that the team would never win on the road – the players were too afraid. Back in Ottawa, with the cheers of 10,500 behind them, with loved ones in the stands and their employers staring down from the corporate boxes, the Senators played one style of hockey; on the road they played quite another. Some who scored at home scored rarely, if at all, on the road. Some who checked ferociously at home stayed away from the corners on the road.

There were a few exceptions – Marsh, for example, whose reputation made opponents tentative no matter what rink he was in – but no one stood out like Loewen, who played with the same reckless, hysterical abandon even in Chicago Stadium, the most intimidating arena in the NHL. He had been cut from teams before, and played, he said, as if every shift might be his last as a Senator.

He came by his work ethic honestly. He told the *Ottawa Sun*'s Earl McRae that before every game he would sit for a while and think about his father heading out to the pumps of his Shell station. "I just think about how hard he's always worked to provide for our family. There are days when he doesn't want to get up for work, when he's feeling down or has a sore back, but every day he gets up before dawn to go to the gas station. I've never, ever, heard my Dad complain. So, I look at my job and I ask: How can I complain when I'm doing something I love? Sure, there are days when I'm tired or down or sore, but big deal. Like my Dad, I just shut up. I go out and do the job the best I can do it every second I'm on the ice. I can't help it. It's in my nature."

His nature was like no one else's. In Tampa, the older players joked that they'd give him $100 if he'd jump into the hotel pool in his suit. *Splash*. He had grown up that way – wild, reckless, intensely loyal. When coaches and teammates were asked about him, whether they were from Pee Wee or professional ranks, they offered the same analogy: if you had to go to war, Darcy would be the one you'd want in your bunker. He'd either go over the top and do it himself, or else he'd die dragging you back to safety.

"Did we ever expect Darcy to make the NHL?" Patricia Loewen said one day. "My goodness, we never expected him to make Junior!" His own burning ambition was to play one day for the local Senior hockey team. By the time he was eight years old he was working the penalty-box door for the Lakers. His parents remember him sitting around a bonfire in the backyard wondering if he'd ever be good enough to wear a Lakers jersey and play for the hometown.

There were reasons for his limited ambition. He was, after all, always the smallest player on any team. He was born deaf in his left ear and developed a spinal condition at a young age. But nothing could hold him back. For years he was the best as well as the smallest. In Pee Wee he scored, the local paper reported, "an astounding 82 goals and 57 assists" in a 20-game season. When he moved up into Bantam and contact hockey, his parents were certain this would be the end of it. During his first game, he knocked another player out. "Mom stopped worrying after that," he now says with a smile. He didn't look tough – he was tiny, angelic, his helmet so large it wob-bled – but he *was* tough, and he could play the game.

Hard as it may be to imagine today, Loewen was once the one who was counted on to score. If Sylvan Lake came up against Grand Cache, he could get five goals and set up four others. In the provincial playoffs, he scored seven times and had three assists in a 15–2 win over Ponoka. In Midget he insisted on going down the road to play against the better players in Red Deer. His parents agreed to this, but only if they first went shopping for oversized pads – they hoped he would at least look normal. But it wasn't necessary – Darcy again emerged as the team star. He was top scorer in the tournaments, made the all-star team, and was named captain of the all-provincial team.

When he was 14, the Spokane Chiefs of the Western Hockey League put him on their protected list, and when he was 16 he made the Junior team. He would have left home right then, but Gerry and Patricia insisted he give one more year to his education. He did, and then at 17 he went off for good. The Spokane papers were soon writing him up as the "heart and soul" of the Chiefs, just as would be said years later when he joined the Senators.

"I get one chance to make it big time," he said at the time. "I'm going to give it everything I have." He broke his cheekbone, collarbone, nose. He damaged knee ligaments, lost teeth, and once cut his lip so badly "I could stick my tongue through the rip and out the other side." In three years with the Chiefs, he missed only 16 games. Twice he was voted Spokane's most inspirational player.

Even his own family was surprised by his success. His younger brother, Terry, was five inches taller and gifted with the soft hands Darcy would never have: "If only we could have made one player out of the two of them," says their mother. Terry made it as far as Junior but his knees could not stand up to the hammering. Darcy's could, and he wanted to *do* the hammering as well. It was his skill – eventually his only skill.

When a coach sets out to construct the perfect team, he looks for the goal scorers and the playmaker and a couple of steady defenseman and the sort of goaltender who can steal a game – but the ingredients never seem to mix properly without a Darcy Loewen in the roster. What players like him can do is simply shame the more talented into working harder. In hockey this gift is called heart, and it was Loewen's big heart that eventually caught the eye of the Buffalo Sabres.

But he couldn't stick with the talented Sabres. In three seasons he dressed for only 12 games. When he became a Senator he was still, technically, an NHL rookie. To the other players, he was the great surprise of training camp, the one who unexpectedly stayed on when the others were sent down to New Haven. He was the first one the New Haven players asked about when they were checking for openings. No one expected him to stick.

But he stuck. Back in Sylvan Lake, they set up five television sets in the house and worked the satellite dish every night the Senators played. When his parents came home from the gas station, Gerry would spin the dish while Patricia did macramé. Sometimes she'd catch Darcy on one of his assaults on an opposing defenseman – the bull terrier versus the letter carrier. Like everyone else, she'd smile and shake her head as if it made no sense at all. The puck would already have gone up the boards. The defenseman, expecting the forechecking forward to peel off, would suddenly stiffen and flinch as the back of a Senators sweater – No. 10 – came high at his face.

It made sense to Rick Bowness. Loewen did more than stay on – he grew in value as the season went by and ended up dressing for almost every game. He had to sit one out after lacerating his arm running a Hartford defenseman into the boards. Typically, he finished his shift before wondering why a white slice of forearm was hanging from a blood-drenched sleeve.

From training camp on, Loewen had been almost inseparable from a big right winger named Jim Thomson. Both were from Alberta, wore cowboy boots, loved country music, and had the same wet, long-in-back hairstyle. It was Thomson who collected the $100 in Tampa when Loewen's new suit hit the hotel pool. It was Thomson who made the jokes and Loewen who laughed at them. And it was Thomson who made the pass against Pittsburgh that set up Darcy Loewen's first NHL goal.

That was also Thomson's first and only point for the Senators. A slow-skating enforcer whose job was made redundant by Mike Peluso's physical play, he was traded to Los Angeles before Christmas. He and Loewen did not see each other again until January, when the Kings made their only visit to the Civic Centre. The two met at center ice, where Thomson caught Loewen off guard as the Senators rookie was skating to the bench. It was Thomson's first shift of the game, and the Kings' star defenseman Paul Coffey had just been given a rough ride along the boards.

From the seats it looked like a vicious and premeditated attack. Thomson jumped the much smaller Loewen, hurled him to the ice, and leaped on top of him. It even looked like he was trying to bite Loewen's ear as the valiant little Senator struggled beneath him. The crowd screamed and pounded on the glass. The linesmen dove into the pile to claw them apart. Because of the crowd noise, it is unlikely that anyone else caught this exchange:

"Sorry about this, Darce —" *Whap!* "— but I have to do something!"

"It's okay, Jimmy – I understand."

"Still on for that beer?" *Whap!*

"You bet." *Thump!*

LIKE DARCY LOEWEN – LIKE SO MANY NHLERS – BRAD MARSH HAD also been a child prodigy. He grew up in London, Ontario, and learned to skate on the pond down by the Valhalla Apartments. His Novice team went all season without a loss, outscoring the opposition 352–38. And he, of course, was the star of the team.

Back then, Marsh was a playmaking center, and he resisted any coach who tried to switch him to defense. When he was 13, his parents sent him off for a week to the Billy Harris–Dave Keon Hockey School. The school judged his checking only "fair." His skating and shooting, however, were "good" and his attitude and desire "excellent." The game on Marsh's mind was still finesse – the setting up and scoring of goals – not prevention; and he did not much care for the notion of no longer being the offensive star.

But Marsh was moving up, and his style soon shifted on its own. "All of a sudden I was playing against people who were a little stronger than me," he recalls, "a little quicker than me and a little smarter than me. I just went to what I do best." And that turned out to be checking.

When he was 14, and heading toward the 6'3" and 220 pounds he would carry into the NHL, Marsh was called up to the Junior A London Knights for a trial. His teammates called him "Baby Huey" after the huge comic-book character. At 16 he was a regular, a player who intimidated his own team almost as much as opponents. When his teammates complained about his beating up on them at training camp, he answered, "There's no friends at training camp." He became a well-known brawler who loved the attention and was, even then, the favorite of local fans. In London they went wild when he got a penalty, because he'd skate full speed toward the penalty box, stopping just at the door in a heavy spray of ice. The other coaches complained that he carried his stick too high, but they all wished he was on their team, for the other teams were all afraid of him. He had become a fighter, he says, because he felt "I might as well make a name for myself." His battles with the Hamilton Fincups' Al Secord in his second year of Junior were the talk of the league.

At 18, Marsh changed dramatically. He was named captain and virtually stopped fighting. The role he played best, he was discovering, was "to get the guys up in the dressing room before a game." He was a natural leader whose enthusiasm was infectious.

Marsh was the kid who stuffed 121 sticks of gum into his mouth one road trip, the one who initiated the rookies by loading up a rucksack of beer and taking them on a tour of the London sewers. He loved a good time, but he also liked responsibility. It was important to be a captain or assistant captain; it mattered that each week he took his $70 "pay" from the team and gave half to his parents for room and board. He was single-minded about his goal, which was to make the NHL: "I had to simply forget my friends, those kids I grew up with. My teammates had to be my friends."

He was chosen to play for Canada in the 1977 World Junior tournament in Prague and came back with a silver medal. He played again in the 1978 World Junior championship in Montreal and this time won a bronze. In his draft year, 1978, he was rated fourth going in, but the team expected to take him, Detroit, got nervous about his lack of speed and passed him up. With his parents beside him, Marsh sat in the Montreal Forum sweating hard until Atlanta called his name as the eleventh pick of the first round. He came out of his seat at the sound of his name. The dream had come true.

Asked by the Atlanta press how much money he expected to make, he replied, "It'll be $20,000 more than I'll ever need." He moved into a boarding house when he got to Georgia and drove a rental car. Buying a sports car, the traditional bounty of first-round draft choices, he thought "ridiculous – I could afford it, but it's not right."

Marsh came into the NHL as an established character. He scored his first goal on his own net. He lost his first teeth changing a tire when the tire iron sprang up and cracked him. He said he missed the buses, where "you could walk around in your underwear." He wore a helmet at first but it looked ridiculous – the other Flames called him "R2D2" after the robot in *Star Wars* – so he discarded it. Unable to score at this level, he began fighting again and soon had a reputation. Everyone remembered one marathon battle between Marsh and his future general manager, Mel Bridgman. "He got three stitches," Marsh remembers, "and I got three." He did not score his first NHL goal until the following year.

In Atlanta they called him a throwback. Though the son of a London furniture manufacturer, he dressed and acted like a farmboy, chewing tobacco and toothpicks, wearing bib overalls and a CAT baseball cap. The Flames fans nicknamed him "Beaver," as in Cleaver. He married the team owner's daughter – a young woman used to the finer things in life – but the marriage foundered when Marsh decided he wanted to raise pigs in the off-season.

When the Flames moved to Calgary to start the 1980 season, Marsh was voted captain – at 22, he was the youngest NHL captain ever. But a year later the Flames decided he was too slow and traded him to Philadelphia for an older player – the same Mel Bridgman. His revenge came the following March when he scored the winning goal in a 9–8 Flyers victory over the Flames. "I'd never scored a goal that meant anything before," he said.

With the Flyers, Marsh came into his own. The fans voted him Most Popular Player. He began hanging out at a quiet night-spot in New Jersey called The First Fret. One of the owner's children was a dark-haired young schoolteacher named Patty Quaile, recently graduated from Seton Hall. They began dating and soon married.

His years of immaturity were now behind him. He was beginning to discover that he had an unusual ability to get along with people, especially those outside the accepted NHL culture. He had become best friends with the Flyers' Swedish goaltender, Pelle Lindbergh, who won the 1985 Vezina Trophy as the league's top goaltender. On the road they were inseparable. The rest of the team called them "the Odd Couple" – Lindbergh was complex and periodically wild, Marsh was simple and steadfast. They had been in the same bar on the night in 1986 when Lindbergh tried to drive home after too many drinks and died instantly when he wrapped his Porsche 930 around a tree. His death haunts Marsh to this day. He and Patty named their first child Erik after Lindbergh (whose given name was Per-Erik), and there are still photographs of the goaltender in the Marsh house.

After Lindbergh, Marsh became the designated link – the one who roomed with Miroslav Dvorak in Philadelphia, with Vladimir Konstantinov in Detroit. When he came to Ottawa, they put him in with a Czech player, Tomas Jelinek. Marsh was the one North American player who was willing to carry dictionaries and try to bridge the cultural gaps. He and Dvorak became so close that the Marshes have traveled to the Czech Republic to visit.

Marsh's longevity is something of a mystery. He's big and enormously strong but has no remarkable gift aside from his steadiness. Perhaps that was enough – that, and hard work. He began to concentrate on year-round fitness when he was with the Flyers. In

1986 he completed the Liberty-to-Liberty Triathalon on the July 4 weekend, swimming one-and-a-half miles from the Statue of Liberty to shore ("There were boards, bottles and such, but no bodies"), then biking the 103 miles from New York to the outskirts of Philadelphia before running the final 6.2 miles to the Liberty Bell in temperatures that reached 100 degrees. It took him more than seven hours. The real pain, he said, came two days later, the morning after he and another triathlete had been out celebrating.

In 1988, the year Philadelphia decided to pass on him because of his slowness, Marsh went to summer hockey school to improve his game – which undoubtedly was a first for an NHLer. He went to Toronto in that fall's waiver draft and set out, once again, to earn a spot on the Leafs blue line. He was 30 years old. "I'm not some old fart saying that I think I can still play," he said. "I can play." And he proved he could. "I guarantee you," former Leafs captain and coach George Armstrong said at the time, "that in all the years he's played in the NHL, Marsh has seen a thousand guys come and go that had more talent than him. They skated better, passed better, shot better. But they're gone and he's still around. Why? Because he wanted to be, a lot more than they ever did. And he won't ever give up."

Marsh had hoped to end his career with the Leafs. He and Rob Ramage were back playing together as they had in Junior, with Ramage now captain of the Leafs, Marsh an assistant. Their friendship had been growing ever since Ramage's mother taught Marsh at public school and introduced the two so they could play road hockey together. Marsh had been Leaf defenseman Bobby Baun in his imagination, Ramage had been Allan Stanley. Now, nearly two decades later, they had become themselves.

Brad and Patty Marsh loved Toronto and threw themselves into charity work, as they had in Philadelphia and Detroit. Unlike so many players who disdain going to play in Canada, where dollars are worth less and taxes are higher, Marsh had been ecstatic. He was a Canadian, and he wanted his kids to grow up the same way he had.

But it could not last. Though he was a great favorite of coach John Brophy, his throwback style did not appeal to the coaches who followed, Doug Carpenter and Tom Watt. They wanted speed on the blue line. He was asked to give up his "A" to Gary Leeman, and so powerful was Marsh's presence in the locker room that Leeman was too ashamed to wear it. Watt sat Marsh out for 25 straight games before the Leafs dumped him off to Detroit for an eighth-round pick. He bawled when they told him.

It was this wide-open emotion that drew fans to him in every city. If he happened to be chosen a game star, he would streak to center ice and stop in a spray of snow just as, back in Junior, he would race to the penalty box. His attitude made the game real again for those sentimental enough to resent the current obsessions with huge contracts and better leases and pay-per-view television. "Whether you're a hockey player or you're selling gas at the corner station," he said, "there's only one way to do things – and that's the right way."

Marsh has always sought out the different; unlike most players, he is interested in the world. On the night of the 1992 U.S. presidential election, he greeted reporters in the dressing room with a question: "Did anyone get Bush's electoral count?" He was the one who did the *New York Times* crossword while others sat, eyes closed, listening to their Walkmans and portable CD players. He once said that the hardest thing about leaving Detroit for Ottawa was that in Ottawa, it took him less than five minutes to get to the rink for the 11 a.m. workouts, which meant he was losing track of "Morningside" on CBC. On the road he read every page of the newspaper; many other players shook free the sports section as if they were dumping a loaded diaper.

Marsh read the sports as well, of course, but he had one rule: any story on contracts or money he skipped. He liked to think hockey was still a game, not a business.

DARCY LOEWEN WAS BEGINNING TO THINK HE HAD MADE THE SENATORS. He was getting regular shifts; he had been given a few shots at the power play; he now had four goals and three assists; and at the last home game a sign had gone up in the Civic Centre: DARCY LOEWEN – A PERFECT 10. But now, in Boston, while everyone else was talking about the weather warnings and the "Storm of the Century," he suddenly had other things on his mind. He'd been in his room at the Marriott Long Harbor getting ready to catch the bus for the morning skate when Mel Bridgman called and asked to meet with him.

The two-year contract the two had agreed to the previous summer was a two-way contract – Loewen was to get $210,000 if he spent the season in Ottawa, $50,000 if he played in New Haven. All two-way contracts have a clause stating that if the player dresses for a certain number of games with the NHL club, he is no longer deemed to be on a two-way deal. The contract then becomes one-way, meaning the team has to pay the player his NHL salary even if he's sent down to the minors. A one-way contract generally means the player has "arrived" in the NHL.

Loewen's one-way clause was to kick in against Boston – if he dressed. He had been hoping all year that this moment would arrive and had come to think it was automatic – that it would not even be mentioned. He would lace up his skates one night on a two-way contract and take them off three hours later on a one-way deal. It was not the money but that little phrase *one-way* that he cherished. He would gladly have played for $50,000 – hell, he would have played for the chance to take the empties back – on a one-way deal in the NHL.

But Bridgman had another idea. If Loewen would agree to renegotiate the contract, and waive the clause that would make him a one-way player as of that night, he could remain with the team and dress against Boston. If not, Bridgman would have to send him down to the minors for the rest of the season. It was Loewen's choice.

Bridgman talked as if he were doing Loewen a favor, and in his mind he was. The simple thing would have been to send him down and be done with it. Some fans would be upset and the media would whine, but that was all they ever did anyway. The simple fact was that Bridgman had signed too many players to two- and three-year contracts, and room had to be made somewhere for all the young draft choices. The franchise had no flexibility on this. If Loewen made this concession, then at least he could stay on until the end of the year. Bridgman probably felt Loewen would have trouble making next year's team; this way he could at least stay in professional hockey as a minor leaguer. Yes, he was doing the young man a favor.

Loewen asked for time to think and called home. His parents told him to refuse. He said he wanted to, but what if Bridgman called his bluff? He would be sent down and never heard from again. He was told the fans and media would never let Bridgman get away with it, but he could not believe this. Why would they care?

He called his agent, who also told him to refuse. He talked to a few of the veterans, who told him to refuse. Some said he should go to the press immediately, but he could not. He was afraid of losing what he had become – an NHLer. When Bridgman called back, Loewen agreed to waive the clause so he could play that night.

Earlier, in Quebec City, the same thing had happened to Senators forward Andrew McBain. McBain had started poorly, had been injured, and had already been to the minors, but he was extremely bright. He knew what was going on. The talk in Quebec was about what might happen if the dreadful Senators came last over-all and gained the first selection in the June 1993 draft. The Quebec journalists were convinced that the new Quebec sensation, Alexandre Daigle of the Victoriaville Tigres, would go first, and that Ottawa was cooking up a deal with the Nordiques for as many as five quality players in exchange for the hottest French-Canadian prospect since Mario Lemieux. The Senators were already beginning to trim the roster, and McBain knew he would be among the first to go.

McBain was 28 years old. He was four seasons from his last good NHL year – a 37-goal performance with the Winnipeg Jets – and had spent most of the last two seasons in the International Hockey League. He knew that if he fought Bridgman he was finished, but he fought anyway. They can't do this, he believed.

But they *were* doing it. McBain knew it was wrong. He also knew that he was playing better hockey than he had all season. Against Quebec he'd had a goal and an assist and been the Senators' star of the game. Now he was headed for the minors if he did not cooperate. He screamed at Bridgman. He called his agent. He called the NHL Players' Association. He decided, for an hour, to go public and fight it. But then he looked at his position – 28, slow, only five goals so far – and realized he had no position at all. So he too caved in.

The story of Loewen and McBain might never have got out if a relative of one of the players hadn't phoned *The Ottawa Sun*'s Chris Stevenson. The story grew in prominence as Ottawa fans began to understand what was happening: the franchise was already writing off its inaugural season and planning for the next. The players were expected only to finish out the year so the organization could get on with its plans. On a team that liked to say the one positive it had going for it was the work ethic, Mel Bridgman had just proved that hard work counted for nothing at all.

In 1986, WHILE HE WAS PLAYING FOR THE PHILADELPHIA FLYERS, AND while his wife was pregnant with Erik, Brad Marsh had one of those dreams that makes perfect sense until reality sets in. He dreamed that he was still playing, and that the baby was now old enough to go to the rink with him, and that the two of them were sitting in the dressing room. The child was four or five and was laughing and proud to be there, because he knew what his father did for a living. He played in the NHL.

Since Erik had been born, four teams had written Marsh off, one of them twice. He had been a Flyer, a Maple Leaf, a Red Wing, and a Leaf again. The Leafs had finally lost interest in him and offered him to the new Ottawa franchise for "future considerations." On a June day 14 years earlier he had been a first-round draft choice; now he was lucky to get one last chance.

Marsh had come to Ottawa on a one-year contract for $225,000. He was, as usual, the slowest player on the ice. He was losing another step in a year when the NHL, because of the incoming Europeans, had picked up a step. He was 35, yes, but in the best shape of his life. On his own he had assessed the club's depth charts, and he saw himself as the third defenseman behind Norm Maciver and Brad Shaw. He had the experience; he had the will; he could still do the job. He began to resent it when the press brought up the topic of retirement, yet he brought it up himself almost constantly when he and Patty were alone.

In many ways Marsh's dream had come true. Erik Marsh was now old enough to know where his father went when he left for work. Patrick, Erik's younger brother, also knew now. Even their third child, Victoria, was beginning to know. "The real test," Patty Marsh said, "is will he play long enough for Madelaine to know?" Madelaine was the fourth. As far as she was concerned, her father worked nights, and his job was to warm the formula and burp her when she was finished.

Patty remembers perfectly the moment when "the light went on" in her oldest son. She had been driving home to their rented home in Kanata, west of Ottawa, and Erik was sitting, as usual, in the back of the van sorting through his stack of hockey cards. He had his heroes and his Brad Marshes, one of which he had recently traded to a young Senators fan in the neighborhood for a Gretzky. He began reading the back of a "Milestone" card that had, on the front, the smiling face of his father. The milestone in this case was 1,000 games in the NHL, a feat Marsh had accomplished in Detroit.

"Geez," Erik said. "Daddy's pretty good."

"Well," Patty called back. "Didn't you think he was good?"

"Yah – but not *that* good."

By then, Marsh's fifteenth season in the NHL had become, he said, "my fantasy year." There were signs in the Civic Centre claiming BRAD IS GOD. Section 14 had adopted the big defenseman as a favorite son after they heard another fan booing him. The frenetic endorsement of that one small seating area reverberated throughout and beyond the arena. In Renfrew, up the Ottawa Valley, a few of the locals got together over coffee in the back of Ray's Flowers and started an official fan club. Barry Breen, a local insurance salesman, had set up a register in his Main Street office. Soon after Christmas there were nearly 2,000 members, including Hall-of-Famer Darryl Sittler and several European fans who had written. They had a newsletter, official meetings, official jokes ("What do you call a guy after Brad lands a bodycheck on him? – A *Marsh*mallow!"), and even

a Brad Marsh Day, when he came up to receive an honorary citizen-
ship from the mayor and to take a few circles during Sunday-after-
noon public skating.

When his fan club announced that it would be raising funds to
put in a new room at Renfrew's Victoria Hospital, Marsh put in
$1,000 of his own money to start the ball rolling. From then on,
every Sunday, Father Steve Ballard would add a small prayer for
Brad Marsh and his teammates during the offering at St. Francis
Xavier parish. For those fans who were looking for someone to
believe in at a time when sports made less and less sense, Brad Marsh
had already answered their prayers.

Marsh had always been popular. As the years passed and
fewer players went without helmets (every player who came into the
league after 1979 had to wear one – the rule was technically lifted in
1992), Marsh's big Jethro grin and galumphing skating style became
more recognizable. By 1992–93, he was one of only five helmetless
players in the league (the others being Doug Wilson of San Jose,
Craig MacTavish of Edmonton, Randy Carlyle of Winnipeg, and
Rod Langway of Washington). Because of this, and because his style
was so peculiar – he moved up the ice like a man pushing a car out
of a snowbank – Marsh had become, on the ice, one of the most recognizable faces in the game.

Marsh was perfect for Ottawa, and Ottawa perfect for Marsh.
The fans were savvy enough to want only what the coach, Bowness,
wanted: effort. The players, led by Marsh and Loewen, were giving
all they had every night. Once Marsh began playing regularly, he did
his job with such style, with such pride, with such determination and
good humor and pure joy, that he was able on his own to ease the
pain of many defeats. Playing like Wayne Gretzky was the dream of
every child; playing like Brad Marsh was the more realistic fantasy

of most of the adults in the Civic Centre. It was not just Brad Marsh slapping the goaltender's pads in encouragement, it was the fan. It was not just Brad Marsh blocking the shot from Pat LaFontaine, it was the fan. When he shot, everyone prayed it would go in – which it never did.

It became, over time, the sweetest sound of the season – a great, growing roar of delight whenever Marsh stepped onto the ice. Even his teammates began to cheer for that one goal that would make his fantasy year complete. The moment he touched the puck the cheers would swell, and keep swelling until he lost it. Everyone knew that his next goal would be his last, the one he would always remember. He came to love the sound, even if he hated its message.

On December 17, 1992, on Long Island, Marsh played in his 1,051st NHL game. It put him in first place among active players. He had started with Orr and Howe and had survived until the era of Lindros and Bure. In honor of this, NHL president Gil Stein named him to the Prince of Wales All-Star team. When they called to tell him, he wept.

He wept because, in all those years, in the three decades that had taken him from minor hockey to the Ottawa Senators, he had never won any honor entirely on his own. He had been an all-star defenseman in Junior but never a champion. He had been named the Ontario Hockey League's best defenseman but shared the award with his teammate, Ramage. He had been to the finals in the World Junior Championship in Prague, and twice to the Stanley Cup finals with the Philadelphia Flyers, but he had never won. In 1987, when the Flyers won the sixth game of the final 3–2 over Edmonton, he had flown his parents from London to Edmonton for the seventh game so that they might, finally, see their son victorious. The Flyers, however, lost 3–1. "He cried like a baby," his mother remembers.

But for an act of God, he would have played in the all-star game a decade earlier, but even then the honor would not have been his alone. His Philadelphia teammate, Mark Howe, had been selected to play, but he had been injured and the team had named Marsh as the replacement. He flew from Philadelphia to Toronto en route to Calgary, but a snowstorm struck Toronto and the airport had to be closed. He watched the game from a bar stool, he says, "but I only remember up to about the third period." Patty Marsh says, "That's Brad's career – just coming short. It's a curse."

He went off to the All-Star Game in high excitement. He flew his parents in from London and took them to all the functions even though, at times, he seemed more spectator than participant. When the practice session for the old-timers overlapped with that of the 1993 all-stars, Marsh stood by the boards chatting with the likes of Darryl Sittler and Gordie Howe. He was more comfortable with them than with Brett Hull and Pavel Bure and Adam Oates.

During the Friday evening skills competition the organizers did not know what to do with him. They could not have Brad Marsh enter for fastest skater or hardest shot. They could not pair him with Teemu Selanne or Wayne Gretzky in a goal-scoring test. They put him in the simplest of the showcases: a test of accuracy, with each player taking ten shots at targets placed in the four corners of the net. Marsh failed to hit a single target.

During the game itself, Marsh looked no more out of place than Chris Chelios or Kevin Hatcher or any other defenseman. The game was an offensive absurdity – a 22-goal shinny match – with the Wales Conference outscoring the Campbell 16–6. But it was a triumph for Marsh, who, with his team up 14–3 in the third period, took a pass on his skates near the boards and kicked the puck ahead to Mark Recchi. Recchi passed to Kevin Stevens in the corner while

Marsh broke for the net. Stevens passed to Marsh, who shot and, to his own astonishment, went down in the record books as having scored in an NHL all-star game.

YOU KNOW YOU'RE IN BIG TROUBLE WHEN MARSH SCORES ran a headline the next morning in Montreal's *Gazette*. The game itself had been a bust. Real fans lost interest; potential fans, if they had tuned in to the American broadcast and happened to be won over, wouldn't see another such game for the rest of the season. It was an NHL image disaster, and typical of a league that does not know which of several games it should be selling.

None of this mattered to Marsh. He went to the officials' room to ask for the puck that had scored the fifteenth goal for the Prince of Wales side. Someone said it would be sent to the Hockey Hall of Fame, where it might one day be on display. *Goal scored by Charles Bradley Marsh, February 6, 1993, NHL All-Star Game.*

After 15 seasons, the curse had been lifted. The roar of the crowd would last forever.

CHAPTER FOUR

THE POWERS THAT BE

West Palm Beach, Florida

THE SMELL OF OLD MONEY IS EVERYWHERE AT THE BREAKERS — A COM-bination of the slightly musty odor of the thick carpeting, the scent of the fresh-cut flowers that grace the rattan tables, the polish in the cloth of the uniformed young man buffing the brass, and the aloe vera and cocoa butter that the guests baste themselves with before heading out into the south Florida sun for the Gucci and F.A.O. Schwartz outlets on Worth Avenue.

The scent contains more than a hint of scandal. Henry Morrison Flagler, who built The Breakers, died 80 years ago after (some say) he collapsed in a women's powder room. The truth is difficult to get at — it usually is when the very rich gather — but the record does show that Flagler was the partner of John D. Rockefeller in Standard Oil and a man who, at the annual ball on Washington's birthday, liked nothing so much as to dress in drag, light a fresh cigar, and swirl about the porticos.

The Breakers opened on December 29, 1929. It was intended as a winter retreat for the privileged of New York and Chicago, as a Mediterranean-style resort that could be reached by private Pullman car. It was modeled on the Villa Medici in Rome; 75 Italian artisans were brought in to hand-paint the frescoes. The sand was white, the sea azure. The servants dined to their own orchestra. Vanderbilts and Whitneys wrote their names in the register. Isadora Duncan came. Sir Harry Oakes, Canada's gift to rich boordom, was despised here before he was murdered in the Bahamas. John Lennon took over the big beach house to the south once West Palm rid itself of Larry Flynt, publisher of *Hustler*. Robert Kennedy's son, David, died of a drug overdose in the Brazilian Court Hotel just down the way. The Kennedy family's compound – site of the 1991 dispute between William Kennedy Smith and Patricia Bowman – is just to the north.

The owners of the NHL's 24 teams had come to The Breakers for the league's annual winter meetings. High on the agenda was the question of how they might go about getting an American TV network deal. Television, the owners believed, was the fabled goose that had yet to lay a golden egg for their league. None saw the present circumstances as a blessing in disguise that had kept salaries and expectations – perhaps ticket prices as well – from spiraling out of control. Players were getting more, and wanted more, and owners expected more – especially under the new leadership of Bruce McNall.

McNall had come along at a most propitious time. Since joining the NHL Board of Governors in 1988 – the year he bought the Los Angeles Kings and then Wayne Gretzky – he had been viewed as a young, progressive thinker, and as a possible leader once he had gained an appreciation for the way things are done in hockey.

The NHL has always fought change. It had only four presidents between 1917 and 1992 and one of them, Red Dutton, had only been filling in. At 58, John Ziegler, president since 1977, was still a young man by the measure of most board members. Bill Wirtz of the Chicago Blackhawks was five years Ziegler's elder and had been board chairman three times since 1970, and continually since 1978. If the pre-McNall NHL had had a corporate mission – as most modern organizations do – it would have been the one stated by Ziegler himself: "If it ain't broke, why fix it?"

In 1992, however, hockey broke. Ziegler had been under fire in the past, especially in 1988, when he switched the league's American cable contract from ESPN to Sports Channel America. By doing that he reduced the potential audience from 60 million homes to 15 million. After his botched handling of the 1992 strike, Ziegler could hang on no longer. With Alan Eagleson no longer controlling the NHL Players' Association, the 564 players who made up that union called the bluff of the owners and went out on strike just before the playoffs. This timing was the master stroke of new NHLPA executive director Bob Goodenow, for hockey's endless playoffs are endless for one reason: it is the time when owners make so much money that those who own baseball teams now wonder why the World Series, which ends magnificently for the fans, ends so quickly for those who stand to profit most.

Players have been bred to believe that the Stanley Cup is about glory alone. Most do not even consider the monetary value of the Stanley Cup race. Before the strike the most ever paid out in prize money to the players was $3.2 million. After the strike this amount more than doubled, to $7.5 million. In 1993 it rose to $9 million. The Stanley Cup–winning team splits $1 million among 25 or so players, which works out to around $50,000 per player, or $2,000 per game for a Stanley Cup champion.

For the owners, the take is of a different magnitude. It is difficult to determine exactly what winning a Stanley Cup is worth to a team owner, for beyond the ticket and souvenir sales, beyond the parking and concessions, beyond even the television revenues, there is the intangible added value that accrues to the championship franchise. On rink gross alone, however, it's possible to take an educated guess. The Greater Pittsburgh Convention and Visitors Bureau did an economic-impact study on the Penguins during the team's successful run for its second Stanley Cup in 1992. It found that a sellout crowd of 15,500 spent $976,500 on game night, assuming expenditures of $63 per fan – $38 for a ticket, $5 for parking, $15 for souvenirs and food, and $5 for miscellaneous. Thus, the value of "going all the way" was placed at about $7.8 million if there were eight home games and roughly $13.7 million if there were 14 home games. (The Penguins won the cup after 11 home games.) This is why potential owners line up to buy sports teams, and why the NHL playoffs will never be shortened.

Ziegler's performance during the strike was his undoing. Not only did he predict outlandish losses for coming seasons, but he also stated that the financial impact of canceled playoffs would be negligible, amounting to 11 percent of the league's gate and broadcast revenues for the year – roughly $8.8 million. Anyone with a calculator could have shown that if, say, the New York Rangers had reached the Stanley Cup final, ticket sales alone would have reached $14.3 million. Ziegler had at one point claimed that making the playoffs was worth a mere $400,000 to the average team.

What little credibility Ziegler possessed evaporated during the spring of 1992. Those board members who did not want him out for allowing the strike to happen now wanted him out for the image he had projected during that strike. The owners were being ridiculed by the public for everything from pleading poverty to, at one point, threatening to finish out the Stanley Cup with minor leaguers – in effect, with scab labor. Under pressure from the rising number of progressives on the board – McNall foremost among them – Ziegler oversaw a hasty one-year settlement that saw the players make a number of small gains, including the increase in playoff prize money.

Players also maintained control over the $11 million in trading-card royalties. Recallable waivers were eliminated, the entry draft was shortened by a single round, and there were slight changes in the free-agency rules. The owners gained four extra games during the regular season, two of which would be played in neutral sites, with the owners and players to split the profits.

Though Ziegler managed a tear of appreciation during the formal announcement of the settlement, it was the end of his 15 years as president. He would oversee the expansion drafts to stock the new teams in Tampa Bay and Ottawa and then "retire" to a handsome settlement and a pension. He would be joined in retirement by Wirtz, whose iron hand had controlled the NHL board for so many years.

In many ways, Wirtz's departure was more symbolic than Ziegler's. Wirtz represented the game's link to its past, a link that for him went all the way back to the Depression, when his father, Arthur, in partnership with James Norris, owned Chicago Stadium, the Detroit Olympia, and the St. Louis Arena, and held controlling interest in New York's Madison Square Garden. With this background, he had little interest in modern marketing strategies. Marketing to a man like Wirtz meant throwing open the doors to Chicago Stadium. Critics like *Chicago Tribune* columnist Bob Verdi ridiculed this attitude – "The Hawks couldn't sell a can of beer in the desert" – but Wirtz was the one doing the laughing. At 63 he had a personal fortune estimated at $450 million, and *Worth* had just named his hockey operation the most successful sports franchise in North America. (Football's Washington Redskins came second, basketball's Phoenix Suns third.) That magazine listed these as the four reasons for the selection: "Large, passionate fan base; competitive team; new arena to open in 1994; increased concession revenue."

Worth heavily stressed the value of the fan base to any sports team – *especially* a hockey team. There is a big difference, it argued, between having the "best franchise" and having the "most valuable and profitable team." For example, as magazine rival *Financial World* explained, the New York Yankees do not make their money on astute business practices or on fan draw – the team was eleventh in major-league baseball attendance in 1992 – but rather by the sheer good fortune of residing in a rich local-broadcast market. The Yankees' luck was in signing a 12-year, $500 million local cable deal with the MSG Network. "Attendance carries more of a burden in hockey," *FW* explained, "because any ancillary revenues are minuscule compared to basketball, baseball and football." In *Worth's* opinion, Wirtz had been going in precisely the correct direction for his sport by catering to the loyal fans who show up at the door and never taking them for granted.

That was not the direction McNall had in mind when he considered the future of hockey, nor was it the desired direction of those who were caught in the dreams he spun. When Wirtz announced he was stepping down as chairman, McNall was widely viewed as the only choice to succeed him. As far as anyone in hockey was concerned, he was the Messiah. McNall tapped into the envy the hockey owners had for other sports owners, especially basketball owners. The 13 million NHL fans who came out each year – those loyal fans who guaranteed a warm body in nine out of every ten seats – were a given. The focus for some time now had been on the next dollar. In an arena that might hold 17,000, the seats were occupied, the parking lots full, the concessions busy, the souvenirs moving, and the corporate boxes booked. No longer was there much anyone could do for the fan coming in the front door. The time had come to look elsewhere for the next buck, and if anyone could show them where it was hidden, it was McNall, who had a vision for the league that entranced those who listened to him.

McNall was the direct opposite of Wirtz and Ziegler. "It is true that our last priority is image building," Ziegler had told *Sport Inc.* in 1988. The old Rodney Dangerfield line – "I went to a boxing match and a hockey game broke out" – said all that needed saying for most Americans, and for American television. McNall knew that hockey's image was, at best, a joke. In 1992 he wanted to move image building from last priority to first.

MCNALL'S RISE HAD BEEN UNLIKE ANY OTHER OWNER'S. HE HAD NOT come from family money. He was a collector – first of coins, only lately of athletes – and he had rather different notions about what creates value. His mother remembered how her son, even as a five-year-old, used to play Monopoly: "His basic philosophy even then was that you had to spend money to make money. He always went for the high-priced stuff like Boardwalk and Park Place. And he would always beat us."

McNall was born in 1950 in Venice, California, a comfortable beach community near Los Angeles. His father Earl taught bio-chemistry at the University of Southern California, his mother Shirley was a lab technician. Bruce was gifted. He entered kinder-garten a year early. Unathletic and heavy, he was a loner. When he was 13, his parents took him to Europe, where he became obsessed with history. When he returned to California he began studying the past and collecting it through old coins and stamps. When his par-ents would not front him $3,000 to buy a coin collection, he talked his grandmother into giving him the loan, made the purchase, and then turned the investment into a $10,000 profit.

At this point the biography grows fuzzy. He told *U.S. News & World Report* that he was making $1,000 a week in the coin markets when he was 12, a year before the trip to Europe. He did, apparently, drive to high school when he was 16 in a Jaguar XKE, and own a Rolls-Royce while attending UCLA. He claims to have been making $300,000 a year on the side while he was working on a doctoral thesis on Roman history (never completed).

There is no doubt, however, that in 1974 he made a permanent mark on the coin world. Having determined that the Athenian Decadrachma, circa 400 B.C., was the most valuable coin in the world, he went after it at an auction, outbidding both Valery Giscard d'Estaing (then France's Minister of Finance) and Greek shipping magnate Aristotle Onassis. At the age of 24 he had set a world record by paying $420,000 for a single coin.

Again the record grows fuzzy. According to some accounts he sold that coin for $1 million. In another version he says he turned it over a week later for a profit of $50,000. Whatever the case, he did drop out of university and begin his own business, Numismatic Fine Arts International Inc., which grew into the largest coin trader in the world. He claimed that his customers included Howard Hughes and J. Paul Getty, whom he referred to as his "mentor." *Forbes* later determined that he had no dealings whatsoever with either Getty or Hughes, but McNall was unapologetic. "I am a salesman," he has explained. "So from time to time, maybe I do get carried away."

Out of his early interest in coins he built an empire that eventually included racehorses and Hollywood movies. He had pieces of *Mr. Mom, Blame It on Rio, The Fabulous Baker Boys,* and *Weekend at Bernie's*. He and his wife Jane, a classics professor at USC, entertain in a $10 million mansion. He also has homes in Palm Springs, Kauai, New York City, and Deer Valley, Utah. His private plane is a Jetstar 731. He drives a Rolls-Royce Corniche and an Aston Martin. His personal worth is sometimes listed at $100 million, sometimes

$200 million. Everything he has touched has turned to gold.

Or has it? The hockey world is a bubble, and those caught up in it have little interest in what goes on outside. In the NHL the measure of McNall was based entirely on what happened to the Los Angeles Kings once Wayne Gretzky arrived. The other owners had not noticed McNall much when he purchased 25 percent of the Kings from Jerry Buss. They did not notice him much in 1987, when he increased his portion to 49 percent, and they barely noticed him in 1988, when he bought out Buss and became the sole owner of a hockey team that never went anywhere in the playoffs and played to fewer than 12,000 fans a night in a 16,005-seat facility. But they paid attention on August 9, 1988, the day Wayne Gretzky broke down in tears in Edmonton and, a handful of hours later, broke into a wide smile in Los Angeles.

The idea of buying Gretzky originated with Buss, whose Monopoly prowess outshines even McNall's – Buss and a friend used to play without a board, money, or plastic hotels, to sharpen their memories for real estate. It was Buss – who also owned the NBA Lakers and the Great Western Forum – who applied the Bill Veeck rule of baseball to hockey. Players, Veeck had once argued, are an asset to a sports team just as machinery is an asset to a manufacturer, and as such had a fixed useful life. Buss had spent two years trying to convince Peter Pocklington that he should trade Gretzky before he wore out and was worth little or nothing. McNall merely pressed Buss's argument until Pocklington, in desperate need of cash to support other holdings, buckled.

That other players were involved in the deal is irrelevant; Gretzky had been bought for $15 million cash, then given an eight-year contract at $2 million a year. The grand total was $31 million. In other words, for a single player heading into the far side of his career, this chubby coin dealer was willing to pay more than most owners thought their teams were worth. Was McNall insane?

They soon decided he was a genius. Gretzky had the face and talent and demeanor to change hockey overnight in California. The man Buss had purchased the Kings from, Jack Kent Cooke, once said, "There are 200,000 Canadians in Southern California, and I now know why they moved here – they hate hockey." Gretzky's appeal reached far beyond the expatriate community. Jack Nicholson, a regular at Lakers basketball games, showed up to see him; Tom Hanks became a regular, as did comedian John Candy; and sprinkled throughout the crowd on any given night might be actors Goldie Hawn, Robert Wagner, and Jim Belushi, tennis star John McEnroe, and golfer Craig Stadler. The Forum began to sell out.

But Gretzky did much more than merely sell out the Forum. McNall was now able to land a better television deal so that he could go after the fans who did not come out. (He had, of course, fully anticipated this.) Through increased merchandising he went after tomorrow's fans. In Gretzky's first year the franchise took in an additional $5 million at the gate, $1 million in increased advertising revenue, another $1 million in television rights, $500,000 in increased jersey sales alone. Gretzky's salary was covered, McNall was able to pay off the $4 million loss from the previous year, and there was more than enough to handle the principal and interest payments on the $15 million that had gone into Pocklington's coffers. He gave Gretzky a hefty raise and declared him "my *de facto* partner" in the Kings. "Wayne does so many things to bring in money," McNall bragged. "I have him say two words and sign a stick to some guy and it comes back as a half-million worth of advertising."

Like Zelig, McNall began surfacing in every photograph of Gretzky and his glamorous wife, actress Janet Jones. McNall drew closer to this game he had never played – he even briefly took over the "coaching" of the Kings during an exhibition match – and Gretzky began, gradually, to become the *de jure* partner of McNall.

Hockey's odd couple even began collecting together, purchasing a 1909 Honus Wagner baseball card for $451,000 – another world record. "You can never go wrong buying the best," McNall said. With John Candy, they bought the troubled Toronto Argonauts of the Canadian Football League for $5 million, with McNall taking 60 percent and the other two 20 percent each.

McNall set out to do for the Argos what he and Gretzky had done for the Kings. He went after the hottest football prospect in the United States, Raghib "Rocket" Ismail, and outbid NFL teams for his services by offering an unbelievable $18.2 million over four years. With built-in bonuses – $8 million for drawing fans and providing promotional services – the deal worked out, in Canadian dollars, to $30.1 million, of which $20.7 million was guaranteed. It ridiculed the CFL's salary cap of $3 million a team, which McNall had sidestepped by making the deal with Ismail a personal-services contract.

Within three days the Argonauts had sold 1,300 season's tickets. Janet Jones, who now had her own workout video on the market, was going to oversee the tryouts of the team's cheerleaders. Gretzky stated that the Ismail deal gave the league "credibility" and held the key to a television arrangement that would make the team and the league profitable. McNall's connections with Prime Time, a regional cable network that carried Kings games, might help them land an American television outlet. They were speaking already of expansion – not to Halifax or back to Montreal, but into the United States.

The Argos won the Grey Cup in the Rocket's first year but collapsed in his second. He was a promotional disaster, terrible with the media and ignorant with the fans. During one game he kicked another player in the head. Gate increases did not come close to covering his $4-million annual salary. The imagined television millions never arrived. Losses for Gretzky, Candy, and McNall were running at $3.5 million a year. The investment was a disaster, and McNall began working furiously to dump the contract and get Ismail into the NFL. Gretzky had never lost money as a businessman, and the experience seemed to sour his relationship with McNall.

The Argonauts were not McNall's only financial worry. The coin market was going flat. Between 1970 and 1990 – essentially the 20 years of McNall's greatest profits – rare coins had been appreciating at a 16.6 percent annually compounded rate. It seemed that coins were as safe a gamble as investors could take. McNall himself had avoided setbacks, but those he dealt with sometimes had other tales to tell. In 1979 he sold a friend's coin collection to Texas millionaire Bunker Hunt for $16 million. The Hunt brothers would eventually claim to have invested $50 million in coins and antiques purchased from McNall. After the brothers were forced into bankruptcy by their scheme in 1980 to take over the silver market, the items they bought from McNall brought only $34 million at a Sotheby's auction. Bunker Hunt was furious, claiming that McNall had told him coins were an absolutely safe investment which would "always beat inflation." Another high-profile investor, music magnate David Geffen, also claimed that he lost substantially on coins he obtained through McNall.

Forbes magazine looked at McNall's dealings and concluded that he was worth "only a fraction" of the hundreds of millions he claimed. Between 1986 and 1990, McNall had used Merrill Lynch to raise $50 million for three limited partnerships aimed at investing heavily in the coin market. In the first partnership, called Athena, investors bought units of $5,000 and McNall was able to raise $7.25

million. In 1990 Athena began losing money; it was being liquidated, on schedule, in 1993. The second endeavor, Athena II, was started in 1989 with the purpose of raising $25 million. In 1993 it was in the process of being wound up as well. McNall's third partnership, NFA World Coin Fund, was to raise $70 million but managed only $16 million by the time *Forbes* investigated. It was also losing money.

The *Los Angeles Business Journal* has speculated that McNall may have been in a conflict of interest through this third partnership. To push NFA he bought a majority stake (51 percent) in Superior Stamp & Coin Inc. (now known as Superior Galleries), one of the world's top coin auctioneers and dealers. Since McNall was also managing general partner of the limited partnerships, the *Journal* suggested, it was impossible to say which coins he would buy for himself and which for the partners. In McNall's filing to the Securities and Exchange Commission, he admitted that the size of the partnership could considerably influence prices. "In other words," the *Journal* explained, "the McNall partnership, as an elephant in the rare coin markets, could end up buying high now in over-heated coin markets and selling low in 1997."

During the 1992–93 hockey season, speculation began that McNall might be in financial difficulty. The coin market was flat; his partnerships were in trouble. Gretzky had suffered a back injury that had the potential to end his career. Crowds were thinning again at the Great Western Forum. The Argos were miserable.

But for those looking for chinks in the McNall armor, the most telling clue was item No. 17727 in the Upper Deck Authenticated catalog, which goes out to wealthy collectors. The item was an "autographed" airplane, the sumptuous Boeing 727 that McNall had purchased to ferry his beloved Kings about North America. The plane had been mothballed – taken away from the Kings, ostensibly until their play improved – and the team was again flying regular routes. The 727, complete with massage facilities, VCRs, and CD players, was listed for $5 million and, the ad claimed, had been signed by Gretzky and the other Kings. The market for luxury jet-liners was at the time nonexistent, and McNall's hopes of selling the plane in the middle of a brutal recession were negligible. When word got out that the jet was in the catalog, he dismissed it as a lark, a wealthy collectors' inside joke. All the same, he was meeting with other sports moguls in the hopes of at least sharing the cost of the expensive aircraft.

One of these meetings was with Wayne Huizenga, a wealthy video-chain owner who had recently been awarded a major-league baseball franchise for Miami. Although no deal was struck for the jet, their conversation would take on huge importance for McNall.

THE ELECTION OF BRUCE MCNALL TO THE CHAIRMANSHIP OF THE NHL Board of Governors in 1992 marked a profound shift in philosophy for the league. With the ouster of Ziegler and Wirtz, professional hockey dropped its conservative attitude and embraced McNall's stated assumption that sports are "in their infancy of exploitation." The other owners now had a dreamspinner in charge, one who understood, as Wirtz did not, that there is much more to the hockey business than filling seats.

With McNall at the helm, the children of America would swap their Chicago Bulls caps and LA Raiders jackets for Pittsburgh Penguins caps and St. Louis Blues jackets. The league would move into the lucrative world of sports gear, which was bringing in $30 billion a year in retail business – 20 times the gate receipts of the four big sports combined. Network television would be possible. Pay-per-view, which McNall had been promoting for years as a $100 million cash cow during the playoffs, would make them all richer still. In other sports some people were saying that PPV was going to triple television revenues for teams, and hockey planned to get its piece of the action. When Chicago White Sox co-owner Eddie Einhorn called free television broadcasts of baseball games "a stupid giveaway to spoiled fans," most hockey owners would have applauded. One of them, Peter Pocklington, was already on record as saying hockey could do better if it did not put the NHL playoffs on public television.

If the NBA could broadcast its playoffs in more than 100 countries, the NHL would go one better. The game would not only be seen around the world – it would be played around the world. McNall would expand the league into Great Britain, Sweden, Finland, Germany, and perhaps even Moscow. Money would flow from new television opportunities, pay-per-view, new licensing deals, and, of course, from expansion itself – there would be multimillion-dollar pots to split every time the league expanded. All knew that new revenue flows were the secret; all understood what Phil Esposito meant when Tampa Bay was brought in for $50 million and he dared to ask out loud, "How much more money can you charge somebody coming into a building?"

McNall's first public performance as the new chair came at the winter meetings in West Palm Beach. Naturally, he wanted to make a splash. It was the 75th anniversary of the league's formation, and his goal was to launch hockey in its new and necessary direction. It was public knowledge that the league would name its first commissioner at the meetings, and that this commissioner would come from the NBA to do for hockey what David Stern had done for basketball. But McNall had even greater plans for his moment in the Florida sun.

That the main interest of NHL owners was cash had been established two years earlier, when they accepted the two shakiest franchise bids solely because both Tampa Bay and Ottawa were willing to pay the full $50 million fee, no questions asked. With North America in a full-blown recession, some of the owners were hurting in their other endeavors, and a few – for example, in Winnipeg, Hartford, and (already) Tampa Bay – were hurting in their hockey operations. Ticket prices were at the upper limit, and player salaries were rising. To complicate matters dramatically, Mr. Justice George Adams of the Ontario Court General Division had ruled six weeks earlier that the NHL owners had illegally taken nearly $30 million from the players' pension fund during the 1980s. With inflation and legal fees, the owners had just been dinged for the equivalent of one $50 million expansion fee. They were about to launch an expensive legal appeal. They needed cash.

The $100 million from Ottawa and Tampa Bay had come in handy in 1991; another $100 million would be even more welcome now. Expansion, however, takes time. John Ziegler had announced in 1989 that the league would consider applications for the 1992–93 season: buck to puck, that was more than three years. But McNall and his new executive committee – made up of Pocklington, Canadiens president Ronald Corey, Red Wings owner Mike Ilitch, Flyers owner Ed Snider, and McNall himself – had other ideas. Why not avoid the messy, wasteful process whereby groups applied for franchises and battled it out for two years before expansion payments could even begin? Wouldn't it be much simpler to select potential franchise owners, "invite" them to apply, grant them franchises, and then announce the *fait accompli*? There was more control that way, and less risk of offending potential fans and perhaps even future franchises in cities like Hamilton and St. Petersburg (both still steaming over their treatment in 1991). As North Stars owner Norm Green, one of the new progressive owners backing McNall, put it,

"We were very democratic the last time. I want us to be undemocratic this time."

AT THE BREAKERS, MOST NHL GOVERNORS HAD LITTLE INKLING OF what was coming. The press was called to the Starlight Room, which two years earlier had been headquarters for the Ottawa bid. McNall, in a white open-neck shirt, and interim NHL president Gil Stein, in a light suit, took their seats on a raised dais. "There aren't too many words that can describe the pleasure," Stein said. He then announced that the NHL had just awarded two new franchises – one to Orange County in California, which would be owned by the Walt Disney Company, the other to south Florida, which would be owned by Wayne Huizenga, whose name Stein still hadn't mastered – "I hope I'm pronouncing that right." The franchise fee would be $50 million, and the new teams would start up in 1993–94 or 1994–95. "It's a great day for hockey," McNall said. "It's a great day for hockey fans." It was also, as it turned out, a great day for Bruce McNall.

A door opened and in bounced a tall man wearing a "Coach Goofy" baseball cap and a green, purple, and yellow hockey sweater with "The Mighty Ducks" on the front. He was followed by a bald and much shorter man in a dark blue suit. Behind them, handlers carried a huge stuffed Mickey Mouse and Minnie Mouse. Mickey was hoisted onto the table, spilling McNall's glass of water onto his pants. All eyes were on the man in the cap, the one with a simian brow and nearly translucent blue eyes. McNall was shaking his hand and jiggling like Santa handing out the Christmas bounty. And why not? The two men who had just entered were about to put $3.1 million in each owner's pocket – and considerably more in McNall's.

"Our company has been involved with hockey through Goofy and cartoons," said Michael Eisner, the chairman and chief executive officer of Disney, who had cashed in stock options worth $197.5 million only two weeks earlier. "We made a movie called *The Mighty Ducks*. It did $50 million box office. That was our market research."

In fact, the lead-up to the Anaheim franchise was this: Eisner's corporation had been anxious to build the DisneySea theme park in Long Beach, California, to complement its Disneyland and Disney-World attractions. The previous March, the project had been scuttled. Disney had then turned its attention back to Anaheim, where the original Disneyland was built in 1955. Disney Co. was now planning a $3 billion rebuilding and expansion program for Disneyland that would involve a new amphitheatre, three new luxury hotels, and a World's Fair theme park called Westcot Center. There would be $1 billion earmarked for public works projects. But the city of Anaheim did not, as expected, get down on its knees in gratitude. Eisner, it was said, had threatened to abandon the project, so put off was he by the regulatory complexities and California's chilly 1990s business climate.

"The hockey team is partly a political ploy to convince Anaheim officials of [Disney's] commitment to the city," the *New York Times* quoted one financial analyst. Another told the *Times*, "Is Disney starting this hockey team with the idea of winning a Stanley Cup? I seriously doubt it. There is much more at stake here." Anaheim, one Disney official said, would become "a 'destination resort,' and the hockey team would fall under the vacation tree."

Eisner was anxious for a successful megaproject. Euro Disney had opened near Paris and was heading for disaster. (In March 1993 Disney would confirm six-month losses from that park of $201 million.) Meanwhile, Anaheim was building a $103 million, 19,200-seat arena even though the city had no team to play in it. The natural choice was a basketball team, but buying an NBA team and moving it to Anaheim would cost more than $100 million as well as indemnification fees to both the Lakers and the Clippers. So a hockey team in Anaheim could serve Disney's purposes by making that city instantly grateful. Westcot Center would be far more likely to meet with civic approval.

And what could it do for Bruce McNall? Several things. Not only would he be bringing in welcome cash, he would also be bringing in the Disney magic – in effect, he would be acquiring for hockey the entertainment industry's seal of approval. And he would be doing it less than three months after the launch of the Tampa Bay Lightning, with Esposito's mysterious backers, and the Ottawa Senators, who had all but collapsed meeting their payments. Disney was worldwide presence, marketing genius, television certainty. The contrast would be delicious.

Eisner and McNall were old friends, even though Eisner was a lifelong Democrat and McNall a lifelong Republican. They traveled in the same wealthy circles – Eisner's bonus on his 1988 salary alone had been $40 million – and had long known each other through the entertainment business.

Eisner had come to Disney from NBC, where he was instrumental in the development of such shows as "Happy Days" and "Gummi Bears." Despite a privileged childhood in an upper-class New York City apartment, he was interested in hockey. His two boys, Eric and Anders, had fallen under the spell of Wayne Gretzky and played in the Junior Kings organization. Gretzky had even been pegged to participate in Disney's MVP advertising campaign – thought up by Eisner's wife, Jane – that had star athletes turning from their championship celebrations and telling the world, "I'm going to Disneyland!" In the fall of 1989, Disney offered to pay Gretzky $100,000 for shouting this toward a camera the moment he scored the point that would overtake Gordie Howe's all-time NHL scoring record. Gretzky said he would, if the point came in overtime and ended the game. It did not come in overtime and the commercial was never made, but Eisner's company gave the hockey star a parade anyway and made him an honorary citizen of Disneyland.

McNall planted the idea of a hockey club in Eisner's mind. Disney at the time was cash-rich. A hockey team would still have to fit its corporate targets, which were 20 percent growth and 20 percent return. Not long before, John Ziegler had projected $102 million in losses for the NHL in the year that Disney was now preparing to launch a team. Clearly, Eisner didn't believe him any more than anyone else did. "We wouldn't have made this investment," he said, "unless we believed it had [the required financial return]."

As the owner of the nearby Kings, McNall announced his full support for a hockey team in Anaheim. But there was one wrinkle: Minnesota owner Norm Green had been investigating the new rink in Anaheim and was talking about moving his North Stars to California. Green, a Calgary millionaire, had taken over the North Stars from the Gund brothers in 1991. He had hoped to develop the land around the Met Center, where the North Stars played, but those plans had never worked out. The team was struggling, and although attendance was up, Green was bitter over his leasing arrangement with the city and the lack of corporate support. Besides, he was 58 and beginning to think of retirement. His second home was in Palm Springs, California. Anaheim made perfect sense to him.

In McNall's mind, however, Anaheim made much better sense to Disney. Quietly, Disney began making inquiries about the new rink in Anaheim. Green says he was never told about this, though he gradually grew aware of another force lurking "in the shadows." He was told that the NHL had other plans for Anaheim and that he should consider another site. A number of cities – Anaheim and Seattle among them – were said to be "off limits" to established teams considering a move; other cities – Dallas and Hamilton among them – were declared "open." Green was granted permission to move to one of these open sites. He would not be required to pay a penalty, as the Gunds had when they left Minnesota.

It was in November, when the wooing of Eisner was at its most intense, that McNall had gone to Van Nuys airport to meet with Wayne Huizenga about the $5 million Boeing 727. Apart from the pale-blue eyes, Huizenga was the opposite of Eisner. Bald, conservative, and quiet, the 55-year-old Huizenga had started out with three garbage trucks and a collection contract for Pompano, Florida, and was now worth $600 million. He had built his first empire out of waste management and his second out of video sales and rentals, buying 35 percent of Blockbuster Entertainment in 1984. For someone who had been forbidden to watch movies as a child – he was raised in the strict Christian Reformed Church – Huizenga was as prescient as Disney when it came to family entertainment. Under his direction, Blockbuster grew to 3,000 stores. Gradually, he sold off his shares and spent millions on a new passion: sports. By the time he met with McNall, he owned 15 percent of the Miami Dolphins of the NFL; he owned half of Joe Robbie Stadium in Miami, where the Dolphins play; and he had just committed $130 million in franchise fees and start-up costs for the Miami-based Florida Marlins, a new National League baseball team.

McNall found the low-key Huizenga hungry for more; it was he, not McNall, who brought up the subject of an NHL franchise. Again, Huizenga's reasoning ran counter to Ziegler's pronouncements that the NHL's straits were growing dire. "It wasn't my lifelong dream to own sports teams," he would explain later. "This is just a business decision for me. We're in this to make money."

So, of course, was McNall. He informed Gil Stein of the

unexpected development. Stein met with Huizenga and convinced him to write a letter of interest to the NHL board. On November 6, the date of a crucial meeting between Eisner and McNall, Stein flew to California to join the discussions. McNall wanted this expansion as a mark of his leadership; Stein wanted it as a mark of his interim presidency and as a boost to his campaign to become permanent president.

Eisner told them he would not pay more than the $50 million entry fee. Nor would he pay a surcharge for territorial invasion, as the New York Islanders and the New Jersey Devils once had to, and as Hamilton would have had to. McNall and Stein accepted this condition. "That was the area he was tough on," Stein said later. "He wasn't going to pay more than the $50 million. He knew the value of the Disney name to us."

Stein and McNall knew that the NHL could not let Eisner come in for less than the going rate of $50 million. By permitting Eisner to pay, say, $35 million to enter and $15 million to compensate McNall, the league would in effect be setting the expansion fee at $35 million; this would devalue all franchises and reduce what the league would be able to charge Huizenga. The other owners would be furious rather than grateful.

Even so, McNall felt that he had to get an indemnification payment from Disney. No matter that the new franchise would be approximately 30 miles from McNall's franchise, on the other side of greater Los Angeles, which is an urban sprawl with a population half the size of Canada's – it was still within the distance defined by the NHL as Kings territory. No matter that only 17 percent of Kings fans came from the Anaheim area, and that another team would probably benefit the Kings by raising the profile of NHL hockey – McNall was going to be as tough as Eisner.

Together, the three came up with a solution. Disney would

pay an "expansion" fee of $50 million, all right, but half would be passed back to McNall as an indemnification fee. For the first time, the NHL rather than the invader would foot the cost of invasion – to the enormous benefit of the NHL chairman, Bruce McNall.

Since no minutes were kept, it is impossible to say precisely how this scheme was sold to the Board of Governors. According to one source, it was presented by Stein and McNall as a done deal – the league would be wise to accept the conditions as stated or risk a walkout by Disney. It is also clear that not all owners were aware of NHL precedent. Six months later, Norm Green would state that "invasion" fees had always been paid out of league funds. He knew nothing about the $6 million the Islanders and the $11 million the Devils had paid other teams and seemed genuinely surprised to learn that the Disney–McNall arrangement was unprecedented. John McMullen of the Devils saw the difference, however, and he thought the league should be offering his team a full refund of the $11 million he had paid in 1982 to the Rangers, Islanders, and Flyers.

That McNall was going to pocket $25 million out of this deal seemed certain to become an issue. The negotiations had taken place entirely behind closed doors, with no list of candidates, no bidding, no interviewing, no investigating, no contemplation time – all of this in direct contrast to all previous expansions. "This is a completely different process than the last expansion," Stein would helpfully explain. "Bruce and I reached out on a selective basis." Why were no other sites even considered? "We've just gone through a recent expansion," said McNall. "We don't need to reinvent the wheel."

On Monday, December 7, Wayne Huizenga submitted his application, which was basically a blank page, with all details to be ironed out later. When he'd applied for a baseball franchise, he had spent $500,000 on the presentation alone, for a professional video brochure, leather-bound fact books, and gifts of Tiffany paper-weights to the other owners, who would later decide in his favor.

On Tuesday, December 8, Disney sent its application, though it didn't even have a lease arrangement with the new Anaheim arena. Both "applicants" paid a token $100,000 application fee.

On Wednesday, December 9, the expansion committee – technically the Market Development Committee – met in the Sandrift Room of The Breakers and approved the two new entries. Word quickly leaked out to other owners, and in some quarters panic set in. Phil Esposito had considered Florida his territory; now he was going to have to share it with a team that was well outside the 50-mile indemnification ring. He would have direct competition but no compensation.

The Ottawa Senators were also concerned. They were now firmly in last place and were beginning to think about the advantages inherent in coming dead last: first pick in what everyone was saying would be the best draft year since Mario Lemieux had come along. Alexandre Daigle was emerging in Victoriaville as a franchise NHL player. For the Senators, whose first season on the ice was already a disaster, Daigle would be a chance to start over and do things right. Now, with the prospect of two new teams starting up as early as next season, that strategy was in jeopardy. McNall busied himself making assurances. The Senators came away from that evening's conversation believing they had been guaranteed that, no matter what, they would not lose their place in line at the 1993 draft.

McNall also called Eisner and Huizenga, telling them to get to West Palm Beach as quickly as possible. Eisner was in New York on business but was able to change his plans. Huizenga, however, was in shock: only the day before, Carl Barger, his Blockbuster partner and Marlins team president, had died suddenly of a ruptured abdominal aorta. Huizenga was at home in Fort Lauderdale and drove up alone to the press conference at West Palm Beach. He seemed out of place at the gathering, uncomfortable with the stuffed dolls and "Goofy" caps.

The press conference caught the media off guard, so sudden and unexpected were the entries of Disney and Blockbuster. When the question of violence and Disney's vaunted family values came up, Eisner dismissed it lightly: "I can show you a couple of cartoons where Goofy plays hockey pretty aggressively." Eventually someone thought to ask the obvious: would Disney be paying any sort of invasion fee to the Kings?

Bruce McNall swallowed once and took the question. His voice softened to a whisper. We have agreed, he said, to split the franchise fee. Half will go to the NHL, half to the Kings. Evidently no one remembered that, only weeks earlier, Norm Green had been talking about moving to Anaheim.

"This is huge," McNall later told the *Los Angeles Times*. "The magnitude – I don't think most people in sports realize how big this is. Even me, I'm not sure I understand. Disney and Blockbuster have made a commitment to hockey. You have two of the greatest companies in American history involved in hockey. We have their clout, their marketing abilities and their creativity. It's huge."

The other owners were ecstatic about sharing an unanticipated $75 million – even if it was $25 million short of what they thought two new franchises ought to bring. They also were enthralled with the idea of tying in with Disney – with what Eisner would later call "the halo effect" of credibility. "I really think," McNall said, "the value of all of our franchises has increased because of this." And because of that, no owners were going to raise any ethical questions relating to this highly unusual expansion procedure. They were all too busy thinking about the $3.1 million that McNall had just placed in each of their pockets for doing nothing more than coming to West Palm Beach and agreeing to let in two new club members, one of them the Walt Disney Company.

Because of Disney, the network television and pay-per-view fantasies were suddenly within grasp. Disney owned television station KCAL in California, which broadcasts the Lakers games. The Disney Channel was already going into millions of American homes by cable. Disney might even reinvent hockey, just as it has reinvented everything from Pinocchio to King Arthur. "This is, after all, Southern California, where remaking images is a way of life," said the *Los Angeles Times*. "Who better than The Walt Disney Co. to present a game that, in its natural habitat in places like Saskatchewan, is played in a deep freeze?"

On top of that, the owners now had their longed-for "footprint" in the American Sunbelt. No longer could the major American networks dismiss hockey as a "regional" game of marginal interest. Now there were five teams in California and Florida, with Norm Green talking about moving his Minnesota franchise to Dallas and Peter Pocklington dropping hints about leaving Edmonton, perhaps for Phoenix. Americans now owned 18 of the 26 NHL teams.

"Hey Canada," Al Morganti wrote in *The Hockey News*, "this is going to hurt, but you might as well admit the obvious: you've lost control of your game ... The fact of the matter is the sport has gotten too big for you. Small markets, thin wallets and lack of vision don't cut it anymore. The new order is marketing, marketing, marketing – and it doesn't make much sense to sell the game in the mini-markets north of the border ... The rules of hockey expansion have become like the three rules of real estate: Location, Location, Location. And Canada just is the wrong location."

As for the $25 million that McNall, chairman of the board, had negotiated for McNall, owner of the Kings, it was quickly yesterday's news. There was new business to move on to, including the matter of Gil Stein's future. Stein had hoped his efforts on the expansion would win over enough owners to earn him the prized job of commissioner. It didn't happen. Bill Wirtz and his allies resented Stein for sweeping the NHL office clean of the old-guard staff, and they were offended by his open courtship of McNall's favor. They wanted Stein out the league, not just the job. Stein read the wind and quickly withdrew in favor of the candidate of choice, Gary Bettman. "Gil decided he would remove himself as a candidate in a show of unity," said McNall. "I'll never forget it."

Neither would Stein. After six months as acting president, he would receive a five-year consulting contract at $500,000 a year and a $250,000 pension for life.

GARY BETTMAN WAS THE ANTITHESIS OF STEIN, 40 TO STEIN'S 64, SMALL and energetic beside the rumbling grandfather Stein. Tightly wound but determined to be casual, Bettman could be described as hyper-relaxed. He had himself wired for sound and hooked to a remote loudspeaker for his first meeting with the press. At least the effort was there, and after 15 years of the robotic Ziegler, a talking human being was a relief.

Bettman – "Gary, please" – had just spent 12 years with the NBA, where he had risen to third in command. He'd been a devoted hockey fan while attending Cornell University in upstate New York. "I have a reputation in the NBA," he told those assembled, "for devoting myself 190 percent."

One of Bettman's early priorities was, as it turned out, to distance himself from whatever had taken place behind closed doors the day before he was named commissioner. Every time he was asked about the assurances given to any owner regarding team movements, his stock answer was that it had taken place before his appointment so he could not be held responsible. He would sound that refrain again and again.

To get Disney and Huizenga operational as quickly as possible, the Board of Governors had to take quick action. No one disputed the view put forward in *The Hockey News*: "One thing is certain, the NHL can't afford to have an Ottawa Senators situation —" read: a hopelessly dismal team "— in Orange County or South Florida." Stein had further complicated matters by declaring that the new teams must be competitive immediately. "It's no secret," he said, "that one of the reasons for this expansion into major U.S. areas is to help hockey grow to the point where it will be attractive to the networks."

South Florida and Anaheim, it seemed, could reasonably expect different treatment than had been offered Tampa Bay and Ottawa. The longer matters went on without a statement from either McNall or Stein – Bettman would not officially come aboard until February 1 – that Ottawa would retain its draft position, the more Ottawa and other lowly teams began to panic. "Why is their market any more important than our market?" Rick Bowness asked one afternoon at the end of practice. "Our market is just as important as any market in the league. We're a team in the nation's capital. Just because we're in a Canadian city they're taking us for granted because we have all our tickets sold."

McNall's Market Development Committee proposed dramatic changes to the usual method of expansion. The committee decided, essentially, to scrap the past and redesign the league completely for the immediate future. The Disney and Huizenga organizations were both aware of the critical importance of drafting first in this high-quality year. If they went first and second, however, something would have to be done to compensate Ottawa and the others. One idea was to have the three newest teams – Ottawa, Tampa Bay, and San Jose – draft ahead of the two new franchises if the three did indeed finish at the bottom of the standings, then have Anaheim and South Florida flip for the fourth pick. Also discussed was a redesigned expansion draft that would permit the new franchises to pluck quality players from other teams, rather than just the dregs, which is what Ottawa and Tampa Bay had been offered. Perhaps other teams would not be allowed to protect more than one goaltender or any of their second-year players.

When it came time to decide, self-interest overwhelmed fairness. In particular, the idea of being able to protect only one goaltender irked some of the owners. Wirtz wrote to Stein on December 24, claiming that the expansion committee had no authority to make such changes in the draft. He had been led to believe there would be only "technical changes," not sweeping ones. He included a list of nine owners and executives who, he claimed, backed him: Marcel Aubut (Quebec), John McMullen (New Jersey), David LeFevre (Tampa Bay), Art Savage (San Jose), Peter Pocklington (Edmonton), Steve Stavro (Toronto), Mike Shanahan (St. Louis), Abe Pollin (Washington), and Barry Shenkarow (Winnipeg). Wirtz was furious that the issue had not been settled by the board as a whole.

Stein tried to mollify Wirtz in a letter in reply, but Wirtz was not buying. He wrote to Stein:

> Your letter of last night reminded me of a scene from *Cat on a Hot Tin Roof*. When Burl Ives, playing "Big Daddy," said "there's a lot of mendacity in this room," one of the children asked "what's mendacity?" Big Mama said, "that's Big Daddy's word for bullshit." The League's position regarding

the Committee's authority has a lot of mendacity floating around it ... Merry Christmas.

FIVE DAYS LATER THE SAN JOSE SHARKS WEIGHED IN WITH THEIR OWN confidential letter to the board. If Disney and Blockbuster were going to get preferential treatment, Sharks president Al Savage argued, then the "onerous" conditions under which the Sharks had been created two years earlier must be "compensated for." Why, he wanted to know, had the Gund brothers been forced to pay a penalty of $19 million for moving to San Jose when, at West Palm Beach, Norm Green had been granted permission to move "without cost so long as he does not move to the cities where the League desires to expand or to other cities where there might be a conflict with other franchises"? Savage called the treatment "extremely unfair" and demanded compensation.

A day later, Boston Bruins manager Harry Sinden, tongue firmly in cheek, faxed the governors to demand compensation for a wrong he felt was committed in 1967 when the Bruins lost Bernie Parent in the expansion draft. Parent helped the Flyers win two Stanley Cups and earned a place in the Hall of Fame. "It is our estimate," Sinden wrote, "that this treatment of our club in 1967 has cost us $25,100,964." Pittsburgh Penguins owner Howard Baldwin also rallied behind McNall and the expansion committee. "The time has come," he faxed his fellow owners, "to follow new leadership – let's do it – now!"

The most serious threat to McNall's leadership, however, did not come from Wirtz and was never put down on paper. The Senators, certain they would be denied first pick when they finished last, held an emergency executive meeting in Ottawa. Rod Bryden was already gathering legal opinions; now Bruce Firestone was dispatched to a Board of Governors meeting in New York to make sure the verbal assurances made at West Palm Beach became a documented commitment. He was to let it be known that if the NHL board failed to guarantee that the first pick would go to the season's last-place team, the Senators were prepared to launch legal proceedings. They would charge the league with breach of contract. They might also consider contending that McNall had been in a conflict-of-interest situation when the Disney franchise was admitted.

At 9 a.m. on January 5, the board convened at the Plaza Hotel in New York City. The gathering was brief and businesslike, and broke up with McNall's announcement that "the committee came away with a full vote of confidence." Phil Esposito left angrily. "I have nothing to say," he shouted by the elevators. "You'll have to ask what's-his-face ... Gil Stein." A smiling Bruce Firestone reported happily that no changes would be made in the order of the 1993 draft. Bill Wirtz had already departed in a huff. He had not been able to deliver enough votes to stop the changes to the expansion rules. He could not even deliver all the people he'd listed in his letter of December 24.

Bruce McNall was now the established power in the NHL. It was confirmed in the New York meeting, but it had been known since the final Friday in West Palm Beach, when Stein had called an early adjournment that left the important matters in the hands of McNall and his expansion committee. Before the month was out, McNall would nominate Stein for election to the Hockey Hall of Fame.

Out on the croquet lawn that day in Florida, workers had been preparing for what had always been the highlight of the gathering – Wirtz's annual croquet tournament, with competitors attired in leisure whites and beautiful young women officiating in NHL referee jerseys. The sun was out, the sea air clear, the orange-and-black NHL balloons had been tied. Waiters were putting out the champagne and strawberries. An aging five-piece Dixieland band was already swinging its way into "Bourbon Street" – "You'll meet all the big shots ..."

None of the big shots even bothered to show. Those not racing for the airport were heading for the tennis courts or the golf course. Washington's David Poile, swinging a tennis racket as he cut across the croquet area, predicted this would be the last time the NHL would ever gather at The Breakers. Wirtz himself didn't even bother showing up. Along with 82-year-old Tommy Ivan, the Blackhawks' general manager in 1961 – the last time Chicago won the Stanley Cup – Wirtz wandered down and sat on the beach, staring out over the azure waves as they rolled in and died at his feet. The tide was going out.

IN THE NEW YEAR, A PRESS CONFERENCE WAS CALLED IN ANAHEIM, California, to announce that the Mighty Ducks would begin play in the fall of 1993. The rink would be known as the Pond. McNall was on hand for the ceremonies, as was the newly installed commissioner, Bettman.

Two weeks later, Gil Stein announced that, as president, he was overhauling the selection committee of the Hockey Hall of Fame, which was scheduled for a gala reopening in June in Toronto. Stein removed Brian O'Neill, whom he had already fired as executive vice-president of the NHL, and Alan Eagleson, who was in disrepute and under investigation by both the FBI and the RCMP, and old Tommy Ivan, the Blackhawks' vice-president, who had remained on the board only as long as his friend Wirtz had remained in power. A fourth voting member, former broadcaster Danny Gallivan, had recently died.

Stein chose as replacements Boston businessman Leslie Kaplan, Washington lawyer Lawrence Meyer, former Canadian prime minister John Turner, and Toronto lawyer Larry Bertuzzi. Boston Bruins president Harry Sinden had never even heard of Kaplan. *Sports Illustrated* suggested that no one had ever heard of Meyer. Bertuzzi, who does arbitration work for the NHL, had contractual ties with Stein's office. Three other board members – Jim Gregory, the vice-president of hockey operations, and Scotty Morrison and David Taylor of the Hockey Hall of Fame – were NHL employees, which meant that seven of the 12 members were beholden to Stein. Stein then changed the ground rules for election to the Hall of Fame from a 75 percent majority of the board to a simple majority. The secret ballot he changed to a show of hands.

The nomination letter was from McNall, stating that, during Stein's tenure, "he has been responsible for directing more innovative thinking and changes than the League has ever experienced in such a compressed period." McNall praised Stein for his work in bringing about "the complete turnaround of the League's low public image" and for his critical role in bringing in Disney and Blockbuster. A vote was taken, The show of hands enshrined Stein in the Hall, supposedly for the eternal edification of all hockey fans.

One of the members of the Hockey Hall of Fame selection committee who had not been replaced – Murray Costello, president of the Canadian Amateur Hockey Association – resigned in protest. When *Toronto Star* columnist Bob McKenzie began getting the story out, the reaction was outrage. In a fax to fellow board members, Bill Wirtz described the appointment of Stein as "despicable." Senator Hartland Molson of the Canadiens suggested, "Maybe we have overlooked the guys who drive the Zambonis." Within days, Bettman had his first scandal to defuse. He immediately announced that an impartial panel, composed of Yves Fortier, former Canadian ambassador to the United Nations, and New York lawyer Arnold Burns, would begin an inquiry into the matter.

In August, Fortier and Burns tabled a 100-page report. Stein, they had found, had "engineered his own election." They used words and phrases such as "improperly manipulated" and "misled" and accused Stein of "misusing and abusing the governance process of the Hall of Fame and the prerequisites of his office."

According to one of the more intriguing sections of the long report, McNall told the investigators that the idea that he write the letter of nomination had been entirely Stein's. McNall maintained that Stein had made this request near the end of 1992, shortly after the two had succeeded in arranging the unexpected expansion into south Florida and Anaheim. The way McNall saw it – Stein would take immediate issue – he had been "sandbagged" by the man he described in his nomination letter as "the epitome of a team player."

Stein would not be going to the Hockey Hall of Fame. Bruce McNall, on the other hand, was now widely considered to be well on his way.

THE SENATORS' FIRST DRAFT: FROM LEFT, RANDY SEXTON, MEL BRIDGMAN,
ALEXEI YASHIN, BRUCE FIRESTONE, CYRIL LEEDER, AND JIM DURRELL.
(ALL PHOTOS COURTESY OF *THE OTTAWA CITIZEN* UNLESS OTHERWISE CREDITED.)

THE LION MASCOT: FIRED AT MID-SEASON.
THE NHL'S FIRST COMMISSIONER, GARY BETTMAN,
UNDERWENT A TRIAL BY FIRE.

MEL BRIDGMAN'S "STATE OF THE UNION" ADDRESS: RICK BOWNESS
CHECKS HIS HEARING WHILE JOHN FERGUSON STUDIES THE FLOOR.

NEIL BRADY SCORES THE SENATORS' FIRST NHL GOAL IN 58 YEARS.

MARIO LEMIEUX: HIS BATTLE WITH CANCER AND A SCORING TITLE
ADDED UP TO A SEASON FOR FOLKLORE, NOT THE RECORD BOOKS.

WAYNE GRETZKY: ON RETURNING FROM HIS BACK INJURY HE SAID,
"I WISH I WAS JUST BEGINNING."

THE 1992–93 SEASON SAW THE EMERGENCE OF TORONTO'S
DOUG GILMOUR AS A SUPERSTAR.

Eric Lindros in cuffs: after a night out, the worst
public relations disaster imaginable. (*Canada Wide/Greig Reekie*)

OTTAWA'S DARCY LOEWEN: "IF YOU BLEW UP A BALLOON
AND LET IT GO – THAT'D BE DARCY."

VETERAN BRAD MARSH AND HIS FAMILY: ERIK, VICTORIA,
MADELAINE, PATTY, AND PATRICK. COULD HE PLAY LONG ENOUGH
FOR MADELAINE TO KNOW WHAT HE DID FOR A LIVING?

MIKE PELUSO AT WORK: THE HOCKEY PLAYER HE FANCIED HIMSELF,
OR THE ROLE PLAYER HE WAS HIRED TO BE?

JOHN KORDIC: WAS THE PUMPED-UP ENFORCER DESTROYED BY HIS
DRUG USE OR BY THE SYSTEM? (*CANAPRESS PHOTO SERVICE*)

BRUCE MCNALL AND ROCKET ISMAIL: THE WORST CONTRACT
IN THE HISTORY OF PROFESSIONAL SPORT?

PETER POCKLINGTON: IF HIS FRANCHISE WAS LOSING MONEY,
WHY DID HE TURN DOWN $65 MILLION FOR IT?
GIL STEIN: ALMOST A HALL-OF-FAMER, WITH A LITTLE HELP
FROM HIS FRIENDS, AMONG THEM BRUCE MCNALL.

DON CHERRY SIGNS WITH THE ONTARIO LOTTERY CORPORATION AS
SPOKESMAN FOR SPORT SELECT-PRO LINE, "THE NEW ON-LINE, SPORTS GAME
BASED ON PREDICTING THE OUTCOME OF PROFESSIONAL TEAM SPORTING
EVENTS" – THAT IS TO SAY, GAMBLING. (CANAPRESS PHOTO SERVICE)

PAVEL BURE: THE RUSSIAN ROCKET SINGLEHANDEDLY REJUVENATED
THE VANCOUVER CANUCKS. (*CANAPRESS PHOTO SERVICE*)

TEEMU SELANNE: HIS SCORING HEROICS MADE HIM THE GREATEST
ROOKIE OF ALL TIME. (*CANAPRESS PHOTO SERVICE*)

ALEXANDER MOGILNY: NO MORE QUESTIONS AFTER HIS SPECTACULAR PERFORMANCE IN 1992–93. (CANAPRESS PHOTO SERVICE)

CANADA DAY, 1993: WHEN THE NEW STAR, ALEXANDRE DAIGLE,
OUTDREW THE NEW PRIME MINISTER, KIM CAMPBELL, THE
SENATORS KNEW THEY HAD "ADDED VALUE."

THE SENATORS' BRAINS TRUST: RANDY SEXTON, BRUCE FIRESTONE, AND ROD BRYDEN.

ALEXANDRE DAIGLE: THE DIFFERENCE BETWEEN HIM
AND ERIC LINDROS? "I *DRINK* MY BEER."

CHAPTER FIVE

THE ENFORCER

Kanata, Ontario

MIKE PELUSO WAS PULLING HIS PUNCHES FASTER THAN HE HAD THROWN them. The video of the Senators' last meeting with the New York Islanders was on the overhead monitor in fast reverse, the third-period battle between Peluso and the Islanders' Mick Vukota like a cartoon as Peluso snapped back off the ice, Vukota pulled a punch, Peluso pulled a punch, sweaters went on. Gloves flew up onto hands and then dropped again as the bout began for the sixth identical time. No one watching was laughing. No one would dare laugh.

Peluso sat in the dressing room of the Ottawa Senators' practice facility with a scowl on his face. His hair, soaked from the shower, trailed down a back that Nautilus machines and boxing lessons had built into a stone fence. He had a white towel around his waist and the remote control to the overhead VCR in his hand. Every few moments Peluso stabbed the remote in the direction of the monitor: reverse, forward, reverse, forward. He kept shaking his head as he watched again and again his fight with Vukota. He was searching for something he could not find. He wanted to know why he had fallen.

It was no surprise that Peluso and Vukota had fought; it had been inevitable. They had fought twice that night – the first time, early on, Peluso got off a flurry of punches before the linesmen broke them up; the second time, he lost his footing and Vukota was able to throw him to the ice. Two fights in a night had once been normal for Peluso, but so far this season the fights had been rare. The two with Vukota had been his response to being benched by coach Rick Bowness. "Our problem is not with work ethic," an angry Bowness had said after a loss to Washington. "It's with aggression." And aggression was in Mike Peluso's job description.

The season before, as a Chicago Blackhawk, Peluso had led the league in penalty minutes with 408 – almost seven hours in only 63 games – that total rendering insignificant his six goals and three assists. He had led the league, as well, in fighting majors with 34. Vukota, shorter but heavier, had had 273 minutes and 31 fights (no goals, six assists). Vukota had set himself an objective for the 1992–93 season: he would have 40 major penalties for fighting. He would, he predicted that summer, lead the league. But the new rules, especially the automatic ejection for instigating a fight, had been playing havoc with his plans. Peluso himself was hardly fighting this year, and had it not been for the benching, he might have failed in yet another game to do what everyone had come to expect of him.

The fights in Long Island had not amounted to much, but for most fans they were the highlight of yet another bad night on the road for the Senators. Vukota had been named one of the game stars only because he had dumped Peluso. The punches he threw had enlivened the crowd, and the cameras had stayed on him for a long time after Peluso went down.

Peluso was furious with his performance. He wanted to know *why* he had fallen. A slip he could accept; he would not want it to get around the league that he'd fallen to a punch. In his line of work reputations rise and fall on late-night sports highlight shows, and he fervently hoped that if the tape of the fight happened to make a late-night package, those watching would see the result for what it was: a slip, an accident, an aberration.

Those same three words could be used to describe Peluso's presence in the NHL. He was born in Pengilly, a village of 2,000 outside Hibbing, Minnesota, in 1965, the same year another area son, Bob Dylan, recorded "It's Alright, Ma (I'm Only Bleeding)." Peluso's family and Dylan's family, the Zimmermans, were steelworkers and acquaintances. The Pelusos lived just outside Hibbing in a village so small that when an ambulance came down the street everyone dropped what they were doing and followed.

Peluso was, by his own measure, "a short and fat kid" who liked sports but hardly excelled at them. He went unnoticed until the summer between grades 9 and 10 when, suddenly, he shot up to 6'4" and thinned out. He became, on size alone, a presence in hockey. He was not a playmaker – his skating was so cumbersome that other teams could hardly wait until he came on the ice because, it was said, "he can't turn." But he could hit and he could work the corners and, as a defenseman, he could clear-cut a crease in short order.

In Peluso's senior year with Pengilly's high school team, he played only 15 games because of a teachers' strike, yet in the 1985 entry draft he was selected by the New Jersey Devils. It was a complete shock to him. He had gone in the tenth round, 190th overall, long after Mario Lemieux, the first pick, had gone home. New Jersey was taking a flyer. "It was just on size," he says, "just because of my size."

Peluso was astute enough to realize he still did not know how to play the game. Instead of chasing the NHL, he headed for Anchorage and a hockey scholarship at the University of Alaska. For four years he studied sociology and developed as a college player. He became captain of the Seawolves, often playing 40 minutes a game, and was known as a "defenseman's defenseman." Even so, after four years he was the school's all-time leading scorer among defensemen with 133 points. He finished his final year a few courses short of a degree but with a respectable 10 goals and 27 assists in 33 games. He had 75 minutes in penalties, none of them for fighting. In the NCAA, fighting is not allowed. "I was an offensive player in college, if you can believe that," he said later. "My first two years in Chicago I probably averaged about 30 fights each year. All of my buddies I played with in college couldn't believe I was doing that sort of thing."

Chicago had signed Peluso as a free agent and then sent him to Indianapolis in the International Hockey League. There he fell under the influence of coach Darryl Sutter, who in 1992 was named coach of the Blackhawks. It was Sutter, a grinding forward during his eight years in the NHL, who explained to Peluso that NHL teams are made up of role players and that the key to success lies in finding a role to play, understanding it perfectly, and executing it better than all the players who would like to replace you. Peluso heard him clearly. It was the steelworker's credo applied to hockey: you get your job, then you hang on to your job.

Peluso got called up to the Blackhawks for two games in 1989–90 – no goals, no assists, 15 minutes in the penalty box. In 1990–91 he dressed for 53 games and scored six goals and an assist while spending 320 minutes in the box. The goals were bonuses, unexpected of him. He understood that. He was no longer even thinking of himself as an offensive player: "I got away from that style and the only thing I concentrated on is what I added to the team." In 1991–92 he led the NHL in penalties.

Peluso remains grateful to Sutter and his first Chicago coach, Mike Keenan, for making him an NHLer. "Mike pushed me," he says. "He made me intense night in and night out." Peluso changed from a player who was, as he said himself, "a bit too polite on the ice" to someone whose heart pumped what Keenan called "Black-hawk blood" through a weight lifter's body. He worked out with a boxing club twice a week. The Chicago Stadium organist began playing the theme to *The Godfather* one game while he was fighting, and that tune became Peluso's anthem, the organist often striking the menacing chords even before Peluso was sent out.

"At first it used to bother me that some people thought I was just a goon or an animal," he told the *Ottawa Sun*'s Earl McRae. "But not now. I know who I am. If people think that, I can just say, 'I'm in the NHL.' That's the top. How many of *them* can say they've reached the top?"

He thought he had bottomed out when Ottawa selected him in the June expansion draft – the second forward taken by the Senators, a protector for their first forward, sniper Sylvain Turgeon. His season with the Blackhawks had ended 17 days earlier. Chicago had gone all the way to the Stanley Cup finals, and he had come to believe he was an integral part of the team. The Blackhawks, however, were reacting to the rumors about the coming rule changes. If battlers were suddenly going to be less important, then they would have one instead of two, and they would stick with Stu "The Grim Reaper" Grimson, who was the same age as Peluso, 27, but an inch taller and 20 pounds heavier.

Ottawa turned out to be a pleasant surprise. He arrived with his role clearly defined in the eyes of eager fans. His reputation, his size, his rock-star hair, and the easy roll of his name off the tongue made him an instant celebrity. And he was eager to play the role. He arrived in Ottawa scowling, his glare intimidating the media, his performance on ice intimidating the other players. In a preseason scrimmage he caught Jody Hull at center ice with his head down. Hull limped off and did not come back. After that, no player would dare challenge Peluso for the role of team enforcer. That role was taken.

His attitude was an act. Gradually the real Peluso emerged, the glare dissolving into a childlike grin he often could not hold back. He became the dressing room's disc jockey, the one tall enough to reach the portable CD player on the high shelf and keep it running with AC/DC and Guns N'Roses and Aerosmith. Many players could not stand the choices. "The music in this dressing room is the worst I've heard in my life," said Norm Maciver, who had come from the Edmonton Oilers, who dress to the Doors and Rod Stewart. Country fans like Darcy Loewen and Ken Hammond grimaced and shook their heads. But Peluso would never change the music; instead he would crank it up even louder, prancing around the room and, when the song ended, grabbing a stick and holding the taped end to his mouth like a microphone: "Thank you, thank you, Ottawa. We're Bon Jovi – thank you and good night."

Of all the Senators, he had the best relationship with the children who showed up at practice with their Sharpie pens and hockey cards. The younger and more timid the child, the more Peluso seemed able to relate, stooping down from what seemed like a mile overhead and often giving far more of his time than an autograph or a question warranted. It sometimes seemed he wanted to play with them, as he did each summer back at the daycare center his mother, Anita, runs outside Pengilly. It is part of the summer ritual there that Peluso, the biggest kid of all, lies down and pretends to fall fast asleep while the tiny ones poke and prod and tickle and call to wake him, Peluso stirring and snoring until, suddenly, he bursts awake like a surfacing whale, sending the little ones shrieking from the room. "I get them all wound up," he says, "and then I leave."

Peluso was eating alone at a restaurant in Ottawa one night in December when a family came in and the children recognized him.

The youngsters worked up the courage to ask for an autograph and ended up asking if he'd like to eat with them. He said he'd love to. He picked up his food and joined their table; the parents were dumb-founded. The children asked about the next game, and Peluso asked if they were going. He offered to get them tickets. The next day he called them and left a message on the answering machine. The parents thought it was a prank. Peluso called again and left the same message. Finally one of the children called back. Peluso had arranged tickets for the entire family. At $325,000 a year he could afford to – but such stories are rare in hockey.

Children were not alone in seeing Peluso in a new light. The Chicago organization had turned him into an enforcer with but one role to play. Ottawa, on the other hand, had few forwards whose skills could keep Peluso on the bench. He played a regular shift. He scored against Quebec City in the Senators' first road game. He scored twice against Boston in their second road game. He was, a week into the season, the team's top goal scorer. In Chicago he had rarely seen the ice in the third period of a close game. In overtime, he once said, "I might as well have taken off my skates."

Peluso was going through what all the Senators were going through in the team's first year. Every player's role was expanding. Fourth-line wingers found themselves on the second line, fifth defenseman were suddenly working point on the power play. And, of course, the enforcer was taking a regular shift – and scoring. Mark Lamb, a good third-line defensive center in Edmonton, was moved to first-line center, a more offensive role. He found the switch diffi-cult, and at one point he took Rick Bowness aside and apologized for his lack of scoring. No apology was necessary, Bowness told him. Some players, like Norm Maciver, flourished by being moved up the depth chart, while others got confused.

Success with the puck changed Peluso. When he returned to Chicago for the first time, in early March, the Chicago reporters seemed baffled by his change in attitude. Why was he was trying to move the puck up the ice? He told them he used to run into old college friends who would ask, "Why are you fighting all the time? Why don't you just play hockey more? You know you can." "I don't regret what I did in Chicago," Peluso continued. "There were so many good players ahead of me. But with Ottawa I've fallen back on the abilities I always had, and things couldn't be better."

So it seemed. He had become a pinup boy after the team's game program featured him on the cover in a black tuxedo with a red bow tie and sash. He would end up scoring 15 goals, fifth on the team behind Turgeon (25), Bob Kudelski (24), Jamie Baker (19), and Maciver (17). In late March, when the final trading deadline loomed, Peluso's name was the one that came up most often, for by then he had become the team's hottest property. Three teams were interested in having him for the playoff run: Detroit, Vancouver, and Los Angeles. The Kings offered the most – a player and two draft choices – but the expected trade never happened. It may be, as the Senators said, that not enough was offered. It may also be that management botched the paperwork at the last minute and could not complete the trade they wanted. The result left Peluso of two minds: he was delighted to learn that he was wanted, but he also wondered if he wasn't better off staying in Ottawa, where he could play a part instead of a role.

The suggestion that other teams might only be interested in his fists deeply offended Peluso. He had already shown how deep his pride ran when he blew up over a newspaper photograph that showed him being dumped by Montreal enforcer Todd Ewan. ("It made people think I lost. That was, like, half a second of action. I didn't lose – I won.") And when it was said he might be going to the Kings to return to his old role, he argued that another team would not want him to fight but rather to continue scoring the way he was in Ottawa. "I scored six goals in Chicago getting less than six shifts a game," he said. "I've been able to show there's more to my game here." But the reality was that there was more to his game in Ottawa because there was less to everyone else's game. Ottawa had given him two roles: enforcer if necessary and player by necessity. Nowhere else would he be so fortunate.

Peluso would not buy this. He believed Ottawa had given him the opportunity he needed to establish himself as a genuine NHLer. It had made him proud and happy and understandably vain. "I think I'll stick around a couple of weeks," he said at the end of his finest season. "Talk to the fans a bit, see what they thought about my play this year."

It did not matter what the fans thought. Peluso was a genuine NHLer, but the rest of the league was not the Senators – and the rest of the league tends to stick by its initial job descriptions.

VIOLENCE IN HOCKEY IS NOTHING NEW. IN 1904, JOHN ROSS ROBERTSON, president of the Ontario Hockey Association, warned that "we must call a halt to slashing and slugging, and insist upon clean hockey in Ontario, before we have to call in a coroner to visit our rinks." Three years later, on March 6, 1907, the coroner was called. In a brawl-filled match in Cornwall, Ontario, Charles Masson killed Owen "Bud" McCourt with what the inquest determined was "a blow from a hockey stick." The jury recommended "that legislation be enacted whereby players or spectators encouraging or engaging in rough or foul play may be severely punished." Like most recommendations that come out of coroner's inquests, it was ignored by the legislators.

In 1907 the original Ottawa Senators and the Montreal Wanderers met in what the papers later described as "the most sordid exhibition of butchery ever seen in hockey." Two Ottawa players, Harry and Alf Smith, were subsequently arrested and hauled off to jail for assault, but not before they had cut or knocked unconscious several of the Montreal players. Harry had slammed his stick across the face of Montreal's Moose Johnson, breaking his nose, and Alf had knocked Hod Stuart cold with a slash across the forehead.

Nor is it a new theory that violence fills arenas. When the New York Americans played in the NHL in the years leading up to the Second World War, owner Tex Rickard arranged for ambulances to be parked outside Madison Square Garden on the theory that the sight of them brought in fans. Conn Smythe, who built Maple Leaf Gardens, was once asked his opinion on violence. "We've got to stamp out this sort of thing," he said, "or people are going to keep on buying tickets." Harold Ballard, his successor as Maple Leafs owner, once announced, "I'm looking for guys you toss raw meat to and they go wild." As far as NHL owners were concerned, there was nothing wrong with violence – so long as the fans wanted it.

The novelist Hugh MacLennan once described the relationship between violence and hockey this way:

> Next to the Swedes and Swiss, Canadians in their daily lives are probably as self-restrained as any people in the world. By comparison, Americans sometimes seem as volatile as Latins. Yet the favorite sports of Americans are neat, precise games like baseball and college football. Baseball I dearly love, but after growing up with hockey, I find American college football as slow as an American finds a week-long cricket match; even its violence seems cold to me. But the violence of hockey is hot, and the game at its best is played by passionate men. To

spectator and player alike, hockey gives the same release that liquor gives a repressed man. It is the counterpart of the Canadian self-restraint, it takes us back to the fiery blood of Gallic and Celtic ancestors who found themselves minorities in a cold, new environment and had to discipline themselves as all minorities must. But Canadians take the ferocity of their national game so much for granted that when an American visitor makes polite mention of it, they look at him in astonishment. Hockey – violent? Well, perhaps it is a little. But hockey was always like that and it doesn't mean we're a violent people.

MacLennan was writing in 1954, at a time when professional hockey was played only by Canadians and the only fans of concern to the NHL were those coming in the doors. Radio and what little television there was were considered vehicles to arouse interest in the teams and draw bigger crowds to the games. By the time Mike Peluso was drafted 30 years later by New Jersey, the tables had turned: hockey owners wanted to reach the fan who *wasn't* coming in the door. They just couldn't agree on how.

The issue of fighting and violence in hockey has long defied resolution. In 1974 an Ontario Royal Commission laid the blame for hockey violence, at every level of the game, firmly on the doorstep of the NHL. Yet many NHL owners of the time considered periodic mayhem a vital part of the entertainment mix.

John Ferguson played eight years for the Montreal Canadiens and is generally regarded as the first "enforcer" of the modern era. "I was the villain who made the game interesting," he said in his autobiography, *Thunder and Lightning*. "Without me, they'd have nobody to hate." The Canadiens brought him up from the minor-league Cleveland Barons, he said, "to maintain decorum" if other teams tried to intimidate Montreal stars like Jean Beliveau and

Bernie Geoffrion. Twelve seconds into his first game, Ferguson knocked out Boston's Ted Green with three punches. In the 1965 playoffs Ferguson's one-punch knockout of Chicago's Eric Nesterenko led the Canadiens to the Stanley Cup, the first of five they would win with him in the lineup.

The peak of Ferguson's career as an intimidator coincided with the NHL's largest expansion, in 1967, when the league went from six teams to 12. Each new team naturally included a "cop on the beat," which is how Ferguson once described himself. By the time he retired from the game, in 1971, the enforcer's job description was well established, and each team was constantly searching for the edge in intimidation.

"To be a winner," Ferguson said in 1976 when he went to the New York Rangers as general manager, "a team, like an individual, must have some killer instinct." Ferguson's first act as Rangers GM was to say, "Get me Nick Fotiu." Fotiu, a champion boxer, would spend almost 24 hours in NHL penalty boxes.

Ferguson was 53 when he came to the Senators as director of player personnel, and he had mellowed with time – he now considered it impossible to run a power play without a European, and he now valued speed above all in a player. Still, Mike Peluso continued to be his kind of player.

But was Mike Peluso still the NHL's kind of player? Could he change into the kind of player he fancied himself becoming? More importantly, should the NHL change? Was fighting really necessary? Clarence Campbell, whom John Ziegler replaced as NHL president, spoke for all the owners of the 1970s when he said, "They'll never take it out of the game because it is an outlet, a safety valve that allows players to get some built-up tension out of the way and to continue on about their business. If you tried to stop it, animosities would grow and linger and they would eventually lead to some very ugly stick incidents. I am convinced of that." He also said that "without violence, there would be no such thing as hockey."

Ziegler had his own say shortly after a 1987 playoff match between the Canadiens and the Flyers that erupted into a pregame brawl over whether Montreal forward Claude Lemieux should be allowed to shoot a puck into the Philadelphia net at the end of the warm-up. Everyone who attended the game must have found it entertaining, Ziegler said, for no one had complained. As for getting rid of such gratuitous violence, "It doesn't matter to me." He added, of course, "If it ain't broke, don't fix it."

But Ziegler was speaking for a group of owners whose view of the game was becoming increasingly outmoded. "Violence is what keeps the game alive," Harold Ballard had said; but now some were saying it was what would kill the game. It was, ironically, in Ballard's own Maple Leaf Gardens that the validity of violence as a tactic would for the first time be legally questioned. In a 1988 game Minnesota North Star Dino Ciccarelli swung his stick at the head of Leafs defenseman Luke Richardson and connected. Eight months later he was found guilty of common assault, fined $1,000, and sentenced to one day in jail. Ciccarelli declared the whole affair "ridiculous – I don't see where these people are getting involved in the hockey aspect." But the voice that made an impact was that of Sidney Harris, the presiding judge: "It is time a message go out from the courts that violence in a hockey game or in any other circumstance is not acceptable."

Hockey had rarely looked so out of touch with society's values. In the Stanley Cup playoffs that year, Jim Schoenfeld, coach of the New Jersey Devils, attacked referee Don Koharski, pushed him down in front of the television cameras, and called him a "fat pig."

Ziegler suspended Schoenfeld for a single game – this at a time when baseball was suspending Cincinnati Reds manager Pete Rose for 30 games for merely brushing against an umpire. When NHL officials protested by refusing to work the next game of the series, the league brought three people out of the stands to drop pucks and blow the odd whistle. "The league will survive," Ziegler said. "It's not pleasant and we don't like it. But it won't affect attendance and it won't affect our TV audience."

Others wondered if Ziegler's inability to get the NHL an American network television deal might not have something to do with the game's failure to clean up its act. Violence in all levels of society was a major issue of the times. Saturday-morning cartoons were under attack – why not hockey fights? Even Wayne Gretzky, who had long favored the "safety valve" argument, was now backing off from it: "Hockey is the only team sport in the world that actually encourages fighting. I have no idea why we let it go on."

When Bruce McNall took over as chairman of the Board of Governors in mid-1992, the timing seemed perfect for change. At that year's annual rules meeting, Boston manager Harry Sinden had proposed a ban on fighting. Sinden had come a long way in his thinking. "If we are going to expand," he said, "and I think that is our future, this has to be resolved. I'm talking about expansion into Europe, as well as other North American cities. The fact is that a lot of people find fighting distasteful. So, does it make sense to try to win fans that way? Look, I've always had a hard-hitting, physical team. That will never change. That's how we built our franchise and I'll always love hard-hitting, physical hockey. But I hate goons and I hate goon tactics."

Sinden was joined, surprisingly, by Jay Snider, president of the Flyers, the team that won two Stanley Cups through deliberate intimidation. "I don't see how you can justify fighting as a part of any sport," said Snider. "I say throw anyone who fights out of the game. And if they fight in the final five minutes of a game, throw them out for the next game, also." The winds were indeed shifting.

At the league's next Congress, held in June in Montreal, a nine-man committee was established to respond to the issue. In August the governors would meet in Florida to consider any rule changes the committee suggested. Any such changes would require a two-thirds majority. To help the governors make their decisions, two position papers would be prepared, one "pro" and the other "con" fighting.

The "con" paper was the work of Sinden, Pittsburgh owner Harold Baldwin, and Sinden's assistant general manager, Mike Milbury. Their central argument was economic: "We have huge revenue growth potential with television in the United States, but until fighting is PROHIBITED, cashing in on this opportunity will never happen."

The "pro" paper was assigned to Vancouver's Pat Quinn, Edmonton's Glen Sather, and New Jersey's Lou Lamoriello. "There is a misconception," they argued, "that the NHL cannot attract a national TV contract as a result of fisticuffs. Yet Molsons, who is a franchise holder, a TV producer and a rights holder wants fisticuffs in the game."

The "pro" faction claimed that no advertiser had ever said it wanted fighting taken off the air; the "cons" listed two – IBM and Thomas J. Lipton – that had said this. (American Express has also requested that the NHL become more "user-friendly" by cleaning up its act.) The "cons" argued that "European hockey absolutely does not allow fighting. Asian audiences will not accept systemic violence in team sports. Do we think that we will ever really expand into those markets as long as we allow fighting?" The "pros" ridiculed this: "The NHL game will resemble European hockey if fisticuffs are removed. Europeans cannot sell their game, either live or on TV. This is the very reason why all European teams want NHL participation in their tournaments."

"When there is no fear, there is no respect," the "pro" faction continued. "When there is no respect, the rules do not matter." The "cons" countered that "hockey players are quality young men who have a tarnished image because of the public's perception that hockey is a sport with an accepted code of violence. We need to market our hockey players as gifted athletes – not bullies." The "pros" shot back that "the North American psychology in sports favours the man who stands up for himself. He is applauded if he confronts a wrong. The issue comes down to what kind of confrontation is desirable. Hockey players carry weapons. Is the player who is frustrated by illegal tactics to respond with an accepted, safe and natural release of emotions through fisticuffs or is he to resort to stickwork?"

The "cons" argued that games would be shorter without fighting, merchandising sales would increase as the image of the game improved, and, most importantly, favorable media coverage would win new fans. The "pro" faction countered, "The NHL plays to 92-percent capacity. This indicates the season ticket-holders, the casual fans, and sports fans in general like the game as it is ... This is a business. With players' salaries and costs increasing exponentially some member clubs are riding a tenuous line between fiscal failure and success. This is not the time to experiment. Elimination of fisticuffs may be a disaster ... and once removed [it] will be impossible to reinstate without a media backlash."

The "con" side conceded that some fans like fighting, "but we believe it to be a small part ... How many more potential fans stay away because of the fighting? Another key question we would ask is, 'Do we actually think fans would stop coming to hockey games because we abolish fighting?' We feel we open the sport up to many more new fans and families by eliminating the single most negative factor in our game today – the fighting. One other point about those fans that do enjoy the fighting: Are those the kind of fans we want in our buildings anyway?"

At the end of the arguments, six changes were proposed for the league governors' consideration.

1. A game misconduct penalty for fighting except purely in self-defense. If the penalty occurs in the last 10 minutes of the third period, it extends through the entire next game.

2. Linesmen can call any penalty as long as they wait until a play stoppage.

3. A minimum five-minute penalty for cross-checking, butt-ending, high-sticking, slashing and spearing. A greater penalty can be imposed at the referee's discretion.

4. Two-minute hooking or holding penalties do not terminate if the opposing team scores.

5. If a review of an incident is requested, the review and determination should be completed within 24 hours. A panel of hearing officers will be established.

6. A divisional monetary reward will be given to the team that qualifies for the playoffs with the fewest penalty minutes.

IN THE EARLY HOURS OF AUGUST 8, 1992, WHILE THESE DISCUSSION papers were circulating, two police officers were called to a motel in suburban Quebec City to subdue an abusive guest. Eight more police soon followed. The angry young man was 27-year-old John Kordic, and it took all ten officers and two sets of manacles to contain his rage. Kordic died in an ambulance on his way to the hospital.

On one level, Kordic's untimely death was merely another

story of cocaine and alcohol and inevitability; on another, it was a telling account of the life of a hockey goon. Kordic's parents had emigrated from Croatia to Edmonton in the early 1960s; they were hardworking, God-fearing, and dedicated, the priest said in his eulogy, to the pursuit of excellence. The children were expected to achieve, and they did, particularly in sports. John was an altar boy, a lover of animals, a sensitive child, and at one time a very promising young hockey player. His hero was Bobby Orr, who had played the game as it has always been played in the dreams and hopes of the very young.

Kordic believed he had the talent to play the game; others believed there was only one path for him to follow. A scout told him fighting would be his ticket to a big-league career. Big and strong, with a head like a hockey helmet, Kordic learned to fight, and fight well.

To make himself bigger, he began pumping himself full of steroids. It gave him a look that was unmistakable. He was using drugs, and everyone knew it, but this being the NHL, neither forgiveness nor help was available to him. The NHL policy was merciless – use drugs, *any* drugs, and you're gone – so Kordic had to deny his cocaine and steroid use, and those who employed him had to pretend it wasn't obvious. Teams traded him back and forth, each attracted by his violence, then repulsed by what his role turned him into off the ice. His employers failed him as much as he failed himself. They could do little else, given the NHL's drug policy as explained by Gil Stein: "Our program is designed to deter players from ever trying drugs in the first place. It isn't designed to help players who have become addicts."

Kordic grew into a hideous caricature of a brawler, his facial features distorted, his bulk soaring to 238 pounds by the time he died, the steroids raging through a mind that had difficulty coping with life even when clean. There were sides to him that people found attractive – the Senators' Brad Marsh, briefly a teammate in Toronto, said, "There was always so much promise to John Kordic" – but there were also sides to him that he himself despised. He made a half-hearted attempt at suicide. He beat up his fiancée, Nancy Masse, who told the inquest he was afraid of the younger players coming along who might take his job. "That's why he felt obliged to take steroids," she said, "in order to keep his job."

Kordic understood his role perfectly. When Gretzky first began questioning the need for fighting in hockey, Kordic had said, "If they banned fighting I wouldn't have a job. I have no illusions about it. If they ban fighting I'm gone."

In 1986 he had been a 21-year-old called up by the Canadiens. He had ended the year with a Stanley Cup to hold over his head and a $140,000-a-year contract offer in his pocket. Six years after his lungs cheered that Stanley Cup victory, they filled with fluid in the back of an ambulance. Training camp was a month away. He had heard nothing. The Edmonton Oilers, the last team to show interest in him, had decided to wait until the end of the month to see how the vote went in Florida before deciding whether or not to invite him to camp.

WHEN THE NHL MET IN ST. PETERSBURG AT THE END OF AUGUST, those who wanted an end to fighting were disappointed. The sweeping changes on fisticuffs were abandoned, though the "instigator" penalty was improved upon. The player who had started the fight could now receive a game misconduct in addition to a fighting major. This did not, however, mean that someone started every fight; the previous season, referees had been able to determine the instigator in only 30 percent of the fights.

The first hint that the stricter attitude could not last came in, of all places, London, England, where the Montreal Canadiens and

Chicago Blackhawks had been sent to promote the game in Europe. As soon as ticket sales flagged slightly, the NHL advertising quickly changed. Instead of promoting the skills of Jeremy Roenick and Chris Chelios and Patrick Roy and Denis Savard, the new ads promised THE GRIM REAPER IS COMING. After the focus was placed on Stu Grimson, the Blackhawks enforcer, the event sold out. To the "pro" faction this was confirmation that the fans, new as well as old, want to see the game as it has always been played, fights and all.

As the regular season began, the slower teams in the league – the Senators included – were predicting that the zero-tolerance policy for rules infractions would soon be allowed to slide. So it turned out. By the time the 1993 playoffs were under way, holding (including stick holding) was back. So was interference, slashing, and high-sticking. And for all the crease-infringement penalties called in the preseason, by the playoffs' end, "crashing the net" had become the most effective tool of those teams advancing toward the cup final.

There has rarely been much criticism of NHL officiating. One reason is that the league has gag rules and levies heavy fines for all but the mildest criticism. (Tony Gallagher of the *Vancouver Province* calls the NHL "the 'Hear-No-Evil League'.") The resulting "libel chill" keeps even justified criticism at bay. "In this fiefdom," Gallagher says, "speech was never free."

Few people involved in the game have stated openly what many fans believe – that NHL officiating is inconsistent and irrational. Two who *have* raised the issue are former goaltender and broadcaster John Davidson and longtime coach Scotty Bowman. Davidson believes that "eliminating the fouls that hold back the game's speed should be one of the league's highest priorities." Bowman has even called for three referees instead of one: "Too much goes on for one man to handle ... There's interference, there's putting hands on the stick. With the one-referee system, the official only tries to pick out the most flagrant fouls."

Few fans – and so far, no sports pages – realize that the most significant tactical consideration going into an NHL hockey game is not which players on the other team are hot, or cold, or hurting, but *who is refereeing*. The NHL tries to keep the officials' schedules a secret, but that doesn't stop teams from spending considerable time and effort learning (or trying to learn) who will be working their upcoming matches. The Senators, who relied on impediment, would pray for Paul Stewart to referee their games against fast and highly skilled teams like the Sabres, the Jets, and the Nordiques. Stewart calls very little hooking and holding and calls nothing away from the play. Such an approach by the officials is vital for teams that rely on slowing the game down. For the Senators, Stewart was the equivalent to a man advantage.

The "book" on the referees is common knowledge throughout the league. Referee Rob Shick is admired by those teams with superstar players, for he calls the obvious. Andy vanHellemond is the choice for the grinders, as he lets a great deal go, and calls little in the third period and nothing in overtime. Don Koharski cannot be intimidated by stars or coaches, which means that weaker teams appreciate him. Dan Marouelli cracks jokes, Terry Gregson is serious, Bill McCreary gets revenge on players who talk back too often. Kerry Fraser is consistent and will call a penalty in the final minutes as quickly as in the opening minutes. Fraser is unusual in that he has openly challenged the old adage that says the players should be allowed to decide the game. "That's bull," he once told *The Hockey News*. "If I avoid making a call then I'm affecting the outcome of the game. I'm penalizing the other team by not making the call."

The inconsistency of NHL officiating was never brought into

sharper relief than in 1992–93. Throughout the exhibition season and well into October, referees called more penalties than usual, and the game changed dramatically as players and teams quickly adjusted. Suddenly speed mattered more than it ever had, and finesse briefly triumphed over holding and hooking. But by the time the playoffs came around, the situation had reversed so dramatically that at one point, Canadiens coach Jacques Demers was running a practice drill in which his players had to skate, with the puck, from center ice to the net while another player hooked and interfered for the entire distance.

There was no conspiracy here. The owners did not send the officials written instructions to back off. It happened because professional hockey is a very small community. Most owners have teams that rely on the many forms of interference; the conviction filters down that illegal stickwork is necessary to the game rather than unnecessary obstruction. If ten teams want to play one style and 14 want to play another, and there is weak leadership, the majority will inevitably rule. Most coaches also want grinder hockey, and the vast majority of players depend on it to be effective. Officials are human. They travel the same road, stay at the same hotels, and drink in the same bars – they go with the flow, and that flow, unfortunately, dictates a style of hockey in which speed and finesse are generally halted rather than rewarded. All of that is why the new rules policy died.

Playoff penalty minutes declined 44 percent between 1988 and 1992, but no one can say whether this is because the standard of play was higher or the standard of officiating was lower. The NHL likes to say that the league's overall parity shines through during the playoffs. Yet the regular demise in the playoffs of those teams finishing highest in the standings may well be related more directly to the way that the playing style shifts once postseason play begins. Also, playoff season is the time when officials face the fiercest pressure to "let the players decide the game." Ken Dryden has said that goaltenders emerge so often as the stars of the playoffs simply because of the different style of play: players check harder and get away with more interference, shooters rarely get away good shots and never get second shots. As a result, Dryden says, the Stanley Cup playoffs offer the best working conditions most goaltenders ever experience.

By far the most vocal supporter of "letting the players decide the game" has been Don Cherry, the popular host of the "Coach's Corner" segment of *Hockey Night In Canada*. "Who wants all those penalties?" Cherry demanded during Game Two of the Stanley Cup final between the Canadiens and the Kings. "The fans don't want them – you can hear them booing." It was a transparent argument: the Montreal crowd was booing penalties to the home side, as hometown crowds have always done. That same game was largely decided by a call on an illegal stick – a call Montreal requested. For the penalty, the cheering was deafening.

Cherry's influence is so astonishingly great that he has been called "the Prime Minister of Saturday Night." He speaks for much of the nation when it comes to hockey. But like the prime minister, he does not speak for everyone – perhaps not even for the majority. Attacks on Cherry flare periodically. As Mordecai Richler wrote in *Maclean's* in the spring of 1993:

> Creationists, convinced that Darwin's evolutionary hypothesis was heresy, were dealt a possibly mortal blow once Mr. Cherry emerged as the star of Yahoo's Corner on Molson's Hockey Night in Canada. Here, if it were needed, was proof positive not only that man was descended from the baboon, but also that in the case of at least one born in an obscure corner of Kingston, Ont., the evolutionary ascent was far from complete. [Cherry is] an inspirational figure. An appropriate

role model for cretins. He has established that a six-figure income is not beyond the dim-witted, providing they are willing to play the boor and dress like a harlequin.

Cherry is an easy target, larger than life in his Wilfrid Laurier collars and Nathan Detroit suits. He is deliberately provocative, often insightful and humorous, sometimes boorish. His insistence that "Coach's Corner" not be rehearsed has led to any number of awkward moments. With the 1993 playoffs coinciding with the conflict in Bosnia, Cherry defended the CBC's constant bumping of the nightly news in favor of live hockey with an insinuation that true fans could care less about "lower Slobovia attacking Slimea." He saluted Sault Ste. Marie in Northern Ontario as "my kind of city" after the city council there created a national furor by declaring itself an English-only zone during the constitutional debate. And earlier in the season, with the anniversary of the massacre of 14 women students at Montreal's École Polytechnique approaching, Cherry rebuffed a request to wear a white ribbon: "If I wore every ribbon or badge sent to me, 'Coach's Corner' would turn into a public announcement."

Cherry's routine is now familiar: praise the gritty Canadian players, criticize any referee who dares enforce the rule book, bait homosexuals and – of course – run down the foreign players. On air, he once asked for some player to step forward and break Pittsburgh defenseman Ulf Samuelsson's arm between wrist and elbow. It is his conviction that European hockey players have taken away jobs from Canadians; he would protect those jobs through immigration restrictions. "Foreigners have really brought a lot to hockey," he likes to say. "They brought helmets. They brought visors. They brought diving, laying there letting on they're hurt. They brought stick work. They brought advertising on the boards and ice. Beautiful. This is not hockey people like."

This is, of course, merely Don Cherry being Don Cherry – an act that he has perfected and that those who know him well dismiss. "Maybe my mind never got over 18," he says. "I relate to guys 18 to 25." Some of what he says is tongue-in-cheek, much is merely to inspire reaction: "I'm the Anglo redneck of all time. When Patrick Roy joined the Canadiens and they called him 'Roo-ah', I said, 'What's this? Who ever heard of Roo-ah Rogers?'" He can be ludicrous, outrageous, and dumb, but he is also a sentimentalist, a student of naval history, a gardener, and a dedicated charity worker.

At another level, however, Cherry and "Coach's Corner" raise larger questions than whether or not there should be some balance on *Hockey Night in Canada* in defense of referees blowing their whistles and in support of the skills Europeans have brought to the game. There is also the matter of how Cherry profits from hockey violence. For several years now, Cherry has conducted a lucrative side-business marketing video compilations of hockey hits and fights. His first, *Don Cherry's Rock'em Sock'em Hockey*, sold more than 150,000 copies, making it the top-selling video in Canada. Two successful sequels have followed. If no new product were available, the series would come to an end, which means that Don Cherry has a direct vested interest in having fighting continue in the NHL. Fisticuffs is money in his pocket.

Cherry also makes money translating his "Coach's Corner" fame into endorsements. Selling insulation and shaving lotion is harmless enough, but Cherry has also become the pitchman for the Ontario Sports Select lottery, a gambling enterprise that the NHL has so far been unable to ban through the courts. Major-league baseball, highly sensitive to gambling ever since the Black Sox scandal of 1919, once banned two of the game's more renowned Hall-of-Famers,

Mickey Mantle and Willy Mays, from any contact with the game while they worked for Atlantic City casinos, where they were doing nothing more than greeting customers. The NHL has said nothing about the propriety of Cherry urging fans to gamble on sports.

Why have Cherry's business activities never become an issue with the CBC, which does not produce the *Hockey Night In Canada* broadcasts but does carry them? Cherry himself has said, "It's a modern miracle that I'm still on the CBC." And the CBC, as the past has shown, is highly sensitive to conflict of interest or even the appearance of it. In 1988 Dale Goldhawk was removed as host of "Cross-Canada Checkup" because he was also head of a broadcasters' union that had spoken out against free trade. It was deemed that Goldhawk was unable to be unbiased on that issue. Cherry is clearly unable to be unbiased on the issue of hockey violence. Goldhawk received no money for his work on the free trade issue. Yet Cherry makes money out of hockey violence.

That the CBC, a public network, has taken no action against Cherry may well be tied to the fact that it can no longer afford to control the broadcasts it carries. In the same years that Cherry's star has been soaring, the CBC has become strapped for cash. For the network, the Stanley Cup playoffs represent about $60 million a year in advertising. The impact of that much money is enormous: a cutback in federal funding of $108 million in 1990 led to the closure or gutting of 11 television stations across the country. Money from playoff hockey is obviously of critical importance to the CBC. The Stanley Cup involves between 80 and 150 hours of viewing time each year, with an average audience on the English network, where Cherry appears, of 1.8 million viewers. "Coach's Corner" is generally conceded to be more popular with most viewers than the games themselves. Non-hockey programming in similar time slots would bring in perhaps one-quarter of the revenues. On this issue the CBC seems to be driven by the same force that drives the game's owners: money. Don Cherry's potential conflicts of interest go unnoticed by the CBC because the CBC cannot afford to notice them.

THE SAME VCR ON WHICH MIKE PELUSO REVIEWED HIS BATTLE WITH Mick Vukota offered some unassailable evidence that the "spontaneous relief" or "safety valve" argument in favor of hockey fighting is laced with holes. For days after December 2, 1992, players in dressing rooms all over North America had gathered in front of VCRs to watch – sometimes a dozen times at a sitting – a fight in New York between the Rangers' Tie Domi and Detroit's Bob Probert.

What made this fight so fascinating to players and fans alike was that it had been promoted long before it took place. The previous season, in an earlier battle between the two enforcers, on February 9, 1992, Probert had been bloodied by Domi, a much smaller man. As the acknowledged heavyweight champion of the league, Probert was expected to reclaim his title at the first opportunity. He had missed that chance in March when Domi injured his knee and had to sit out a game against Detroit. Over the summer of 1992 Domi bragged to columnist Scott Morrison of the *Toronto Sun* that he had circled December 2 on his calendar. Interest rose as the date grew closer. Domi virtually guaranteed a sellout at Madison Square Garden when he said, "You know how much I've been looking forward to this game. If it's a good fight, it still may pick up the league and get the real game back."

In the week before the fight, the NHL announced that fighting penalties were down 60 percent over the season. That statistic must have disgusted Domi, but it was welcomed by at least a few other enforcers. Peluso had been in only two scraps before he hooked up with Vukota, and people were saying he was turning into a hockey player. Shane Churla of Minnesota was another beneficiary. "The way they were calling the new rules at the start of the season made me try to change the way I played the game," he said. "It forced me to be a better player and to try and keep my game inside the rules."

But Domi was determined to get back "the real game." Lacking other skills, he had dressed in only ten games before the match against Detroit. Acting NHL president Gil Stein sent a letter to the Rangers warning them against premeditated fights, but the 18,200 fans at the game were not to be disappointed. Domi, a fringe player best known for the shape of his head – it resembles a ten-pin bowling ball – was sent out to start the game. Probert, who has the body of a giant, the eyes of a tortured child, and far more ability than Domi, started for Detroit. As soon as the puck was dropped, Probert tugged at Domi and then cross-checked him. Both dropped their gloves and the Fight of the Year was on. Domi eventually went down after an overhead right from Probert, but as usual, no damage was inflicted on either player.

"I think it's great," said Domi's coach, Roger Neilson, after the battle. "It's exciting. Part of the reason those guys are in the NHL is because they're such tough players. They drop their gloves; they have their fight; they go off to the penalty box, and the game resumes. I don't think there's anything wrong with that at all."

The premeditated fight had no clear effect on that night's game, which the Rangers won 5–3 thanks to the play of goaltender Mike Richter. As Bobby Clarke, now general manager of the Florida Panthers, had asked, "How many times do fights ever change the momentum of a game any more?" Domi was already talking about a rematch and ridiculing the league's new rules. "All the new rules have done is given guts to guys who never had them before," he insisted. "Guys aren't fighting any more, guys aren't even hitting any more. It's brutal. It's a joke. We might as well be wearing skirts out there. It's like we're in the Ice Capades."

For all the macho sentiment, hockey fights always end quickly and rarely hurt the participants. The one throwing the punch slides back, the one receiving it slides back; the players' skates act as shock absorbers. Sweaters get pulled, fists rap off helmets – in rare cases heads – and the "fight" evaporates into a testosterone standoff while the linesmen separate the brawlers and the referee sends them to the penalty box. Those who have played the game understand that the laws of physics render most hockey fights meaningless; perhaps that's why they are so much more exciting to American than to Canadian fans.

At first, it was uncertain whether the league would even take action against Domi and Probert. The NHL's first official comment was that "there were two willing combatants in that fight ... there was no incident that would be forwarded to the president ... it wasn't anything out of the ordinary. It was a spontaneous hockey fight." But it very soon became apparent that this stance would not hold. The fight made the news. *The Hockey News* made it a cover story. Bruins manager Harry Sinden was saying, "We move five steps forward and then ten steps back."

Finally, a month after the incident, Stein tabled a bizarre, 11-page report on the Domi-Probert affair: "On December 2, 1992, a boxing match was held in Madison Square Garden. It was one of the most successfully promoted bouts in MSG's history ... Oh, yes, there was also a hockey game played that night ... However, the NHL is not in the fight promotion business." Stein eventually got around to laying the blame for the fight on Domi and Neilson. Domi had been warned "not to engage in premeditated fighting" but had chosen to ignore this warning. And Neilson, he wrote, "planned to and did send Domi on the ice to engage in a premeditated fight with Probert." Each was fined $500. Neither was suspended.

Domi's value went up because of the incident. A free agent who had signed a three-year, $1.225 million contract during the summer of 1992, he had barely played for the Rangers. Yet in one 48-second battle he had regained his "form" and his reputation. Very soon after, he was traded to Winnipeg, his new assignment to protect the Jets' European stars. By January the clumsy, ever-grinning Domi was skating alongside the elegant Alexei Zhamnov and the swift Teemu Selanne. When the Jets briefly became the hottest team in the NHL, in some hockey circles the credit was given as much to Domi as to Selanne.

Domi and Probert are lucky they aren't basketball players. When the New York Knicks and Phoenix Suns fought in March, the NBA fined 21 players and both teams a total of $160,500. It was not the largest fine ever levied by the NBA. That league's attitude toward fighting, as stated by one league official, is breathtakingly simple: "If you throw a punch that connects, you're suspended for a game – it's automatic." Probert connected for 47. He was not even fined.

The Domi-Probert fight and Stein's waffling brought the debate again to the forefront. "The fans," wrote the *Toronto Sun*'s Christie Blatchford, "clearly, not only *want* fighting, they adore it ... It seems the only folks who are truly against fighting are a handful of owners, a smarmy segment of the media, and the handwringers who rarely bother to watch the game but remain convinced it is too violent."

In an interview with *Hockey Stars Presents*, Vancouver general manager Pat Quinn, the author of the profighting discussion paper, suggested that "if the league ever was successful in [ending fighting], the game wouldn't sell in North America. North Americans like contact – just look at football. We've been at 93 percent capacity for the past few years. You know what that means? People like our game. The fans who put out hard dollars accept fighting as part of hockey. I don't know of anybody who has said we should go after the family crowd."

That, of course, is precisely the crowd Disney and Blockbuster have identified as the future of hockey. Quinn, however, sees nothing but looming disaster in such thinking. "Hockey was meant to be a physical game. [Fighting] can act as a nuclear deterrent by settling the game down, or it can get the whole team pumped up. If things keep going the way they are, we may not see any of that. All we'll see is the ugliness of stickwork, a lot of penalties, skilled players playing four-on-four, and a lot of goals scored."

Quinn was falling back on the argument of preference for supporters of fighting: stickwork would increase if hockey's "spontaneous safety valve" were removed. This argument has two flaws. One is that less fighting does *not* lead naturally to more stickwork. The Canada Cup tournaments, the world championships, and – for that matter – the Stanley Cup playoffs are evidence that fighting all but vanishes when games count for something or when (as in international play) fighting leads to expulsion. In such games stickwork does not replace fighting. It could in fact be argued that the single greatest cause of fighting is meaningless games – and most of the NHL's regular-season games *are* meaningless.

The second flaw in Quinn's argument is that fighting is *not* a necessary "safety valve." If that were true, surely it would hold true for all players, yet it is the same two or three on each team who do all the fighting. If fighting is nothing but the release of frustration, then a very few players get frustrated almost every time they step on the ice, and most players don't get frustrated at all.

If the 1992–93 season proved anything, it was that players can easily adjust to new working conditions. The new rules did not increase frustration; rather, they reduced it by eliminating so much hooking, holding, slashing, and high-sticking. Fighting declined dramatically under the new system. So it seems, then, that whatever Cherry believes, the real problems arise when infractions are *not* called. Calgary coach Dave King recently told Carleton University journalism student Matthew Fox, "Tell the referees, 'You've got to call stickwork.' If you think this is going to proliferate stickwork, then we're telling you, 'call it'." The NHL now has proof that it can work.

The very notion of role players goes against the notion of "spontaneous explosion." Every enforcer from John Ferguson to John Kordic has at some time or another said, "I know my job." Fighting is a learned behavior with a formal code. It stands apart from the rest of the game. It has its own values, its own ritual dance, even its own subgroup of fans. The code is strict: tough players must drop sticks and gloves and must never wear face protection. The *appearance* of toughness matters as much as toughness itself; willingness to fight counts as much as fighting skill. Social scientists have called it a "face game" – two role models engage in a dynamic exchange in which each seeks to gain or save face at the expense of the other by appearing to be tougher. If this sounds like the vocabulary of animal behavior, that's because it is.

Clearly, fighting is far more a learned response than a spontaneous reaction. "There's a sense it's going to happen," believes Marty McSorley, the Kings' enforcer. "A real mood will have been created. You better have that sense, know it's coming." That does not make fighting sound remotely spontaneous.

It's arrogant and narrow-minded for hockey players to presume their game is inherently more frustrating than others. Football is surely as aggravating to the players, yet fighting has been banned in that game. Fighting is not permitted in soccer or basketball, two other sports where tempers flare easily. Defenders of fighting in hockey like to say it will never be banned completely, as if this somehow argues in favor of allowing it. The real issue is how a sport deals with fighting – and in this, hockey stands alone.

THE CONNECTION BETWEEN FRUSTRATION AND FIGHTING WAS THE SUBject of the thesis submitted by the Senators' assistant coach E.J. McGuire to the University of Waterloo in 1990 for his doctorate in sports psychology. He chose a typical NHL season, 1987–88, and examined 24,326 penalty minutes that could be classified as "aggressive." Of the penalties involved, 1,806 were for fighting and 233 for being the instigator. The "frustration" argument collapsed under McGuire's analysis: losing teams were not more aggressive than winning ones. "The high level of aggression by teams while winning was not expected," he wrote. "Clearly, winning is not a frustrating experience."

McGuire did find a direct correlation between frustration and aggression in games in which one team was losing by three or more goals. In other words, in games that got out of hand, fights were more likely. If a penalty could hurt a team, fights were far less likely to happen. If neither coach nor players much cared, enforcers felt more free to fight. McGuire could only conclude that "ambiguity of outcome may act as a deterrent to aggressive behavior." In other words, hockey players have no problem controlling their frustration when it matters. A prime example is Peluso himself. The season he led the league in penalties, he averaged 6.5 minutes per game in the box. In 17 playoff games, he averaged less than half a minute and did not have a single fight.

Can fighting and violence in the NHL ever be ended? It would require, more than anything else, a tightening of league discipline, the recent laxness of which was highlighted by Stein's limp ruling on the Domi-Probert fight. Suspensions have been rare in hockey for incidents involving violence. Discipline was hardly the strong suit of John Ziegler – except when players were caught with narcotics. Even so, tighter discipline was a possibility until Stein went public with his belief that "it is not necessary to take players off the ice to deter conduct."

Certain owners had convinced Stein that they could not afford to lose their stars – and by stars they meant Domi and Probert as well as Gretzky and Lemieux. As league president, Stein devised a system whereby players could be fined and suspended, but with the suspensions to take place on nongame days only. This meant a player suspended by Stein would miss practices only. Many NHL players would gladly pay to miss practices.

In November, Doug Gilmour of the Maple Leafs slashed the Kings' Tomas Sandstrom, putting him out of action for more than a month with a broken bone. Stein suspended Gilmour for eight practice days. While the suspension cost Gilmour $28,984 in lost salary, he did not miss even the next meeting with the Kings, which took place during the "suspension."

Stein's curious system of punishment also turned out to be tax-deductible for more than half the players in the league. Gilmour, playing in Canada, could not write off his fine; Revenue Canada had ruled that such fines "will be viewed as punishment or deterrent in connection with the infraction and will not be deducted from income." The Kings' Marty McSorley, on the other hand, playing in the United States, was able to write off the $14,130 he lost while suspended for six nongame days for a vicious cross-check. The Internal Revenue Service had decided to view such punishments as fines imposed by a professional group against its members, and therefore a cost of doing business.

The real issue is not the cost of violence to the players, but its cost to the game. Shortly after Stein's ruling on the Domi-Probert fight, The Sports Network commissioned a poll which found that 74 percent of Canadians believed the NHL would be more entertaining if it were less violent – a surprising figure given that the Canadian audience was thought to be far more tolerant of fighting than the elusive American audience. Further, 50 percent of those polled said that, despite the NHL's recent crackdown on violence, they believed the level of unnecessary violence had increased over the past few years.

A month later, another voice was unexpectedly added to the antifighting side: that of Brian O'Neill, who had spent 27 years with the NHL and been in charge of discipline for most of the contentious years before Stein removed him from office in the summer of 1992. "The aspect of violence has caused us grief," he told a class at Montreal's McGill University. "Not in Canada but in the U.S. I know because I was at the center of it for a long time ... We can change our image. We can't do it via public relations. We have to do it on the ice."

The man hired to change the image of the NHL, Gary Bettman, indicated clearly in his first disciplinary act that he would look for precedent to the National Basketball Association rather than to Stein. Early in the 1993 playoffs, Washington's Dale Hunter deliberately blindsided the Islanders' Pierre Turgeon after Turgeon had scored. The attack separated Turgeon's shoulder and put him out of the lineup. Bettman's decision was quick and clear: a 21-game suspension to Hunter to start the 1993–94 season and $150,000 in lost salary. The Stein era was officially over.

Bettman also announced after the playoffs that he would immediately analyze the league's officiating and bring to a close the endless debate on fighting. As he had come to realize after only five months on the job, "the debate on fighting is too much of a distraction."

While the debate continues as to whether fighting and violence are hindering the NHL's efforts to land an American TV contract, the real future of the game – youth – is being profoundly affected by the acceptance of intimidation in hockey. The Canadian Amateur Hockey Association, the largest developmental program in hockey, has recently concluded that systematic intimidation is now as much a part of hockey as learning to skate and the mandatory-helmet rule.

"The problem," said Murray Costello, president of the CAHA, "has to do with the forcing from the game of almost every player of average or modest structure because of minor hockey coaches recruiting and presenting size and intimidation in order to win hockey games." In 1992 the CAHA concluded that the violent style of NHL hockey – as carried by television and celebrated by such commentators as Don Cherry – had trickled down to and thoroughly saturated minor hockey. "In branch or regional championships at the Bantam and Pee Wee levels of play," said Costello, "it was apparent this year that the recruitment of size for intimidation and neutralizing skills is proving successful." Sadly, he concluded, "many smaller in stature who are often blessed with the highest level of skills are being urged more directly and forcefully with each passing season to leave hockey."

IN A CORRIDOR OUTSIDE THE VISITORS' DRESSING ROOM IN PHILADELphia's Spectrum one afternoon, Mike Peluso stood with a blowtorch and a new stick, working to achieve the exact curve that might lead to another treasured goal. He had never scored so often, never played so much, never been so popular as he was with the Senators. Some were saying that it was his career year, that he would never again rise so high. If he did not go to another team at the trading deadline, they said, he would surely go over the summer while his value was still high. On another team, he would be reassigned to his original role. The smile that was becoming so familiar as the year went on would vanish, once again, into the practiced grimace he had brought with him to September camp.

Peluso hated such talk. He now fancied himself playing many roles. He could score. He could hit. He had found that his natural intensity rubbed off on the younger players even if, at times, it rubbed some of the veterans the wrong way. His exhortations had sometimes led to rolling eyes farther down the bench, but he didn't care. He kept coming at them, talking about "pride" and "heart" and pushing, pushing, pushing. If he had to fight, he would. That was still part of his game, but now only one part.

Fights, Peluso believes, just happen. "Maybe he says, 'You wanta go?' and you go. That's it. You go. You just *go*." It was not a subject for further discussion.

He turned off the blowtorch and set it down. "Have you ever played at this level?" he asked. It was a rhetorical question. "Then you can't possibly understand, can you?"

Nor could Peluso understand when his phone rang on June 24, 1993. He'd been traded to the New Jersey Devils with goaltender Peter Sidorkiewicz for goaltender Craig Billington and left winger Troy Mallette. Billington, the Senators explained, was a fine goaltender three years younger than Sidorkiewicz.

As for Mallette, he was more than four years Peluso's junior and could play the same role. And he would not make the mistake of thinking his job was to put the puck in the net.

CHAPTER SIX

THE SUPERSTARS

Montreal, Quebec

THE MOST CURIOUS THING ABOUT THE ALL-STAR GAME IN ANY SPORT IS that the game itself is unnecessary. Anything memorable is usually found in the surrounding ceremony, when for a brief few moments the old game belongs again to the fans, when sentiment matters more than money, and the past has more pull than the future. The 1993 NHL All-Star Game in Montreal will be remembered, if at all, for two men who could not play and one who – it seemed so obvious – should not have been playing. Heading into the 1992–93 season, there were three North American superstars around which the league and its ambitious new commissioner could fulfill their dream, which was to celebrate and market the game's heroes the way basketball was doing with such extraordinary success. One of the three was aging, one was young, and – appropriately, since hockey fans are said to worship their heroes – the third was at this moment the game's Holy Ghost.

During the opening ceremonies the towering man in the dark suit stood hidden in a back corridor while familiar names were announced amid polite applause and uneven cheering. He heard the crowd roar when the hometown hero, Patrick Roy, was introduced, and he heard the more familiar cheer – the sudden snap of sound only the real heroes bring forth – when Wayne Gretzky's name was called. When he heard the lead-in to his own name he moved through the doorway and into sight of those nearest the entrance, and the sudden snap was replaced by a roar of surprise, the sound building as the fans spotted him and reacted to the presence of a god they feared might be dying.

It was a wonderful moment – the fans first confused, then stirring, then rising slowly to their feet as they began to understand who this was – and how well he looked. Even before the name "Mario Lemieux" was called, old men and young children were rising to their feet cheering, the Prime Minister of Canada, Brian Mulroney, was rising to applaud, men and women were wiping tears away as the tall man in the dark suit raised one arm to the roar.

The roar built and held. The aging one, Gretzky, leaned on his stick and watched. He had heard such cheering before, but rarely for anyone but himself. The only other who could raise such noise as this was the youngest superstar, and in this province the noise would have contained far more anger than admiration. But that player, Eric Lindros, was not even here. Injured and unable to play, he was waiting for an Ontario judge to rule on whether or not he had assaulted a young woman at a bar in Whitby, Ontario.

Lemieux stood to one side of center ice waiting for the roar to subside, but it would not. He seemed nervous, embarrassed by the attention. Finally he turned toward Gretzky and pointed his finger at him. And the roar built another notch.

Lemieux had always been a hero in Montreal. He came from a working-class section of the city known as Ville Émard, the youngest of three sons of Jean-Guy Lemieux, a construction worker, and his wife, Pierette. The spring he was 18, he began taking Berlitz courses in English. He had to – the rest of Canada was suddenly waking up to a fact that was already common knowledge in Quebec: a new Lafleur was among the people, a new Beliveau. In 70 league games for the Laval Voisins, he had scored 133 goals and 149 assists to break the record that Lafleur had set and that Alexandre Daigle would later challenge. He was the sensation of the Memorial Cup tournament that spring and the talk of the NHL entry draft, where the last-place Pittsburgh Penguins would have first pick.

Naturally, Lemieux was of great interest to the Canadiens, who would draft eighth that year. But when Eddie Johnston, then Pittsburgh's general manager, was asked what it would take to pry this extraordinary draft choice free, he had answered, "Up front, a million dollars in a suitcase – plus $200,000 a year for the rest of my life." Montreal should have accepted. Lemieux went to Pittsburgh reluctantly.

In his first season attendance increased at the Civic Arena by 46 percent. Soon every game was sold out. "We used to leave here for the last time every season," Canadiens broadcaster Dick Irvin told *Maclean's*, "and we'd wonder whether we were going to be back the following winter. The rink was only half full. There was no publicity. The media coverage was sparse. We used to ask ourselves, 'How can this team last?' The whole atmosphere is different now, and it's all due to Mario."

English came slowly to Lemieux, and he was reluctant to try it out. When he played (brilliantly) for Team Canada in the 1985 World Championships in Prague, English-speaking reporters arriving late on the scene were told that Lemieux was refusing to be interviewed. The problem, it turned out, was that he had a terror of saying the wrong thing in a language that was still new to him. He found that his reputation for being a difficult interview worked in his favor – it kept reporters at bay. Even as his English improved, he made no effort to regain lost ground with those who had already dismissed him as cold, aloof, and uncooperative.

Being a French-Canadian hockey star outside Quebec is no easy task. Lafleur is said to have stumbled in his early years because expectations were so high. Lafleur, at least, had his own friends and language to retreat to in Montreal. Lemieux was alone in another city in another world, as so many Quebeckers have been through the years in the NHL. André Lacroix, who played for three American NHL teams between 1967 and 1980, says the stress placed on francophone players is extraordinary, the discrimination undeniable. He adds that the all-French lines he played on were sometimes broken up simply because other players were irritated by the three working together in their own language. Early in Lacroix's career, when he was with Philadelphia, coach Vic Stasiuk took his five francophone players aside when the team arrived in Montreal and told them they were no longer to speak French, even among themselves.

The Senators' Sylvain Turgeon was selected second overall by the Hartford Whalers in the 1983 entry draft. Turgeon, who is from Noranda, arrived in Hartford not knowing a word of English. He boarded with an English family and soon became proficient in the language as well as a rising young star. But when he came down with a mysterious injury – it turned out to be a torn stomach muscle, requiring surgery – his teammates turned on him. They called him a "frog" and said he was faking the injury to avoid the tough games. To this day, Turgeon – a loner who keeps to himself on the bus and at the rink – will not discuss the experience.

Lemieux was heading to an anglophone American city *and* the worst team in hockey. It was five years before the Penguins even made the playoffs. Finally, in 1991, they won the Stanley Cup. In 1992 they did it again. In 1992–93 they were without question the class of the league, as well as the NHL's biggest draw. That they were knocked out of the playoffs by the Islanders proves either that anything goes in playoff hockey or that God, if a hockey fan, has a twisted sense of humor. Lemieux was at the peak of his talent, which is arguably as high as anyone has ever risen.

It should have been the perfect marriage: Mario and the new NHL. He was still young. He was handsome. In the fall of 1992 he got off to the most dramatic scoring start since 1985–86, the season Gretzky set the all-time record of 215 points. Lemieux's English had improved dramatically over the intervening years. And if he was shy and reluctant to step into the limelight – while other players spent their summers traveling around to celebrity sports events, Lemieux gardened in his yard and golfed at his private club – that was something he could overcome.

On October 5, 1992, at a downtown Pittsburgh hotel, he celebrated his 27th birthday by signing the biggest contract in league history. Lemieux, now the premier player in the game, would be paid $42 million over seven years. For that investment the Penguins would own both Lemieux the player and Mario the celebrity. His image would be a part of the total package the Penguins were buying. With Gretzky fading, Lemieux's image, like his talent, was soaring.

The relationship between Gretzky and Lemieux has long been somewhat strained. Lemieux's number, 66, is "99" upside down, in deference to the older player. "Wayne is the best hockey player in the world," Lemieux has said. "He still is my idol. He does a lot of things better than I do them. That's why he is my idol." Gretzky has been credited with bringing Lemieux's enormous talents to maturity: when they played together in the 1987 Canada Cup, Gretzky's playmaking made Lemieux the star of the tournament. Gretzky, it was said, taught Lemieux how to win.

Gretzky himself has always been gracious about the younger star. He disputes what others have said about that 1987 Canada Cup:

"People would end up saying that I got him to bloom that Canada Cup," he said in his autobiography, "that I *taught* him how to score, but that's ridiculous. He was already on his way. It was just a matter of time before Mario became one of the great players in history."

Perhaps Lemieux felt patronized by Gretzky's comments; certainly he felt shut out of the chosen circle when, a year after their fabulous Canada Cup triumph, Gretzky married Janet Jones and did not even invite him to the lavish wedding. Then Gretzky, in his first season with the Kings, 1988–89, was awarded his ninth Hart Trophy as the league's most valuable player. Lemieux was furious: he had scored 199 points, 31 more than Gretzky, and had the best season of his career. He'd been selected to the league's first all-star team while Gretzky was the center on the second team. "Nothing in this league makes sense," he said with bitterness. "In the past, they gave it to the best player or top scorer. I don't know why it should change."

Lemieux kept chasing Gretzky into the next season. Among all Gretzky's astonishing NHL records, three stand out: 50 goals in 39 games, 215 points in a single season, and the consecutive scoring streak of 51 games, which he set in 1983–84 while with Edmonton. In 1989–90 it seemed that Lemieux would set a new consecutive-game mark, but then he suffered the herniated disk that would haunt his career from then on. He continued playing in pain, icing his back down between periods and sitting out shifts, and his scoring streak continued. His teammates were fully aware of the agony he played through each night and could not believe how important the record was to him. Finally, at Madison Square Garden, in the 47th game of his streak, he pulled himself out of the lineup between the second and third periods. He hadn't scored but was in too much pain to continue. The streak was over, five games short of the record.

The question would remain whether Lemieux was Gretzky's

equal, but Lemieux's will to win would never again be doubted. In 1991 and again in 1992, when he hoisted the Stanley Cup and won the Conn Smythe Trophy as the playoffs' most valuable player, he proved he also had that ability – which for the past decade Gretzky alone had seemed to possess – to win when it counted.

In 1992–93 Lemieux began another challenge against a Gretzky record – 215 points in a season. After only eight games he had 27 points. His pace slackened, but never enough that Gretzky's record seemed out of reach. Scoring two and three points every night, sometimes more, Lemieux was having a career year that was perfectly timed with his ground-breaking contract. Everything was going right – even his back was cooperating. The herniated disk had been removed after the 1989–90 season. Back spasms still periodically bothered him, but he had learned to play with the restrictions they placed on him. (The team physiotherapist was now doing up his skates for him.) Team physician Charles Burke believed Lemieux was playing at only 60 to 70 percent of capacity – but that was still the best hockey being played in the world. His fiancée, Nathalie Asselin, was pregnant with their first child. They were planning a June wedding. There was a small lump on his neck that he kept nicking when he shaved, but even that would soon be taken care of – as soon as he had a chance, he planned to show it to the doctor.

But barely a month after he had signed his $42 million contract, things began to unravel. The Penguins had played Sunday in Chicago and were to play Tuesday in Minnesota. With Monday night free in Bloomington, three Penguins – Rick Tocchet, Bob Errey, and Lemieux – had gone to Hooter's, a bar in the Mall of America that featured finger snacks and young waitresses in neon-orange shorts and torn T-shirts. They were joined by the North Stars' Dan Quinn, a former Penguin and a good friend of Lemieux's.

They passed the evening joking and flirting with two underage women – both 19 in a state where the drinking age is 21 – who were waiting for a third, one of the waitresses, to go off duty.

The women agreed to go back to the Marriott, where visiting teams stay. The three women and three of the players ended up in Lemieux's room, 1001. (Errey had called it a night.) What happened in 1001 is still in dispute. Later that night, the women gave statements to the police alleging sexual assault by Quinn. The players also gave statements to the police. All of the parties' statements and the evidence collected were subsequently sealed by court order. In news reports of the episode, police said they had a "strong case" and that they would be laying charges of first-degree criminal sexual conduct.

Lemieux was at first identified in news reports only as "a Pittsburgh player"; later he would be clearly identified. The charges, if laid, would be against Quinn, but Quinn was just a hockey player – Lemieux was the game's greatest star.

The news caused a firestorm in Quebec. It became a major issue on the talk shows and in the papers, and there were devastating attacks on Lemieux's role in the sordid incident as well as, at times, passionate defenses of him. The Penguins lost to Detroit 8–0 the day it was leaked that Lemieux had been the Pittsburgh player involved. Penguins coach Scotty Bowman admitted he would have to do some serious "psychological restructuring" of his charges to get them over this incident.

Others, of course, were far more concerned for the women. The revelations had undermined Lemieux's godlike status in his home province, particularly among younger, more socially progressive fans. At the very least, something troubling had gone on in room 1001.

Hockey's sexual mores in 1992–93 were largely stuck in the

1950s. When a woman accepted an invitation back to a hotel room for a drink, most hockey players assumed that she was tacitly approving whatever might follow. Road women – groupies – were for quick use and quick disposal. A woman who let herself be placed in such a situation was asking for it. In the world of hockey, real men conquered unreal women. The 1990s were still a time for snide jabs at the sexual proclivities of players who had not yet displayed their "manliness." During the playoffs the media got caught in an war of absurd innuendo against the Maple Leafs' Wendel Clark and Glenn Anderson. On national television, Don Cherry kissed the cheek of hard-nosed Toronto center Doug Gilmour to prove he was "a nineties guy." In fact, even the more enlightened in hockey were a decade behind society.

Quinn's lawyers were prepared to argue that the activity had been consensual, not forced, and that their client was not guilty of anything except poor judgment. On November 24, however, the Hennepin County attorney's office announced it would not be filing charges against Quinn, even though police chief Bob Lutz had previously called what had happened an open-and-shut case. Quinn's lawyers were informed of the decision before the police were.

The matter was dropped in the courts but not outside them. On the same day, North Stars general manager Bob Gainey released Quinn from the team on the grounds that he had violated the team curfew on the night in question – a violation that is typically ignored or results, at most, in a small fine. The North Stars, however, had taken the precaution of installing a number of "morality clauses" in Quinn's contract when they signed him as a free agent the previous summer. Three times during the 1992–93 season the team would have the right to terminate the contract without being liable for a full season's salary, which meant that the curfew charge was wonderfully convenient. Quinn didn't play again all season.

The larger concern for the NHL and the Penguins was, of course, the public fate of Mario Lemieux. His image was tarnished, but had it been shattered? Would parents want their children wearing sweaters with "66" on the back while they were still wondering what exactly had gone on in room 1001? And how would his play be affected – could he still reach Gretzky's record? These were pressing questions in light of his $42 million contract, which was tied directly to marketing rights for his image.

These questions were, however, rendered moot by a wildly unexpected development. The Penguins played at home on January 5 against Boston. Lemieux, still on line to challenge Gretzky's record, felt his lower back going into spasms, and during the second period he went to the dressing room. Dr. Burke happened to be in the stands with a friend who was an ear, nose, and throat specialist. Burke remembered that Lemieux had recently mentioned the annoying little lump in his neck, and so he had the friend come with him to the dressing room. The back spasms were nothing new; rest would ease them. The tiny lump, however, worried the other specialist, and he recommended a biopsy. It was done that Friday.

Part of Gretzky's allure is his inability to mask his feelings. Lemieux, on the other hand, is remarkable for his sphinxlike ability to hide both pleasure and pain. When Burke met with Lemieux on Monday, the doctor was more nervous than the patient. Lemieux took the news calmly and then drove back to the house he shared with his fiancée in the town of Sewickley. It was during that drive, alone in his BMW, that he began crying.

In one of the season's more striking coincidences, Gretzky began his comeback, with a game against Tampa Bay, the day after Lemieux left the Boston game. The excitement was precisely what the NHL had been hoping for: the return of the Great One in the same season that Lemieux was challenging the all-time scoring record. That same day, however, the Penguins announced that Lemieux's back problems would keep him out of the lineup for two or three weeks.

On January 12 the Kings skated onto the Civic Centre ice for their only game of the year in Ottawa. It would be one of the better efforts of the year by the Senators – a 3–2 loss, the home players shaking their heads over a hit crossbar that would have tied the game in regulation time. But the final score became secondary as soon as a curt, four-paragraph statement found its way into the press box:

Pittsburgh Penguins superstar center Mario Lemieux is suffering from Hodgkin's disease, the team announced tonight.

Lemieux was diagnosed with an early stage of the modular lymphocytic form of the disease, which team officials described as the most favorable form. When diagnosed at an early stage, the disease has a 90 percent cure rate.

The diagnosis was made following the removal of an enlarged lymph node from Lemieux's neck. The disease is confined to the abnormal lymph node, the team said in a one page news release.

"Subsequent tests have shown no evidence of any other problems," the statement said. "Further treatment in the form of radiation for a one-month period has been recommended."

Paul Coffey – once the quarterback for Lemieux's magnificent rushes, now back with Gretzky in Los Angeles – heard the news while sitting on the bench during the second period. He said it made him not want to play the third period. A hockey game suddenly seemed so meaningless, cheering so inappropriate. For Gretzky, who had played poorly – he had barely been able to skate or even keep a puck on his stick – there was a press scrum waiting after the game that choked the hallway. It was his second press conference of the day; his first now seemed brutally ironic. "The saddest thing that happened in the NHL this year," he had said only hours earlier, "was Mario getting hurt." He had also, in a touching moment, hurried off the ice after the Kings' morning skate to fetch one of his special silver aluminum-shafted sticks for Kirk Blades, a seven-year-old cancer patient who had come to see his idol practice.

Still soaking from the shower, Gretzky came to the door and stared, stunned, at the now-familiar lights and cameras and microphones. There was nothing to ask, nothing to answer. His green eyes mirrored the emptiness everyone felt at that moment.

On January 15, Mario Lemieux appeared in front of even more lights and cameras and microphones and calmly let the world know, for the first time, what was going on inside. He spoke of the tears, of the difficulty he had telling his fiancée, of how frightened one feels the moment a doctor pronounces the word "cancer." Dr. Burke talked of the disease, saying that one early report had seemed to indicate that it had spread to Lemieux's lungs but that the X-ray had merely been picking up indications of a low-grade pneumonia Lemieux was also suffering. The prognosis, the doctor explained, was excellent. The lump in the neck had turned out to be "stage one" Hodgkin's disease, which has a 95 percent cure rate. Lemieux sat on Burke's right wearing a gray-blue blazer and a light-blue dress shirt unbuttoned at the neck, his Stanley Cup ring playing with the light whenever his hands moved. He would begin radiation treatments immediately. "My health is more important than playing hockey," he said. "Hopefully, I'll be able to help us win another Stanley Cup. But first things first."

The day after the press conference, the Senators played in

Pittsburgh. The Penguins were still in shock. Rick Tocchet said he felt "a mystery inside me – of not knowing what to do." Others spoke of the team's history, of the way bad things kept happening to the Penguins. A small pewter plaque on their dressing-room wall now seemed more haunting than touching: it was a relief of former coach Bob Johnson, who died of cancer on November 26, 1991, after taking the team to its first Stanley Cup. Inscribed on it was Johnson's best-known quote: "It's a great day for hockey."

Lemieux was not the only player in the NHL with health problems. The 1992–93 season had also seen Islander goaltender Mark Fitzpatrick struggle with a rare blood-and-muscle disorder called eosinophilia-myalgia syndrome. Another goaltender, Flyers rookie Tommy Soderstrom, was dealing with a rare heartbeat condition. Yet another goaltender, Buffalo's Clint Malarchuk, had to contend with an obsessive-compulsive disorder that at one point did not let him sleep for two solid weeks. Defenseman Garry Galley of the Flyers had a misunderstood affliction known as "Yuppie flu," and Bernie Nicholls had an impossible year, first in Edmonton and then in New Jersey, that ended with he and his wife deciding to remove their critically ill infant son from life support.

But among all those afflicted that year, Lemieux was the superstar. "When Mario came into the dressing room and told us," his winger Kevin Stevens said, "there was dead silence. It was an awful silence. No one knew what to say. But we have to believe. Mario has to believe." The players dressed for the morning skate in silence, the empty stall at the far end of the room commanding far more respect than its occupant would have had he been there. Two size 11¼ CCM Tacks hung by their blades. The white No. 66 helmet sat on a high shelf, the CCM Supra pants hung from a peg, the Koho 600 gloves and Jofa shin pads sat on another shelf. A roll of hockey tape and small tubes of lip balm and nasal spray lay on the bench below a framed photograph of a smiling Mario. The scene resembled a closed-casket funeral.

Then Jaromir Jagr came in off the ice, giggling, his face flushed from exertion, and began singing as he undressed opposite the instant shrine. Jagr kept looking at the other players, who were quiet with their thoughts, and at the reporters taking notes for the next edition's big pathos story. He could not suppress his giggles. Naked, bolting for the showers, he stopped directly beneath Lemieux's picture and turned to lecture the room. "He will be back," he promised. "He will be back – don't worry."

Lemieux had been scheduled for 22 radiation sessions over the next month. Each day of treatment, he arrived at the clinic around 8:45 a.m. and entered a shielded room, where he was fitted into an immobilizing shell. His head was placed in a molded mask that had been bolted to the table to ensure stability, and the radiation was aimed at a small circled area where the lump had been found. It was, Lemieux later said, the only time he thought about cancer. On the drive back to the huge, First World War–era house he shared with Asselin, he erased the disease from his mind and got on with his day. He later signed the molded mask as a memento for the clinic. Everyone who dealt with him would remark on his calm.

The radiation made him tired. He was bored and he wanted to play. His requests to return to the ice met with warnings that the radiation might make him temporarily more susceptible to injury. A bone might break more easily. There was no point in taking a chance until, at least, the treatments were finished. He missed 23 games, during which time Buffalo's Pat LaFontaine passed him in the scoring race.

Lemieux returned to action on March 2 in Philadelphia. Though expected to play little, he ended up clocking more than 20 minutes' ice time and scored a goal and an assist. So began a torrid scoring streak that will appear in no record book but will survive forever in the memories of those who watched it. In one 20-game stretch he scored 56 points. He led his Penguins on a record 16-game consecutive-win streak, scoring five goals himself in the sixteenth game. He passed LaFontaine handily and finished the year with 69 goals and 91 assists for 160 points. That effort won him his fourth Art Ross Trophy, his second in a row and by far the most remarkable anyone had ever won. He'd missed 23 games battling cancer! It was an accomplishment for folklore, not the record books.

The Senators returned to Pittsburgh, where Lemieux scored the final goal in a 6–4 Penguins victory. From the way the crowd joined the announcer – 16,164 joyous voices waiting for "by No. 66" before screaming in unison, "Mario *Leeee-mieux!*" – one would have thought he was the only player on the ice with a name and a part to play. No one cared that this was the Senators' 38th consecutive loss on the road, an NHL record. The story, as always, was Lemieux.

To preserve energy that day he had not taken part in the morning skate. Instead he spent that time picking through the several thousand letters he had received wishing him well and offering prayers. The tall, studious-looking man in glasses could not himself explain what was happening on the ice. "I'm tired on the ice all the time," he said. "I just don't have the jump I had a couple of games ago."

And yet he was playing even better now than he had earlier in what was supposed to be his greatest season ever. Part of it, he admitted, was that he was chasing LaFontaine, but LaFontaine had been so gracious about the competition – seeming to cheer for Lemieux himself – that this could not explain all. Lemieux, talking in a back corridor of the Penguins' dressing area, wondered aloud if perhaps it had to do with his mind compensating for his body, with his desperately wanting to prove something to himself and to others. To prove something more than that he could beat LaFontaine. To prove something more, even, than that he could beat cancer. How he could draw such resources when his body was depleted could be understood only if it was understood first that, at this level, mental energy is what carries the day. But where this energy came from, Lemieux himself could not say. "I don't know," he kept saying, "I don't know."

The Penguins went into the Stanley Cup playoffs at the end of an 18-game unbeaten streak and with Lemieux again at the peak of his magical game. A third straight Stanley Cup was generally expected. It had the promise of being the NHL's finest moment. When the Penguins headed into the first round against the New Jersey Devils, hockey was for once commanding more American media attention than basketball. The *New York Times* suggested that Lemieux might be the sort of heroic figure that professional sports needed so badly. "It's kind of tough even to think of myself as a hero," he said. "I've never been too comfortable with any of it. I like to stay in the background and not go out of my way to be on TV or talk to reporters." Yet he was doing precisely this, and with grace and confidence. He was on "Good Morning America," "World News Tonight," and "Wide World of Sports"; he was featured on the front of every sports section in North America.

"I think I'm still the same on the ice and off the ice," he kept saying. "I don't think the cancer changed me." But it had dramatically changed the way the American media treated him. *Sports Illustrated* gave its cover to hockey and Lemieux, something the magazine has long avoided, except for Gretzky. "Remarkably," the magazine reported, "the cancer has made Lemieux greater than the sum of his parts. After being viewed for years as a major figure in a minor sport, Lemieux now transcends hockey. He's being recognized as the world's dominant pro athlete."

Lemieux should not have found such attention surprising, for the culture of sports is built more on sentimentalism than on statistics. In the collective memory of the North American sports fan, Howie Morenz is forever lying in state in the Montreal Forum, Lou Gehrig is forever declaring himself "the luckiest man on the face of the earth" before walking out of Yankee Stadium to die, George Gipp is forever asking the boys of Notre Dame for one final, heroic effort. Such stories are treasured both by children and by adults who cannot stop staring at children's games in search of simple truths. No matter that reality can sour myth (the Gipper liked to bet on the football games he played in), for memory will erase what it does not want to hold. By coming back, by defeating cancer, Lemieux was able to erase room 1001 from memory – a feat all the more remarkable considering the importance North Americans were at that time placing on ending the abuse of women by men. The $42 million investment of Pittsburgh owners Howard Baldwin, Morris Belzberg, and Thomas Ruta no longer seemed foolish. Thanks to the fickleness of fate, they were now part-owners of a perhaps indestructible blue-chip image.

Had Lemieux's team not grown careless during the endless playoffs and let the Islanders steal the second round from them, and had Lemieux ended the season holding the Stanley Cup over his head, it would have been one of the great lingering images in sports history. Even with a different ending, it was *the* big story of the most remarkable NHL season in memory.

"I WISH I WAS JUST BEGINNING," WAYNE GRETZKY SAID WHEN HE finally returned from the injury that at one time had seemed certain to end his playing days. His sentiments were easy to understand: he had been forced to sit out too many of the most interesting moments of a momentous season. For years he had complained – at times a lone voice in the wilderness – about the hooking and the stickwork, and on into October he saw hockey being officiated in a manner he hadn't imagined possible in his time. The new rules policy had collapsed, but the NHL might yet come to its senses again. Also, the North American teams were heavily recruiting Europeans, most of whom played his style of hockey. And there were new franchises promising to end forever hockey's reputation in the United States as a minor, regional sport. And, not least, the NHL finally had a commissioner – a smart young man from the NBA who understood that everyone can benefit from the marketing of a superstar, not just that player's team. It seemed things were really just beginning. Having turned 32 in January, Gretzky felt slightly out of it.

The injury that had sidelined him was a herniated disk between the fifth and sixth thoracic vertebrae. In simple terms, the interior of a disk in his upper back had squashed out through its tougher edges, creating a bulge that could press on a nerve. The problem could easily end his career. It meant that three of the finest scorers in the game – Mike Bossy, Lemieux, and now Gretzky – had all gone down with damaged backs, Bossy retiring permanently in 1987. The reason for all three back injuries, Gretzky said bluntly, was illegal hits. "People who play this game are getting bigger, faster and stronger," he said when his back first began restricting his game. "Hitting from behind is a serious situation. We can't afford to lose a Mario Lemieux or a Brett Hull."

Gretzky's comments were prescient: Lemieux went down first with back spasms; Hull had to leave a game against Detroit with back spasms and did not come back for seven games; and when Gretzky's own back gave out, hockey lost its best-known player – and, in many eyes, the best player in its history.

Ever since Gretzky was a child, people have tried to describe what he does that is so effective. Slight and no smooth skater, he moves about a hockey rink like a weasel in a shed, his turns so sharp and unexpected that they make sense only to him. His vision is more birdlike than human; he's impossible to surprise, aware of everything around him. "Gretzky is like an invisible man," assistant Soviet coach Ivan Dmitriev once said. "He appears out of nowhere, passes to nowhere, and a goal is scored." The American writer George Plimpton described Gretzky's play as "a graceful, swooping style that seemed to materialize him abruptly here and there on the ice." The best book about him remains Peter Gzowski's *The Game of Our Lives*, published in 1981 just as the sports world began to understand what Gretzky meant to the game. Studying Gretzky the winter he turned 21, Gzowski captured him perfectly in a single line: "He is as quick as a whisper."

The winter Gretzky turned 32, the whispers were not so flattering. On September 22, 1992, the Kings had announced he would be out indefinitely. Many believed it would be forever: Gretzky, after all, had said many times that he would retire by the age of 30, and he did not want to hang on beyond his time. And the disk injury, it was said, was more serious than the doctors would admit. Gretzky hated the talk that he was finished and insisted that his back was healing slowly. It caused, he later admitted, some "touchy days at home" – he missed the game dreadfully. "Everything I have in my life," he said, "I owe to hockey. My kids, my family, the money I've made – it's all because of hockey. Getting a second opportunity, you realize how big a part of life it is. You just don't walk away. It's harder than people think." He was adamant that he would return. On December 7 he began skating. On December 26 he had his first practice. On January 6 – the day after Mario Lemieux left the game in Boston –

he came back. It was the 1,000th game of his career.

When the Kings came to Ottawa three games later, it was heartwrenching to watch Gretzky on the ice. His elbows still pumped in that hunched style that is his alone, but he seemed to go nowhere. He had trouble turning, and moved behind the Ottawa net like an old man with a kink in his neck. He could not control the puck; once a yo-yo attached to the end of his stick, it now clanged when he stickhandled, bouncing over the blade.

By the all-star break he had been back 14 games and had 14 points – very modest production by his standards. He had not scored in his last dozen games. He'd had no points in his last three. One NHL coach said he had stared into Gretzky's eyes before a face-off near the opposition bench, and the only conclusion he could draw from what he saw was, "It's over."

The all-star weekend in Montreal was a crushing lesson in what age can do. The Rocket, Maurice Richard, now 72, had dressed in his old Canadiens uniform to carry out the Stanley Cup for its 100th anniversary commemoration. He fell as he stepped onto the ice and dropped the trophy while 16,197 fans closed their eyes. Gretzky, now 32, fared little better. Attending by special invitation of the league, he fell during the first event of the skills competition, unable to dip low enough for a turn around a pylon. The reaction in the Forum was dead – and embarrassed – silence. Meanwhile, on the opposite side of the ice, Buffalo's LaFontaine, 27, was scooting around his pylon effortlessly, skates sizzling, legs certain.

In the all-star game Gretzky fared little better. He could not avoid an early check from Washington's Al Iafrate – perhaps the only check that landed that afternoon. He let New Jersey's Scott Stevens lazily sweep-check him and then stumbled awkwardly, falling out of the play. He was set up by Brett Hull but could not connect with the open net. He fell along the boards for no reason, and when he got up and waved for a replacement, he seemed on the verge of giving up.

It was a miserable weekend for him. His close friend, Paul Coffey, who had joined him in Los Angeles less than a year earlier, had been traded the week before in a six-player deal with Detroit. Gretzky had not been consulted and was furious. Not only was Coffey a friend and a former Oiler from the glory days, but he was also a defenseman with the speed and skill to make those long passes that had led to so many Gretzky goals in Edmonton and Lemieux goals in Pittsburgh. Gretzky considered him essential to the Kings' success. And now there was a report that Gretzky himself was about to be traded to the Maple Leafs – a report he refused to deny. "It's out of my hands," he said at the Forum. "I just heard about it. I don't know what to say, other than I'm not worried about it."

But of course he was. "I don't think I've ever seen him this down," said Coffey. There were now doubts as to whether he could still play; he himself now had doubts that he was even wanted. The great owner-player relationship between Gretzky and Bruce McNall was on the rocks. Coffey himself believed the trade rumor, having already been let down by McNall. "I'm a firm believer," Coffey said, "and Wayne is, too, that where there's smoke, there's a little bit of flame."

McNall arrived at the Forum after Gretzky. It was announced that he would hold a press conference, and reporters waited more than an hour for him to arrive. Perhaps Gretzky really had been traded to Toronto – a simple denial, after all, would have required only a one-sentence statement by the Kings' media-relations department. But McNall wanted to be on display. "I love Canada!" he shouted as he hustled into the gathering like a harried world leader on his way to more important business. With cameras rolling and notebooks rustling, he proceeded to deny the rumor. "It's sort of the most absurd, ridiculous thing I've heard in my life," he said, calling it "a classic case of irresponsible journalism." He said he would never trade Wayne Gretzky, who had done so much for the game. Wayne, he said, had laughed about it himself.

But Gretzky was not laughing. Nor would the star player again praise the star owner, as he had consistently since 1988. From that point on, he would rarely even refer to McNall – not even during the playoffs, when he pointedly praised everyone connected with the Kings' playoff drive *except* McNall. In the hockey world, the rumor of a trade was believed to have had some solid basis – McNall, it was said, was indeed trying to dump Gretzky.

McNall's reputation for deep pockets and extravagance was unraveling. The deal with Detroit – essentially Paul Coffey for Jimmy Carson – made no sense except financially. Coffey was a proven winner, the best power-play quarterback in the business, irreplaceable. Carson was a slow forward with a fine shot, a goal scorer with no other talents. The Kings already had a player with similar weaknesses but far more adept at scoring in Luc Robitaille. But McNall would save $500,000 by swapping Coffey's $1.1 million salary for Carson's $600,000.

Perhaps McNall was taking to heart the argument he'd used on Peter Pocklington – that Gretzky was a rapidly depreciating asset. Gretzky was fading as a player and might soon fade as a personality. McNall needed a superstar in Los Angeles to keep the machine working. He was said to be keen on Brett Hull, who was four years younger than Gretzky, but the price the St. Louis Blues were asking – Kings defenseman Rob Blake and $5 million in cash – made the deal impossible.

McNall denied he was having cash-flow problems of his own,

but few believed him. His Athena II coin investment fund was being wound up ahead of schedule, his Toronto Argonauts were a disaster, and Rocket Ismail, his football megastar, was demanding that his $10 million personal-services deal be paid off in full before he disappeared (McNall hoped) into the National Football League. The contract McNall had offered Ismail was now considered the worst contract in the history of pro sports. On top of that, Toronto seemed on the verge of receiving an NBA franchise – yet more competition for the Toronto sports dollar that the Argonauts had long been chasing without success. McNall's partners, Gretzky and actor John Candy, were already alarmed at the rising loses.

Gretzky was also beginning to make noises about an agreement he and McNall had reached back in 1988, when Gretzky was indeed the best player in the game. According to Gretzky's autobiography, McNall had promised Gretzky's father "that no hockey player would ever make more than me. If somebody suddenly made $4 million a year, I'd make $4,000,001. It's not in the contract, but Bruce shook my hand on it and I believed him." McNall was paying Gretzky $3 million a year, but since $1 million of that was deferred, with no interest, the book value of the contract was more like $2.4 million a year. Gretzky had fallen to fifth place on the money list behind the Rangers' Mark Messier (about $3 million a year), behind the Blues' Brett Hull (about $4 million), behind Mario Lemieux ($4.5 million in the first year of his new contract, with increases in the next five years), and – most insulting of all – behind a rookie, Eric Lindros ($3.5 million a year). Gretzky did not like it – a deal was a deal, and he wanted McNall to live up to his end of it.

His play improved as the season wore on. He dressed for 45 games and finished the season with 16 goals and 49 assists. For any other player, it would have been a good season; had Gretzky played a full year he would have been among the league's top scorers. But clearly he was not what he once was. Some of his old gifts had come back – the feathered passes, the ability to seek out a hole and fill it with opportunity – but he could no longer dominate on skill. Slowed and restricted by his back, he became the first player of whom it could be said that he dominated the play intellectually rather than physically. He found openings that gave him just enough space, and just enough time, to do carefully what he had once done instinctively. His would have been the comeback of the year, had it not been for Mario Lemieux.

In Ottawa, and at the Montreal all-star game, and in Los Angeles when the Kings played the Senators, it seemed as if he was reaching that stage for the first time that most hockey players reach when they are 8, or 12, or 16 – in the snap of a finger, everybody else has caught up, many have passed by. You could see it in his eyes while he played, that look of wonderment – *What is going on?* ... He looked a little confused, surprised, as if hockey was suddenly no longer fun no matter how often he leaned into a microphone and said it was. It was fun in his memory, just as he will always be holding the Stanley Cup aloft in ours, but it was not fun in the moment. The game he was playing was not the game he had once played, and he knew it.

Gretzky's playoff performance, then, was all the more meaningful. The Kings, dismissed as a serious contender by the all-star break, became a team of substance as Gretzky's own damaged game came back together. The Kings finished in third place in the Smythe Division, a point ahead of Winnipeg, then defeated Calgary in the first round, Vancouver in the second, and Toronto in the third to move on to the Stanley Cup final for the first time in the 25-year history of the franchise. Then they fell to the Canadiens, winning the first game but losing the next four.

Gretzky would end the season as the playoffs' scoring leader, but he was not the playoffs' best player. In the Toronto series, 29-year-old Doug Gilmour showed that the Leafs had a late-blooming superstar, just as the Kings had a fading one. Gilmour's work was so intense, and so physically courageous – this, from one of the few NHL players even smaller than Gretzky – that the Conn Smythe Trophy for playoff MVP could legitimately have gone to someone whose team didn't make the final.

The eventual Conn Smythe winner, Montreal goaltender Patrick Roy, put the inevitable tag on this extraordinary season when he picked up the cup, turned in search of a camera and, for $100,000, shouted three times, just to make sure the cameras caught it, "I'm going to Disneyland!"

ABC had agreed to carry a number of the playoff games, but they didn't attract much of an audience. Bruce McNall got Ronald and Nancy Reagan out to a number of games, and Goldie Hawn and Andre Agassi were both seen at rinkside and interviewed on television. Agassi obviously had no sense of the game (he didn't know the difference between a power play and a four-on-four), but no matter – his presence was another stamp of approval for a league that had long sought respect. If celebrities were interested, the world would naturally follow. Gretzky hoisting yet another Stanley Cup was exactly what the NHL had been looking for when it set out to be noticed by the world, but it was not to be.

Gretzky himself did not come out of the 1993 playoffs as he might have. His remarkable comeback was shadowed by a new unease. He seemed cranky. During the Kings' series against Toronto, when *Toronto Star* hockey writer Bob McKenzie wrote that he seemed to be "skating like a man with a piano on his back" – an accurate observation – Gretzky was indignant. The criticism, however, motivated him wonderfully: he scored the overtime goal in Game Six against Toronto and then scored three times in Game Seven. "I don't think I've had this much personal satisfaction during my entire career," he said. "I took the heat. I stood up to it and answered the bell." But in Los Angeles they were saying much the same thing as McKenzie had – for example, that his play was "strictly lower case." Gretzky's nickname among LA writers was now "the Good One." The Great One, apparently, was dead.

Gretzky was acting self-obsessed during the spring of 1993. Perhaps it was to be expected – a premier professional athlete was nearing the end of a remarkable career. Even so, the attitude change was a shock, particularly since Gretzky in public had always shown extraordinary grace and sensibility. When he went on *Hockey Night In Canada* after the Canadiens' victory and turned the interview into a rumination about his own future, it rubbed many fans the wrong way. Gretzky has always been considered a "whiner" by those players who have had to contend with his talents. Such knocks had usually been dismissed as sour grapes; now a whiner is exactly what he looked like.

Gretzky insisted he should be given more money. No one disputes his value to hockey – he has been, over 14 years, the game's greatest natural resource, on and off the ice – but he now sounded more like an owner than a player. He also sounded like a general manager, listing the players on the team he felt should be offered new contracts, foremost among them his personal protector, Marty McSorley. But it was the money that made fans choke. He later let it be known that he felt he should have been more fully rewarded for increasing the value of the Los Angeles franchise by more than $50 million. He felt he was owed for having established the game in the Southwest and that he should have got a portion of the controversial $25 million that had found its way into McNall's pocket the day the

Anaheim franchise entered the league. And he had, of course, taken the Kings to the Stanley Cup final, which meant a lot of extra sell-outs to help McNall refill his pockets.

Gretzky wanted what he considered his fair share; about $8 million a year seemed reasonable for a player of his stature. But his gifts were fading, which made it all seem rather pathetic to viewers struggling through a deep recession. Whatever the validity of his arguments, they should have been put forward in private rather than offered to the media during the Canadiens' triumph. It was as if an aging Mickey Mantle had come to the door of Yankee Stadium to claim back wages.

SPORTS JOURNALISM IS NO LONGER DEDICATED TO FASHIONING "TIN-can gods out of cast-iron jerks," as *Globe and Mail* sportswriter Dick Beddoes put it in 1970. John Kennedy could only have been president of the United States in the decade before Watergate, for out of that scandal came a fundamental shift in the manner in which journalists – sportswriters included – examine public personalities. Babe Ruth would never have become the beloved "Bambino" if he had played in the last three decades of the twentieth century. Ruth was, Robert Lipsyte has written, "the prototype for the cock jock, the loud, vulgar rambunctious male athlete whose excesses, irresponsibility, com-mercialism, and total self-absorption were all excused as necessary parts of the whole." His teammates, Lipsyte noted, considered him "the kind of bad boy it's easy to forgive." This would not hold today: Ruth would hang on to his job for as long as he was hitting so many home runs, but his popularity with the fans would drop once his true nature became public knowledge. And in the era of the superstar-athlete as partner, that could be as devastating to a fran-chise's well-being as an 0-for-40 losing streak.

One of the more curious side-stories in modern baseball is that the performers are stuck with a negative image. Baseball players are generally regarded as greedy, disloyal, obnoxious, and self-centered, and that generalization has hurt even the exceptions. Advertisers tend to shun baseball players when it comes to endorsements. In May 1993, *Worth* listed the top sports personalities in terms of endorsement figures. No. 1 (no surprise) was basketball's Michael Jordan, who picks up an extra $25 million from Nike, Gatorade, General Mills, Chevrolet, McDonald's, Sara Lee, and Wilson Sporting Goods. The others included three golfers and nine tennis players – but no baseball players.

The fastest-rising new star on the sports scene is basketball's Shaquille O'Neal, now in his second season with the Orlando Magic. O'Neal had contracts with Reebok and Spalding even before he signed his first NBA contract ($40 million over seven years). The NBA is counting on O'Neal, *The New York Times Magazine* reported in the spring of 1993, "to lead it into the next generation and a continuation of the spectacular, personality-driven growth of the last decade that has made the league the most astonishing success story in the history of professional sports." The NHL, of course, is hoping to follow basketball's lead. Having missed the boat with Gretzky, the league is hoping that Mario Lemieux will become its Michael Jordan, Eric Lindros its Shaquille O'Neal.

A superstar player is no team's automatic solution. Lemieux did eventually bring a Stanley Cup to Pittsburgh, but he had been a superstar for years by then, and the championship served only to confirm his greatness. Lindros may be many years away from making the Flyers a force in the NHL. Gretzky has not and probably will not deliver a Stanley Cup to Bruce McNall (though it would be absurd to deem him a failure). All three are superstars in every sense of the word. But it is a word too freely thrown around in a game that is desperate for personalities who, like O'Neal, can lead hockey "into the next generation."

Two players have recently come up just short: Brett Hull and Mark Messier. St. Louis's Hull is a one-dimensional player who scored 72, 86, and 70 goals in each of the seasons leading up to 1992–93, when he "fell" to 54. Though he's perhaps the game's most prolific scoring machine, his image disappoints. His own general manager has called him "a floater." He does not bother to hide his disappointment with teammates who fail to get him the puck. At one point during the season he responded to criticism by insisting, "It's not my fault there is no one here to play with." Messier fell from grace when his New York Rangers missed the 1992–93 playoffs after finishing first overall the previous season. A disappointment on the ice, he was said to be a key factor in Rangers coach Roger Neilson getting sacked halfway through the season.

"There's no question superstars can pose problems for a coach," Neilson said in 1991 when Messier came to the Rangers, "but that's part of coaching. To be a successful coach, you have to be able to get along with your superstar."

Superstars are a risk. They are different. What fascinates those closest to the game is the way pure talent flies in the face of conventional wisdom. Guy Lafleur, perhaps the finest skater among the extraordinarily gifted, never did a thing to get in shape or stay in shape. His daily regime, even during the fitness-mad 1980s, was to consume as much coffee and smoke as many cigarettes as he could before a game and between periods. After workouts, Washington's Al Iafrate – the hardest shooter and third-fastest skater in this year's skills competition held during the all-star break – sits on a chair outside the Washington dressing room chain-smoking.

Lemieux does nothing to stay in shape but walk around a golf course. Gretzky only recently began to work out, partly to rehabilitate his back, partly to prolong his amazing career. They make no sense as athletes – until the game begins.

What all this seems to prove is that superstardom is a gift. Training and hard work can improve an athlete's skating, shooting, and passing, but those skills only come together when the gods so decree it. This, and the strong personality that goes hand-in-hand with supreme ability, is what makes a superstar such a risk, but also makes him so valuable to the team's owners. If the talent pans out, he deserves the label. If the image pans out, the opportunities for the owners are basically limitless.

PERHAPS IT WAS FOR THE BEST THAT ERIC LINDROS WAS UNABLE TO PLAY in the all-star game in Montreal. Who knows what sort of reception he would have got. Early in the season, in Quebec City, a young man, with the television camera panning his section, lifted a sign that spoke for the 15,399 Quebeckers who had crammed into the Colisée that night: FUCK LINDROS. Each fan had been issued a baby pacifier on entering, and each time Lindros stepped on the ice those pacifiers pelted down from the stands, along with epithets attacking everything from his ethnic background to his personal greed to his mother. For a 19-year-old it was a brutal start to a difficult season.

Little more than a year earlier Lindros had been tagged the savior who would lead the Nordiques out of the wilderness. Many believed the team had deliberately finished last so that it could claim the massive, mean Junior, then playing for the Oshawa Generals of the Ontario Hockey League. Marcel Aubut, president of the Nordiques, had wanted him desperately, for he could see that Lindros was going to draw. If they loved him he would pack the place; if they despised him he would pack the place. He would attract television, sponsors, and merchandise, and he would build the arena that Aubut had decided the Nordiques had to have.

Lindros had said he wouldn't go to Quebec, but of course under the rules of the NHL it was not his choice to make. He had warned Quebec not to draft him, but of course Quebec did. Lindros had refused the traditional donning of the team sweater at the draft, but Aubut believed he would come around. At one point there was an offer of $50 million on the table, which Lindros and his family and his agent refused, and in the end the Nordiques had been forced to trade him. The resulting deal so strengthened the Nordiques that at the start of the 1992–93 season they were being called the most exciting team in hockey. Still, Lindros had snubbed them, and on this first visit to the Colisée he paid for it.

It is, some players have said, extremely difficult to play in Quebec. John Ogrodnick of the New York Rangers played half the 1986–87 season there and remembered it as "a three-month nightmare." In a city where 96 percent of the population is French, he did not speak the language, and his wife was unable to adapt. American players, who tend to have no feel for second languages, and players from Western Canada, who understand language frictions too well, are the most reluctant to play there. Europeans, who have a greater appreciation for the diversity of languages, adapt far better than anglophone Canadians. "It's such a beautiful city," said Mats Sundin, a Swede. "I can respect people who don't want to play here, but I don't agree with them." Mike Ricci, who grew up in Toronto and came to Quebec in the Lindros trade, fell in love with the city, as the city did with him, and happily signed up for language lessons. His teammate, Curtis Leschyshyn, did the same. On the other hand, when Nordiques captain Joe Sakic – born in Burnaby, British Columbia – signed a four-year $8.8 million contract with the Nordiques in December 1992, one clause stipulated that he finally take French lessons.

That Lindros is potentially a great player will never be questioned by anyone who watched him bully the Ottawa Senators into submission in his first shift of the first game he played against them. His extraordinary size, his mean streak, and his skating, shooting, and playmaking abilities all combine to make him unique. In some ways he is the opposite of Gretzky, who knows how to disappear on the ice. Lindros is pure presence, noted by all every moment he is on the ice.

But a player's off-ice presence can be, to a franchise, just as significant. At 18, Lindros published his autobiography (with the help of writer Randy Starkman). It was not an idle effort, and it appeared on the Canadian bestseller lists. His refusal to cooperate with the system made him more interesting as a personality than as a player, though of course his personality would never have drawn attention if his playing ability had not been so great. The point is that Lindros didn't have to establish himself as a player in the NHL to generate a consuming interest among fans and critics. By the time he was 18 he had inspired enough controversy to become a national personality. For that reason he already had a value far greater than that of most established NHL players. Merely by refusing to become a rookie, he caused the trading-card business to switch its emphasis from rookie cards to prospect cards.

"He has bent the game of hockey to his will," *The New York Times Magazine* declared in its cover feature of March 21, 1993. "For the first time, a single player demanded the right to choose his employer and, by dint of what was essentially a one-man job action, forced the NHL to honor that choice ... By doing what he did, Eric Lindros took upon himself the *de facto* leadership of the sport as it moves into the next century."

In his rookie season he sometimes dominated games the way only Lemieux and Gretzky can at their best. In his first game against the Senators, in which he seemed to score at will, the emotion rising from the ice suggested that he intimidated not only the Senators but his own teammates. He looked, from a distance, like a Bantam all-star playing a Pee Wee game. He was the most dominating player the Senators encountered all year. Ottawa's Mark Lamb, one of the better checking centers in the game, had never seen such strength, such will. "I used to think Mark Messier was strong," Lamb said. "There's no comparison. He's strong as a bull – you just can't stay with him." Lindros was 19, in all likelihood seven or eight years from his hockey prime.

Lindros missed a total of 23 games with a knee injury that also kept him out of the all-star game. In the 61 games he did play, he scored 75 points on 41 goals and 34 assists. If he had played the whole season at that pace, his totals would have been 56 goals and 103 points, and he, like Teemu Selanne, would have broken Mike Bossy's 15-year-old goal-scoring record for rookies. For all the injuries and distractions, he had an impressive debut. The Flyers missed the playoffs by only four points; if Lindros had played a handful more games, they would likely have reached postseason play. With Lindros in the lineup, the team won more than half its games; with him out, it won barely one-third.

LIKE GRETZKY, LINDROS HAD GROWN ACCUSTOMED TO THE LIMELIGHT long before he reached the NHL. When he was 16, he was drafted by the Sault Ste. Marie Greyhounds. When he refused to report, he set loose the first of the controversies that would help rather than hurt an image that was growing faster than he was himself. His parents were worried about school, and worried about not seeing him enough, and the Soo was 300 miles from Toronto. Any parent could understand such a decision.

His parents sent Eric to Farmington, Michigan, where he played in a U.S. Junior league. The OHL knew what a gate attraction the 16-year-old would be, and wanted him so badly that it changed its bylaws to allow teams to trade first-round picks. It marked the first time the hockey system had ever changed its rules to accommodate a player. In return for three players, two draft picks, and $80,000, the Oshawa Generals bought a temporary franchise from the Soo Greyhounds.

Lindros was an instant sensation in Oshawa. The league made him an all-star after he had played only one game – and he packed the all-star game. The Soo players wore black armbands in protest. The OHL officials wore wide smiles. He was the biggest draw the league had known since Bobby Orr, who had also played for the Generals. NHL scouts reported that Lindros would be a great player; the owners already knew he would be a great draw.

No one remembers who came first in the NHL in 1990–91 (it was Chicago), but most fans remember who came last: Quebec. Picked by the Nordiques, Lindros again bucked the system. Quebec's general manager, Pierre Pagé, chose him despite ample warnings from the Lindros family that he wouldn't play for them. The philosophy of the NHL entry draft is that you take the best player available, and in 1991 there was no contest.

A half-dozen theories were offered to explain why the Lindroses were snubbing Quebec. The lack of an English-language university in Quebec City was one, the Lindros family's dislike of Marcel Aubut was another. Only two of the theories really stuck. The first was that the Lindroses were francophobic, and no amount of rebuttal by the family – Brett Lindros, Eric's hockey-playing younger brother, is bilingual – will ever change that perception, particularly in Quebec City. One provincial daily in Quebec hired a psychologist to do an assessment of Bonnie Lindros and found her, not surprisingly, rather like one of the Borgias.

The second theory was that the Quebec market was not suitable for a player of Lindros's market potential. This is what separates hockey in the 1990s from all the hockey that has gone before. The game once meant frozen creeks; now it means revenue streams. And while any team's ultimate goal is still to win the Stanley Cup, today's owners are more likely to break out the champagne over other victories: another row of corporate boxes, another block of club seats, better signage, more dasher boards, in-ice ads, concessions, parking, jackets, caps …

There are two roads to success in the NHL. One is to be like the Montreal Canadiens, consistently challenging for the Stanley Cup. The other is to be a competent team with a dominant personality, like the Los Angeles Kings. As hard as it is to land a franchise player, it's still easier than spending 75 years working toward franchise glory. When the Canadiens and the Kings met in the Stanley Cup final, the emphasis in Montreal was on the tradition of winning. In Los Angeles the story of the day was the postseason revenue the team was generating.

Once Aubut realized that Lindros would never sign with the Nordiques, he set out to peddle Lindros to other NHL teams. Aubut split his sales pitch in two. His own hockey people would sell Lindros's playing ability, though there was little need to do that; meanwhile, New York-based International Sports & Entertainment Strategies would sell Lindros's ability to churn up the revenue streams. Lindros had threatened to sit out for two seasons, thereby regaining his draft eligibility, but Aubut guessed – correctly – that it was not a serious threat. (Had Lindros done so, he would have been available to the Senators in the 1993 draft and, in all likelihood, again have refused to go to a small-market Canadian team.) Utilizing the services of ISES, Aubut concentrated on four markets: the New Jersey Devils for the New York market, the Philadelphia Flyers and Detroit Red Wings for their own rich markets, and the Toronto Maple Leafs as the one potential Canadian market. These teams had a number of things in common: all were rich franchises, or had extremely wealthy owners; all enjoyed large market areas with extensive television potential; and all were in need.

ISES did market studies for the teams and assessed the impact Lindros would have on each market and each franchise. A marquee player, the study argued, would boost attendance immediately in those rinks where hockey fans cannot be taken entirely for granted. Where the fans were a given, the greater demand for seats would justify higher seat prices. The presence of such a player would increase the team's television coverage and lead to more lucrative local-coverage deals. Ad revenues would rise considerably for both the broadcast coverage and the in-rink advertising, the latter being tied both to the number of spectators and to the size of the viewing audience. The team would make more on clock advertising, on corporate sponsorship, on signage, on dasher-board advertising, and on the new advertising vehicle coming on line for the 1992–93 season: in-ice plugs. A marquee player would also have a profound effect on licensing revenues. A New Jersey sweater with "88" on the back and Lindros's name stitched above it would become the hottest seller of the season.

The ISES study used the obvious examples. Attendance in Pittsburgh was up 133 percent since Mario Lemieux had come on board. In Los Angeles, Gretzky had packed the rink. Bruce McNall had hoisted ticket prices from an average of $19.50 to $22 ($25 at the window). Gate receipts rose $5 million in the first year, advertising revenue went up $1 million. Jersey sales alone accounted for another $500,000. Gretzky, the argument went, had been a bargain.

The team most favored by the ISES study was New Jersey, whose fortunes had been sagging since the spring of 1984, when the Devils had lost the race for last place – "the Lemieux Cup," the media had dubbed it – and Lemieux had gone to Pittsburgh. Lindros was their opportunity to recoup; even so, the Devils passed on him, though he might finally have filled the isolated Meadowlands Arena. Two other teams began bidding. One was the Philadelphia Flyers, whose need for Lindros was obvious: owner Ed Snider was setting out to build a new Spectrum to play in and, like Aubut, needed a superstar to break the ground. The other was the New York Rangers, a team that already had the fans and the revenue streams, but also had inexhaustible market opportunities and a desperate desire to win after 52 years without a Stanley Cup.

The negotiations took place during the 1992 playoffs and ended at the Montreal draft; in other words, Lindros became the first player in hockey history to dominate two successive drafts. He also became the first player to be traded to two different teams at once. At 1 a.m. on draft day, Aubut sent a piece of paper to Ed Snider's son, Jay, outlining the deal: six Philadelphia players – Mike Ricci, Kerry Huffman, Ron Hextall, Steve Duchene, Peter Forsberg, and Chris Simon – as well as two first-round draft picks and $15 million for an unproven 19-year-old. But an hour-and-a-half later, Aubut informed Snider that he'd struck a deal with the Rangers. Snider went straight to John Ziegler, who was still the NHL president, and officially protested. The NHL handed the predicament over to Toronto lawyer Larry Bertuzzi for arbitration. On June 30, Bertuzzi ruled in favor of Snider.

Within a week, Lindros had signed the biggest contract in

NHL history. Philadelphia would give him a $2.5 million signing bonus and he would be paid $18 million over six years. His agent, Rick Curran, estimated that over this time, Lindros would earn another $10 to $20 million in endorsements, personal appearances, and other ventures. Not long after, Curran was sacked and Lindros's father, Carl, took over the role previously handled by the agent. More controversy; more added value.

Lindros was perceived to be coming into the game at the right place and the right time. Gretzky was fading and had back problems. Mario Lemieux was too shy or too aloof; his marketing value had to ride entirely on his playing ability, which was – for the moment, anyway – great enough to compensate for his reticence. Lindros's rivals were not Gretzky and Lemieux but the new generation of European players: Pavel Bure, Alexander Mogilny, Teemu Selanne. These players too had built-in problems. One was language. Another was the NHL old guard's reluctance to embrace them. Yet another was location. "Lindros is like none of them," *The New York Times Magazine* reported. "They play in the game's great white hinterlands. He plays in the news media heartland that the NHL so feverishly wishes to conquer."

Lindros would change not only the way the game was sold but also the way it was played. "Little kids across the country are going to want to hit again," predicted the Flyers' general manager, Russ Farwell. "Just like Gretzky and Lemieux made kids want to pivot, he might make kids want to run people over again." Plans were racing ahead for the Flyers' move into the $100 million Spectrum II. The nearly 100 Superboxes were selling out; the facility would have 3,000 additional seats in luxury suites, 21,000 seats in all. The Flyers, and Eric Lindros, would move in by 1994.

Then two unexpected factors came into play. The first was

Lindros's knee injury, which reminded everyone, in case it was necessary, that the teenager considered the biggest, strongest, toughest, meanest player in the NHL was vulnerable just like every other player. Bobby Orr's career had been shortened by at least one-third by knee problems. Could something similar happen to Lindros?

And then there was Koo Koo Bananas. Lindros returned to Ontario in late November to see a knee specialist. On the night of November 29 he went out with some old high-school friends and ended up at a Whitby bar by that name. There was beer, there was dancing, and there was an incident. The next day, 24-year-old Lynn Nunney filed charges against Lindros, claiming he had assaulted her on the dance floor and spat beer over her. On December 5, Lindros turned himself in to the police in one of hockey's all-time public-relations disasters: he showed up unshaven, in jeans, a blue-denim shirt, and a white T-shirt. In a mistake in procedure, the police handcuffed him for the ride to the courthouse where he would be formally charged. When he emerged from the car into a flying scrum of photographers and television camera crews, he looked like a convicted felon being transferred to higher security. Photographs from that scene made the front pages of papers across the country. Guilty, before he was even charged.

Two months later, after a ridiculous court case that proved little except that young adults and beer lead all to easily to boorish behavior, Judge J.R. Morgan of the Ontario Provincial Court found Lindros not guilty. Morgan said everyone involved had been guilty of rude and insulting behavior, but there was reasonable doubt as to whether Lindros had poured beer over Nunney's head and then spat beer in her face. Not guilty, but the damage had been done. As Lindros himself noted outside the courtroom, "I'm glad it's over in some respects, but in other ways it's still going on. It's never done, is it?"

Meanwhile, he had just missed another 12 games with his wonky knee. The Flyers had lost five straight and won only twice in their past ten games. Lindros flew back to Philadelphia, where the Flyers were to take on Ottawa. The Senators were about to play their 27th road game without a single point to show for it, but they were, at that moment, the hottest team in hockey – over the past two weeks they had three wins, a tie, and a loss. That Lindros returned in such foul humor was a happy occasion for the Senators executives, some of whom were beginning to panic over Ottawa's unexpected surge. Alexandre Daigle was beginning to sound increasingly like the next Lindros, and the Senators would only get him if they finished dead last.

When the Senators entered the Spectrum, Lindros was already on the ice for practice, a huge, hulking presence relieved to be back on skates. "The rink was my getaway, my little bit of heaven," he said in his autobiography. "If I ever had a problem in school, I would get out into the rink and blow it off. Being on the rink was the best time of day. You didn't care that your room needed cleaning, that you were supposed to help your brother with a project or anything like that. You just didn't obey." He remembered the sensation of "being swallowed up by the surroundings." He remembered how "everything was so simple on the ice. It was just you, your stick and a couple of pucks." A problem in school, a problem in court – the rink was still sanctuary.

Those who throw up their hands in despair at what hockey has become should skip the games and come to the practices, for it is here – perhaps only here – that the simplicity of the game lives on. There are no revenue streams during practice, no spectators in the corporate boxes, no television crews, concessions, flashing ads, or market penetration strategies. On the Spectrum ice Lindros laughed and did backyard tricks with the puck and hit his teammates' sticks with passes that echoed like rifle shots in the empty rink. Here, at least, for the hour of the morning skate, Eric Lindros was not a corporate entity or a public figure or the future of a franchise. He was a kid with a hockey stick and a puck on a sheet of ice, and he was enjoying himself.

The rewards of celebrity are obvious, the penalties less so. Fans cheer, strangers smile. The bar is always open, the law is often forgiving. But for every Billy Martin there is a drunken salesman wanting to take his best shot; celebrity brings with it risk. Eric Lindros has been learning slowly that you cannot throw beer, cannot show up in prison denim for a photo op, cannot tell a fan at the airport, "Put your camera away or I'll kill you." On this night, after leading his team to an 8–1 crushing of the Senators, he would say. "It's my rookie year, and I'll do a lot of learning on the ice and off as well."

Off the ice he blurs. He is a man, he is a child. He is 6' 4" and 235 pounds, he is 19 years old. He is a player, he is a celebrity. Wealthy beyond a teenager's wildest imaginings, he wears an off-white Oniga sweatshirt, faded jeans, and loose runners. He once admitted that he cried when child actor Macaulay Culkin died in *My Girl*, but he has shown no sympathy for Lynn Nunney – instead he has talked of revenge and countersuit. On the ice he is commanding, off it he seems to shrink into his own bulk, his voice now a soft, teenager's voice, his eyes avoiding contact, the hands nervously twisting a plastic coffee stick.

In January there had been a report of another incident, this time in a New Jersey restaurant. There had been no charges, but it had been confirmed that Lindros had been present. The Flyers were considering putting a watchdog on their young star. (They would later do just that, moving him in with the family of veteran Kevin

Dineen.) Lindros, of course, felt he didn't need one. The day before, he had been asked outside the courthouse whether he had learned his lesson, and he had answered, quite reasonably, "You're telling me to stay inside. Well, I'm a kid, and I like to do things that kids do, and I'm not going to compromise my life." A kid; but not a kid.

Leaning against the wall outside the Flyers' dressing room the following day, he said, "I *don't* need a babysitter ... I'm not going to lock myself up in a house and not go out and have some fun." He did however, acknowledge that when he did go out again, "It's just going to end up in the social columns."

He has long been more than a kid and is now more than a player. He is a celebrity. Macaulay Culkin stopped being a kid the day moviegoers began paying millions of dollars to see his films. Perhaps his emotional reaction to Culkin is a matter of instant identification. The child in Lindros has been destroyed by his talent, and by the opportunity for so many to profit.

The teenage corporate entity that is Eric Lindros twists the coffee stirrer until it whitens along the stress lines, then says, almost in defeat, "You can't control people's minds."

But, under these circumstances, you must control yourself.

CHAPTER SEVEN

THE COACH

Uniondale, New York

CLOSE ON MIDNIGHT, THREE FIGURES SET OUT ACROSS THE EMPTY parking lot of the Nassau Veterans' Memorial Coliseum, the only sound the slight click of leather soles on rainwater. Ottawa assistant coaches Alain Vigneault and E.J. McGuire walked shoulder to shoulder but alone in their thoughts. Vigneault – 31 years old, a proud man who had passed up a job with the Nordiques and the head coaching job with Canada's national Junior team to join the Senators – had a number in his head that he could not shake. "Nine points," he kept saying, sometimes to himself, sometimes to no one in particular. "Nine fucking points."

Vigneault went jogging every day. Sometimes he chanted a number while he ran, the mantra changing so slowly – "five" after seven weeks of the season, then "six," then "eight," then "nine" (thanks to a 1–1 tie against a listless Calgary team) – that he was now sure he would go insane if it weren't for the escape of his daily runs, which had become so much longer that he'd lost 20 pounds since the season began.

Thirty-four games into the season and the Senators had nine points. To beat Washington's 1974–75 futility record of 21 points the Senators had only to maintain this pathetic pace, but recently the team had been playing worse than usual, if that was possible. In Hartford the Senators had fallen 6–2 in what coach Rick Bowness had called "the worst performance of the year." This night's game – a 9–3 humiliation by the Islanders that had them laughing in the stands and chanting "We want ten! We want ten!" – had been no improvement.

Beside Vigneault walked McGuire, video equipment slung over his shoulder. The VHS tape for the game had been handed to him by the Islanders' staff while he was leaving. He would take it back to Ottawa and stack it with the others in the team's practice facility in suburban Kanata. Thieves would later break in and make off with six videocassette recorders, a large-screen television, and a satellite receiver, but they would identify themselves as discerning hockey fans by taking only blank tapes. Not even for free was any-one interested in the video record of what was becoming the Ottawa Senators' season from hell.

McGuire, 40, with seven years and more than 300 NHL wins behind him as assistant to Mike Keenan in both Philadelphia and Chicago, had never seen anything like this. The year before, in Port-land, Maine, where he had coached the Mariners of the American Hockey League, he had dealt with bad losses by going back to his apartment and staring out over the Atlantic toward England, "where no one knew or cared that we'd been beaten 7–2 that night." But now, wherever he looked for escape, he found the Senators' record staring back at him. The presses at *Long Island Newsday* were beginning to print the Island edition, which the coaches would read at breakfast. The lead hockey story would call the Senators "a semi-fraud" as a professional team.

To the right of the assistant coaches walked Rick Bowness, who was even more troubled. Bowness's hunch this night had been that his team would get its first road win in 15 tries. He had started backup goaltender Steve Weeks, then yanked him after one period.

The Senators had been about as aggressive as a child reaching for a garter snake, and the Islanders had charged at will. Even Darius Kasparaitis, the young Lithuanian defenseman that Ottawa had passed on in June, had scored. "That's about as bad as we can play," Bowness told the postgame scrum.

The players were also feeling the frustration, but the ones having the toughest time on this night were the coaches, especially Bowness, whose job required him to take most of the heat. No one spoke – there was nothing to say. Bowness knew that his three-month refrain about "work ethic" was wearing thin. He knew that such phrases are merely tricks, the language that losers speak to avoid reality. The same phrase was the daily line in San Jose and Tampa Bay and Hartford. The coaches in those NHL cities knew as well as Bowness what it meant in translation: work ethic be damned, we need real players.

E.J. McGuire's coaching career had begun at Brockport University in upstate New York, and he was coaching the University of Waterloo team in Ontario when Keenan hired him. His approach was sometimes academic and involved, among other things, applying a ratings system to each game. McGuire assigned a mark between 0 and 5 to each player. A 5 indicated "a good, NHL performance," with the player outplaying his counterpart on the other team. A 4 was awarded for those nights when the player's "good plays clearly outnumbered his bad plays." A 3 was "an average performance," with bad plays canceling out the good. A 2 was "below average," with the bad plays outnumbering the good, and with little effort and an attitude "not consistent with that of a winner." A 1 was "unacceptable," with the player operating well below NHL standards and contributing nothing. A score of 0 was so "awful" the player may well have helped the other team more than his own. If everyone played to a 4, the team would win; by playing to 3 they could hope for a tie.

On a 20-man roster, a perfect team score was 100. When McGuire and Keenan devised this system in Philadelphia, the Flyers regularly scored in the 90s. So did the Blackhawks when they applied it in Chicago. The 1992–93 Senators rarely did better than 50. Even on the night that they somehow beat Pittsburgh 2–1, their score was still only 73 – an indication of how dreadfully the better NHL teams sometimes played when they came to Ottawa.

The Senators had only one thing in their favor as Christmas neared – the new rules experiment was dead. Clutch-and-grab was essential to any success the Senators might conceivably have, and it was back. There was little else to give hope. Bowness was down on the veterans for not coming through. The veterans were down on the young players for lacking "heart" – hockey's most damning condemnation. The coaches, having failed to convince management that an $18,000 computer system would give them better player assessments and scouting details, were despondent over the rumor that the team mascot, the Lion, was making $100,000 a year and had a company car. Worse, the Senators' upper management was bragging that the club would make $13.6 million this season and, even after servicing of debt, would end up the third or fourth most profitable franchise in the league.

The *Newsday* edition the three men would read the next morning would point out that in the previous season, Brett Hull alone had scored four more NHL goals than all the Senators combined. The veterans and coaches were longing for a free agent like Dan Quinn, once a 40-goal scorer in the NHL, who had been released by Minnesota after a November 9 hotel-room incident that had also involved two women and Mario Lemieux. The Senators had considered taking him but in the end declined his services, apparently because of "character." (It may also be that the Senators were quickly coming to the conclusion that they did not want many more points.) "Character's fine," a Senators veteran had said that morning in the hotel lobby, "but it can't fucking score goals."

The style the team was forced to play – dump and chase, clutch and grab, hope the opposition dozes off, pray for a lucky break – was satisfying the 10,500 fans who showed up every night in Ottawa. They were content merely to have the NHL in town. At the same time, it was infuriating the players on the other NHL teams who had to play against the Senators, as well as the spectators in the other arenas who had to watch. Montreal defenseman Mathieu Schneider had called the teams' most recent meeting "one of the most boring games I've ever played in." *Hockey Night In Canada* wit and analyst Harry Neale was making caustic remarks and blaming the Senators' play on the team payroll. How, people were asking, could the Senators brag about a payroll that didn't reach $6 million – less than what Mario Lemieux alone would make – and then pass off what was happening to the team as the natural result of expansion? "This business is the same as any business," Neale said. "If you have the cheapest product on the market, then you probably have the worst one, too." That the Senators were the worst team in all hockey was, at this moment, beyond dispute.

Rick Bowness had the awning down as he headed for the rear entrance of the Long Island hotel after the loss to the Islanders. Play-by-play radio announcer Dean Brown had first noticed this physical oddity in Bowness, this elongation of the forehead caused by a drooping, furrowed brow. If the awning was down, people knew better than to speak to him. The few players still in the lobby scattered. The reporters beginning to gather at the bar turned to their wings and beer. Silently, Bowness crossed to the elevators, entered one and pressed the button for the seventh floor, the elevator hesitating just long enough for one unsuspecting member of the press to slip inside as he hurried to file.

For six floors the elevator rose in chilled silence, Bowness leaning against the back wall, the reporter making sure the numbers were in their proper order as each one lit up. Finally, at the sixth floor, the silence was broken by an enormous burst of held breath. The startled reporter turned to discover Bowness, the awning raised, sliding down the back wall in a heap of laughter. With nine points, what else was there to do?

BIG BOB BOWNESS, RICK'S FATHER, WAS A HUGE, HANDSOME MAN WITH a love of good clothes and a rakish George Raft part to his hair. He was a fine hockey player, a tough winger able to lead a league in both goal scoring and penalties. With a bit more speed he might have had a career in the NHL. He was born and raised in Montreal and played Senior semiprofessional hockey in Halifax and Quebec City. His one great chance came in 1951, when the Montreal Canadiens offered him a two-year contract at $5,000 a year with a $2,000 bonus to sign. Big Bob was on top of the world, newly married to Thelma and headed for the big league. He used the bonus money to buy a brand-new Chevrolet sedan, in which they set out together for Montreal.

The Canadiens' training camp was an experience he would never forget. He skated on a line with Billy Reay and Floyd Curry and even played a few shifts with the great Rocket Richard. But it was over too soon. The Canadiens liked another young forward, and Big Bob, Thelma, and the new Chevrolet set out on a minor-league tour that would eventually land them in Moncton, New Brunswick, where, in 1955, their first son, Richard, was born.

By the time Rick began hockey, the Bowness family – now with another son and two daughters – was living in Halifax. Bob had opened a sporting goods store, and his playing reputation around the Maritimes had the customers pouring in. They still called him "Big Bob" and "Bono," and soon enough they were calling the younger Bowness "Bones." The reasons were obvious – he was tall and gangly and had to spread his arms to reach the width of Big Bob's shoulders. But "Bones" would fill out, and he was as tough as the old man, and had a better shot, and was even hungrier for a chance at the NHL. He would not drink his first beer until he was well past legal age, for fear it might somehow ruin his NHL chances.

At Halifax West High School the younger Bowness began dating Judy Egan. To play Junior he had to leave home at 16 – first for the Quebec Remparts, then for the Junior Canadiens – but, like a young soldier heading off to battle, he promised to return one day and marry. In 1975 the Atlanta Flames drafted him – 25th overall, behind first pick Mel Bridgman – and signed him to a contract that included enough bonus money for him to buy a Corvette. He set off with the same nervous anticipation that Big Bob and Thelma had felt a quarter-century earlier.

The NHL had tripled in size since 1967, and the rival World Hockey Association had opened up even more jobs in the game. Even so, Rick Bowness found it a difficult transition. He'd been tough and effective in the Quebec Junior leagues – he once scored 100 points in a season – but he found the NHL far more intense and the expectations shockingly different. Once the star, he was now the role player. It is the story of all but a handful: the puck carrier becomes the puck chaser, the shooter the blocker, the checker the fighter, the reluctant to change the quickly replaced. Atlanta coach Fred Creighton took a look at the tall rookie's first drill, skated over, and crushed him with two sentences: "Son, you're a little too slow to play center. We're going to take a look at you on the wing."

Bowness never again played center, never again dared consider himself a playmaker. His role was simple: up and down right wing, grind it out in the corners, move the puck to someone who knows what to do with it, be prepared to fight for your teammates and your job. Bowness was a good fighter. He fought, and cut, Mel Bridgman that first year. He was sent down to Tulsa and became, at 20, the talk of the Central Hockey League when, during the playoff final against Dallas, he took on tough guy Dave Logan and knocked him out with one punch. It was the turning point in the championship series, which Tulsa won.

Bowness was one of that multitude of players who get caught between two leagues – too good for one, too weak for the next, frustrated in both. In the minors he had respect. They noticed when be broke three fingers in a fight, came to the rink the next game with his hand swollen so badly the glove would hardly fit, rammed the broken fingers into their slots, then went out and scored a hat trick. But in the NHL he was seldom noticed at all. In Detroit, general manager Ted Lindsay told him he didn't have what it takes, and it seemed he could never get the chance to prove them wrong. He survived till he was 26, spending parts of seven seasons in the league. Atlanta moved him to Detroit the year he and Judy married. Detroit sold him to St. Louis, St. Louis to Winnipeg.

In Winnipeg he had an all-important lesson in losing. The 1980–81 Jets went 30 games in a row without a win, and it marked the players forever, just as the 1974–75 Capitals would be forever branded as losers for their 21-point season. He never again wanted to live through such ignominy.

Winnipeg, where he was a fringe player on the weakest team in the NHL, was his last stop. By then he was a "character" player, as Darcy Loewen and Brad Marsh would be a dozen years later with the Senators. Their skating might be suspect, their shooting dubious, their skills slipping – still, their hearts beat with a hockey rhythm that is pure Canadian: neither snowdrifts nor hurt feelings nor injury would ever keep them from showing up first at the rink and from working the hardest and cheering the loudest even if they never so much as left the bench. Bowness finished his NHL career with a total of 173 games, 18 goals, 37 assists, and 191 minutes in penalties.

Character players have a way of turning into winning coaches. Glen Sather, Al Arbour, and Fred Shero were all brilliantly successful behind the bench. On-ice flair almost never transfers to the chalkboard – witness Rocket Richard, Bernie Geoffrion, and Bobby Orr. (This phenomenon is not unique to hockey: baseball manager Earl Weaver never made it to the major leagues as a player, Sparky Anderson was a dreadful player for one year, and Whitey Herzog once said, "Baseball has been good to me since I quit trying to play it.") Perhaps it is because the stars never spend much time on the bench, while journeymen usually spend years watching plays develop and unravel and imagining how they might improve the patterns.

John Ferguson, then the general manager of the Jets, saw Bowness as coach material. The Jets made him player-coach in Sherbrooke, Quebec, then sent him to their American Hockey League affiliate in his hometown, Moncton, where he turned the team around in only his second season. He and Judy now had three children and believed themselves settled when the Jets organization began to fall apart. Ferguson was fired in December; soon after, with only 28 games left in the season, coach Dan Maloney was also fired and Bowness was named to replace him. It was an awkward, tense situation and Bowness didn't like it. When the team won only eight more games, the new general manager decided to bring in yet another new coach, Bob Murdoch, to take the team into the 1989–90 season.

In Ferguson's opinion, dumping Bowness "was the biggest mistake they ever made."

The Bruins offered Bowness the Maine Mariners, their AHL farm team, and he spent two seasons with them, in both taking the team into the playoffs. In 1991 a shake-up in the parent club again brought him back to the NHL. General manager Harry Sinden decided his fiery-tempered coach, Mike Milbury, should join him in the front office and help him redesign the Bruins for the 1990s. Sinden wanted to turn the Bruins from lunchpail grinders into a more international-style team built on speed and skills. Perhaps they would want another coach later, but in the meantime Bowness would do. He had a reputation as a communicator and was said to be good with young players. And he would be more patient than Milbury during the transition. Sinden offered a two-year contract at $140,000 a season, which Bowness accepted.

Bowness had already decided that "no matter what, I would be the exact opposite to what Mike Milbury had been." His two years in Maine had made him familiar with the players bouncing back and forth between the two clubs. "I knew what was being said. I knew what the players thought. I knew they were fed up with the temper tantrums and the screaming and the whining. I went there absolutely determined they would never, ever hear it from me, no matter what. I would be the nicest, most even, most understanding coach they ever had to deal with. The players would never have reason to feel about me the way I knew they did about Mike."

It was an impossible year. With Sinden and Milbury constantly tinkering, Bowness had to deal with 55 different players over the season. He spent almost the entire year without the team's top offensive player and key intimidator, Cam Neely, who dressed for only nine games. Many players were injured, including, when it mattered most, all-star defenseman Ray Bourque. The team got off to a weak start and there were soon rumors of Bowness's imminent firing. Previous Bruins coaches had all been fire breathers – Don Cherry, Terry O'Reilly, and Milbury, to name three. Bowness was being dismissed as "too soft." The rumors, it was said, came from Milbury himself, whom some thought resented the presence of anyone else behind the bench.

Bowness was indeed different. Unlike O'Reilly, he never took a tire iron to a parked car that was blocking the team bus. Unlike Milbury, he never yanked off his shoes, Khrushchev-style, to pound a point home. Even so, by early December Bowness's self-declared patience was running thin. During a road loss to the Nordiques he ordered two lackadaisical players, Craig Janney and Bob Sweeney, to take off their sweaters after the second period. It was an unheard-of coaching tactic and it made Bowness both a villain and a hero on the Boston radio circuit. Had his team not beaten Montreal two nights later, the local hysteria might have cost him his job. Two months later, after the Bruins were swept by the Blackhawks in a two-game series, the rumors of his imminent firing came back, stronger than ever. It was a terrible time for the Bowness family – the boys were coming home from school in tears – and Bowness could see no sign of confidence from management. When his team began a late-season rush, credit went instead to a trade the Bruins had made – Janney to St. Louis for playmaker Adam Oates – and to the arrival of four Olympic players, including the promising Joe Juneau.

The Bruins could never quite make clear what it was they considered lacking in Bowness. The closest Sinden ever came was to speak of some "slippery ingredient" that some have and some do not. "If I could define it, I would," Sinden said. "It's an element, an instinct." Bowness recalled, "If I was going to be fiery and emotional, it was done behind closed doors." He knew that Sinden wanted him to be more like Milbury, whose temper still periodically caught the spotlight. During the playoff series against Pittsburgh, Milbury grew so infuriated with referee Denis Morel that he verbally attacked the official in the corridors of the Civic Center in full view of the television cameras. "Just another fucking day at the office!" Milbury screamed. "Just take your fucking pay check and go home, you phony ----!" Milbury's 27-second, 11-expletive tirade made five straight newscasts and the *New York Times*. It also earned him a gross misconduct penalty and a $100 fine. "On a scale of Mike Milbury tantrums," Milbury himself concluded, "this was probably an 8 or a 9."

The 1991–92 Bruins finished second in their division, behind Montreal. They went on to beat Buffalo in seven games and Montreal in four – Bowness pumping his fist with the hometown crowd at the end of the sweep – before falling four straight to Mario Lemieux's Penguins, who were marching undefeated toward their second straight Stanley Cup. After the NHL year was over, Sinden pointedly refused to endorse Bowness. "There is an element of instinct in coaching that comes to few," Sinden said. "We hope we can find it. I happen to think that Mike Milbury had that instinctive quality." Put another way, Bowness did not.

No Bruins team had ever swept the mighty Canadiens, but it did not matter. As soon as Brian Sutter became available from St. Louis, Bowness knew he was doomed. He had already been tipped that Sutter had been approached and was going to accept. He and Judy flew home to Halifax for a wedding and a reunion with old high-school classmates, but he refused to tell anyone, including his father, what he was going through. Sinden and Milbury called him in on Monday morning and gave him the news. While driving home to North Reading to tell Judy and the kids, he heard a radio bulletin saying that the Bruins had called a press conference for 2 p.m. to announce that Bowness would be back. "Uh-uh," he said aloud to the radio. "You've got the wrong info."

Judy Bowness was furious about the way Sinden and Milbury had treated her husband. "All this crap about him not being emotional," she told the *Boston Herald*. "There's no more emotional guy in the world – it's just that he doesn't go around screaming in front of TV cameras to put himself in the forefront. He doesn't need that kind of attention. When I read the criticisms it just reminds me that I'm the luckiest girl in the world. They say he's too nice, he doesn't have snake eyes, he doesn't have the 'psycho' look, he lacks some 'slippery quality' – well, aren't I the lucky one!" While Sutter was being introduced at the press conference, Rick Bowness went off to help run his son's third-grade field day, as he had promised he would. He was the only father who volunteered.

Sutter was more in tune with Boston's management: Milbury quickly began to refer affectionately to the new coach as "the nut case." Bowness was offered a scouting job but turned it down. He headed home again to Halifax with his family and began telling friends he was finished with hockey and all its hypocrisy.

But almost immediately there was speculation that he might be in line for the Senators job. The new franchise was a month away from the expansion draft and still had no coach. The Senators had been hoping to land Sutter, but the Boston job had proved too attractive for him. Bowness was free, and with John Ferguson pushing for him, the Senators made contact. Bowness was persuaded to at least talk to Ottawa by his oldest son, Ricky, who told his father he could only stay happy by staying in hockey.

Bowness met with the Senators and liked what he heard. He would have a three-year contract at $225,000 a year and the right to choose his assistants – a right the Bruins never gave him. He immediately hired McGuire, who had succeeded him in Portland; soon after, he decided on Vigneault, the coach of the Hull Olympiques, during their first interview. Bowness was told that the Senators had a long-term game plan, that everyone was in for the long haul, and that everyone would be patient and understanding. After Milbury, it sounded very good indeed.

In some ways it *was* good. The Bowness family fell in love with Ottawa instantly. They bought a new home backing on to a golf course and began planning a pool. The schools were excellent, the kids happy, the fans knowledgeable and certain to be more forgiving than Sinden or Milbury. They would need to be. On a break home to Halifax to see his father, who had undergone surgery for skin cancer, he was asked what kind of a year he was looking forward to. Rick Bowness had buried his head in his hands, peaked through his fingers, and told his father, "Brutal."

Bowness was ahead of the pack. The Ottawa media, most of them also rookies, had left the Montreal draft convinced that Mel Bridgman had handily outdrafted Phil Esposito and Tampa Bay. At the Senators' training camp the conventional wisdom was that the players being cut from the big team would give New Haven the strongest team in the AHL. The Senators, everyone was saying, would be instantly competitive.

Bowness and McGuire and Vigneault knew better. They knew the moment the players skated onto the ice of the Robert Guertin Arena in Hull. They could not skate, could not shoot, could not play at the NHL level. They lacked size and skill and speed. McGuire, who had come from Chicago and Philadelphia, bit his lip. Vigneault wondered if perhaps he should not have stayed with his Junior team. Rick Bowness sighed heavily and went to work.

FOR AN NHL COACH, WHAT EXACTLY IS WORK? "WATCHING THEM from my seat," George Plimpton once wrote of NHL coaches, "I often wondered what they actually did, especially compared to coaches of other sports who always seemed so deeply involved in what is going on." Plimpton eventually concluded that the most important selection a hockey coach had to make on game day was which tie to wear with which suit. Granted, he was writing about a Bruins team then coached by Don Cherry.

Scotty Bowman, who has coached Montreal and Pittsburgh to the Stanley Cup, has suggested, tongue in cheek, that he earns his money by opening and closing the gate to the bench. More seriously, he has said that his most important job is to make sure the right players are on the ice in every game situation. A coach in hockey, perhaps more than in any other team sport, is captive to the talent on the bench once play begins. He cannot create talent, but he can, to a degree, manage it. Though much is made of "systems" and "set plays," the fundamentals of the game are carried in players' minds from Pee Wee days, and the best players make much of it up as they go. A hockey coach can tinker with lines but will rarely send in a play that influences the game. The strategy in hockey is simple and varies little; the play is too fast and unpredictable for set plays to work.

If the one crucial concept in baseball is "the creation of opportunities," as George Will put it in *Men at Work,* then the crucial concept of hockey is turnovers, or – more accurately – mistakes. If football is a game of planning, hockey is a game of surprises – the most pleasant ones surprising the coach as much as the fans. Like basketball, hockey is about openings and fast breaks and rebounds, about coy interference and accurate shooting, but no hockey player – not even Gretzky or Lemieux – can dominate the ice the way the best basketball players can dominate the court.

Once the team has been assembled (which is usually out of the hands of the hockey coach), and once the drills are in place, and the practices are set, and the video breakdowns are under control, and the small game-by-game strategies are determined, the NHL coach is there, more than anything else, to set the tone. There is a "good cop, bad cop" theory of coaching which proposes that all NHL coaches (a) have a lifespan of two or three years with a given team and (b) offer either emotion or discipline – the yin and yang of motivation. Teams that fail with emotional coaches will turn quite soon to discipline coaches, and vice versa.

Much of the 1992–93 season could be seen in these terms, with the disciplinarian Pat Burns going to lackluster Toronto and showing immediate results and the emotional Jacques Demers replacing Burns in Montreal and taking a fairly pedestrian team to the Stanley Cup. Good Cop Bryan Murray isn't working in Detroit? Replace him with Bad Cop Scotty Bowman. In Boston, try replacing Good Cop Rick Bowness with Bad Cop Brian Sutter. Good Cop Rick Bowness ended up in Ottawa and, within a month, wanted to shoot his own team.

The Senators almost defied description. By year's end it was justifiable, at least statistically, to refer to them as one of the worst teams in hockey history – the worst ever, certainly, on the road. And yet there were nights when, to someone merely dipping in and out of the season, they might have passed for a genuine NHL club. Their wins were rare (they beat Montreal, New Jersey, Philadelphia, San Jose, Hartford, Edmonton, Buffalo, Pittsburgh, Quebec, and the Islanders); realistically, they should have had an outside chance only against San Jose, Hartford, and, perhaps, Edmonton and New Jersey. That they could even stay in games against the league's best is a tribute both to their surprising grit and to their ability to lull opponents into such torpor that, from time to time, far better teams could not recover until it was too late.

The problem was less with individual players than with the whole. As a team, the Senators were plodding, inconsistent, and frightened on the road. Overall they lacked speed, skill, and size. Yet each Senator was a gifted player in his own way. Several were clearly good enough to play well in the NHL – Norm Maciver first and foremost, but also Sylvain Turgeon, Mark Lamb, and goaltender Peter Sidorkiewicz. Quite a few would have been fringe players with other teams – Mike Peluso for one, and also defenseman Brad Shaw, center Jamie Baker, and perhaps one or two others. A few, such as the captain, Laurie Boschman, forwards Doug Smail and Andrew McBain, defenseman Brad Marsh, and goaltender Steve Weeks, were aging veterans approaching retirement, whether they wished to admit it or not.

The Senators had said they would go with youth and stick with youth. Much was made of the fact that they had several former first-round draft choices who, for whatever reasons, had not panned out for the teams that had drafted them: Neil Brady (who scored the Senators' first goal), Jody Hull, Rob Murphy, Dave Archibald, and Darren Rumble. They were, management said, the building stones of the franchise.

Brady's career with the Senators went downhill almost from opening night. Hull and Murphy flashed brilliantly at times, faded, flashed again, faded. Archibald – a November addition through a trade with the Rangers – was fast, strong, and promising until he suffered a severe back injury in a collision at center ice with New Jersey's Scott Stevens. Rumble, who began the season carrying his own pillow for road trips, ended with the greatest promise. He was the Canadian child living out his own dream. Right to the end of the season Rumble, with his wife, Jennifer, would slip quarters into the trading-card dispensers at the Civic Centre in the hope that his own card would slide out – proof positive that he had finally made it.

The Senators were endearing, they were sincere, and they were fine athletes – they just weren't much of a team. The problem, Bowness mused, was the Peter Principle: every player had reached the level of his incompetence. Ken Hammond, who might have been the sixth defenseman on another team, was the fourth defenseman on the Senators. Mark Lamb, a third-line center in Edmonton, was on the first line in Ottawa. It meant more ice time than these players were used to, in roles with which they were unfamiliar. It gave the Senators a power play on which no one had an NHL-quality shot from the point. It gave them grinders who were now expected to be playmakers. It gave them a fine backup goaltender, Sidorkiewicz, who would end up playing 64 games. The player with the best shot, Bob Kudelski, had no speed. The player with the best speed, Doug Smail, had no shot. Out of all this, Bowness and his assistants were asked to produce a team.

"Patience," Bowness had told the Boston press as he prepared to depart for Ottawa, "is the operative word." It took him until Halloween to begin losing his. At home the Senators had fallen 7–2 against Pittsburgh for the team's eighth loss in a row. Then, in Buffalo, the team had been humiliated 12–3. Asked for a postgame comment, Bowness would only say, "The score is the comment – we played stupid." For the first time, Ottawa had been blown out two games in a row. For the first time, Bowness lost his temper – in the dressing room and in private. The players responded the following night in Ottawa with a 2–2 tie against the Sabres. He didn't know whether they were ashamed of themselves or afraid of his temper.

Bowness was growing frustrated not only with the players he

was saddled with but also with the employer who had done the saddling. By late October, Mel Bridgman was looking for ways to justify the choices he'd made at the June draft. It was being said that the Senators had set out to build a team of the kind that had been out of fashion since the 1970s. Bridgman and his scouts had gone for the grinders – for a style of up-and-down-the-wing hockey that hadn't been played much since the Flyers teams of the 1970s. The Senators were a dump-and-chase, clutch-and-grab team at a time when dump-and-chase no longer worked and clutch-and-grab was no longer allowed.

On their first western swing the Senators dropped games to Edmonton and then Calgary. Bridgman, along for the trip, was growing irritated with the suggestion that the Senators had botched matters from the start. In private he would admit that he and his people would have drafted differently if they had foreseen the rules experiment. But for political reasons he had to justify his choices, to show the hockey world and his new employers that he could be a general manager despite his lack of experience.

The friction began in Calgary. Bowness had gone out for the evening to visit his sister's family, and Bridgman took Vigneault and McGuire off into a far corner of the Westin Hotel bar. He told them the problem was not the players but the way they were being coached. Bowness's error – and by extension, the error of his assistants – was that they had no "systems" in place. Hockey was a game, Bridgman contended, that could be broken down into its various parts – breakout patterns, two-on-one rushes, penalty killing, power play – and then put together by systems-oriented coaches into a smooth, effective machine: the Wharton Business School of hockey.

McGuire and Vigneault began to avoid Bridgman as much as

possible. Bowness for his part was furious about the meeting, and his relationship with Bridgman took on a permanent chill. Communication stopped between the two. In Vancouver, when Bridgman announced that he had just picked up Archibald from the Rangers and that he would be playing that night if he arrived in time, it was the first Bowness had heard of it. On the next road trip Bridgman had New Haven defenseman Dominic Lavoie and forward Jeff Lazaro join the Senators during a connecting flight, again catching Bowness unaware. In Bowness's opinion, Lavoie could not skate and Lazaro could not make the team. Lavoie was indeed a poor skater, and Lazaro was soon back in the minors.

"Welcome aboard the expansion Ottawa Senators of the NHL," the captain of the U.S. Air flight into Tampa announced over the public-address system in December. "They're the good-looking but kind of gloomy guys." The Senators were quickly becoming the laughingstock of the NHL; the New Haven Senators were already the joke of the AHL. Sidorkiewicz was overworked and losing, and the team had no backup help; Steve Weeks was letting in an average of seven goals a game when they dared let him play. Bridgman's solution was to reach into the Austrian elite league and pluck Daniel Berthiaume from the EC Ottakringer Graz team. Again, Bowness had not been asked his opinion. Had he been, he might have said that there was no player he wanted to see less that Berthiaume. Seven months earlier Berthiaume had run out on the Bruins during the Stanley Cup playoffs. Even before "the Bandit" lost his first game as a Senator, Bowness wanted him gone.

Bowness blew up for the second time as the team bus was about to depart for the Philadelphia airport after a 7–2 loss to the Flyers. Philadelphia rookie Eric Lindros had set the pace in his very first shift, when he drove Senators defenseman Chris Luongo into the boards; the resulting turnover led to the Flyers' first goal. Lindros so intimidated the Senators that the game was painful to watch and humiliating to coach. "You played like horseshit!" Bowness screamed on the bus.

Things were falling apart. The team was losing constantly. The coaching staff did not approve of the roster, yet they had no say in it. The team had no goal scorers and no one to trade. The singular plus was the sure profit the team was heading for in its first year. The conclusion was obvious: the franchise would have to spend money on some real hockey players. There were free agents available; there were probably players available in return for lesser players and hard cash from teams claiming financial difficulty. Surely somewhere there were quality players for sale.

The difference one good player might have made could be seen in the difference Norm Maciver made. He had arrived, almost by accident, only four days before the Senators' first game, picked up in the waiver draft from Edmonton. A defenseman, he'd been the team's leading scorer since opening night. At one point Bowness said that if there had been no Maciver the Senators might not have earned a single point: he was that vital. If they landed a forward as good as Maciver something might start to happen.

But it was not to be. Bridgman had no discretion on spending and, since the draft, little nerve for gambling. He was also distracted by office problems. The budget was already out of control; he was overspent and overcommitted to too many contracts. By December co-owner Rod Bryden was so concerned that he ordered an internal audit of the team's operations. No one was sure even how many players were under contract. Secretaries had quit. Other general managers were complaining they weren't getting their calls returned. The organization was a mess.

Bowness was frustrated but resigned. He and the assistants

worked on extravagant game plans that seldom worked. When Minnesota came to town, Bowness laid out a strategy whereby the Senators would "take away the neutral zone" between the blue lines. The Ottawa defensemen would take up their positions and hold them. The North Stars could have their cross-ice passes but the Senators forwards would keep the North Stars forwards tight to the boards, thereby eliminating the two-on-one break. When a Senators forward was able to hold an opponent with the puck, the puck would sometimes bounce free to the waiting Ottawa defense, with everyone positioned to exploit the turnover. The North Stars won the game easily, 3–1. Asked for an explanation, Bowness could only shrug and state the obvious: "Speed."

Less than a week later, Bowness exploded again. Again, the Senators were playing Philadelphia, but this time the game was in Ottawa and the Flyers were missing Lindros, who was out with a knee injury. They were highly distracted – Lindros had just been charged with common assault over a beer-spitting incident in a Whitby, Ontario, bar. On top of that, the Flyers' second-best player, Kevin Dineen, was out with a bad shoulder. Even so, Philadelphia was leading 2–1 by the end of the second period. In the dressing room, Bowness could take no more – he cursed the players, then grabbed Maciver's stick and smashed it against the wall, shattering it on the third swing. One of the veterans rated the tantrum "eight-and-a-half to nine out of ten." It worked. The Senators scored twice in the third period and got their third win of the season.

Bowness knew there was a limit and wondered if perhaps he had already passed it. In the opinion of Washington coach Terry Murray, a great temper explosion can absolutely have a positive effect on a team, but a coach has only two a year to cash in. Bowness was already at three – and he had 56 games to go.

THE NEW YEAR BROUGHT NO IMPROVEMENT. *THE OTTAWA CITIZEN* was running a daily feature on the Yelnats Puc ("Stanley Cup" backwards) to remind the Senators that they were as bad as – and often worse than – the worst hockey team in history, the 1974–75 Washington Capitals. The Senators lost an overtime heartbreaker to Detroit on New Year's Eve, their best effort on the road all year and still not good enough. On the charter flight home the stewardesses poured champagne while, high over the Canadian Shield, the pilot dramatically counted down the final seconds of 1992. No one counted with him. Only a few players dared wish each other Happy New Year. Laurie Boschman, as captain, thought he should shake hands with everyone.

The team arrived for its first practice of 1993 to find a young man in the stands wearing thick, horn-rimmed glasses and brand-new hockey equipment. His name was Vincent Pun and he said he was a student of economics at the University of Ottawa. On the drive out to the Kanata practice facility he had stopped in at Canadian Tire and purchased more than $1,000 worth of hockey gear – skates, socks, shin pads, garter belt, athletic protector, pants, shoulder pads, elbow pads, gloves, helmet, and aluminum sticks. Then he had dressed without bothering to remove the price tags. All he lacked was a sweater, which he expected the Senators would provide. He had come for a tryout.

Mike Peluso, laughing, invited Pun onto the ice before the rest of the team and the coaches arrived. Pun got up, scraped his new, unsharpened skates across the cement, and fell through the gate onto the ice. Having never played anything but street hockey, he could not skate, but he had heard so many news reports about the team needing help that he had somehow become convinced they would teach him if he was willing to learn. McGuire convinced him to leave the ice before Bowness arrived, but Pun would not leave the building. He scraped about the cement until his feet blistered.

As well as games, the Senators were losing their sense of humor. By midseason only defenseman Ken Hammond – who had come to Ottawa after a year with the expansion San Jose Sharks – was still able to laugh at their predicament. The Senators were trounced 6–1 by the Penguins in Pittsburgh. In that game Hammond had made a bad giveaway to Ron Francis, who relayed the puck to Joey Mullen, who scored a Penguin goal. "Look," Hammond told the press afterwards, "if I'd known Mullen was open, I never would've passed it to Francis."

Bowness was finding it harder to laugh about anything. The awning was down almost permanently. The season was a disaster. He had no communication at all with Bridgman. Once it became clear that the team would neither buy nor trade for better players, the only interpretation Bowness could make was that disaster was acceptable.

He was quite right. Management was already focusing on the next draft and the advantages of picking first. They had become convinced that the Nordiques were determined to land francophone Junior sensation Alexandre Daigle. Through an adroit deal, the Senators could conceivably leap ahead several years. The Nordiques had been able to get several legitimate NHL stars, $15 million, and the rights to Swedish superstar Peter Forsberg in return for Eric Lindros; what would they be willing to give up for a superstar of their own? One day in December, Bridgman had reached for a reporter's pad, written "Forsberg," circled the name, and handed it back without comment.

Bowness understood his dilemma all too well. As an NHL coach, it was his job and his duty to try to win every game. As the long-term coach of the Senators – longevity being the promise made to him on hiring – he couldn't help dreaming of an improved team down the road. As a realist, he was well aware that the NHL had created an opportunity not to be missed for a team bad enough to cash in on it.

Bowness felt he could survive only if he operated as a day-to-day coach dedicated to winning. He could not afford a conflict of interest, even if no one ever discovered it. Of course he wanted first draft pick, and of course he wanted either Daigle or the deal Daigle would bring. But no, he could not work to make that happen – he had to coach to win. If he didn't, and if it were then found out, he would be ruined – no player would ever again respect him, nor would he respect himself.

Oddly, Bowness was not particularly worried about his job. He knew that coaches of expansion teams don't last long – the Capitals went through four coaches in their first two seasons, the Islanders went through two before landing Al Arbour – but he had long given up worrying. He knew what people were saying: that the coaching was better than the team. People were also saying that if anyone was going to go, it would be Bridgman. Bowness knew the fans were on his side; his hunch was that senior management was as well. Bowness had people skills; Bridgman did not. Bowness was funny, irreverent, nervy in his comments; Bridgman was evasive, secretive, suspicious. If the tension between them ever broke, Bowness would not be without his allies.

Bridgman had suffered terribly from osteopolio as a child and had gone through ten operations by grade 5. "That," he once said, "is why my great hero was Mickey Mantle." The Yankee legend had suffered from the same disease and become a great athlete. Mantle, however, could open himself to the public in a way Bridgman never could. Bridgman had a fine young family, and he'd had an admirable playing career, but he'd started badly with the Senators and never recovered.

The simmering feud between the two men erupted in late January. The Senators were leaving on a three-game road trip, first stop Minnesota, when CJRC sportscaster Michel Lapointe went to air with a radio commentary mildly rebuking Bridgman for missing the Junior all-star game in Montreal. Daigle had been playing, and Lapointe suggested to his French-language audience that the man most responsible for the sorry state of the Senators should have been on hand. One listener turned out to be the Senators' public-relations director, Laurent Benoit, who called the station to argue on his boss's behalf. Bridgman's presence in Montreal had not been required, Benoit said, because John Ferguson and his scouting staff had taken in the game.

According to Lapointe, Benoit then suggested that the real problem with the Senators was that they were being outcoached, as opposed to outplayed, and that their pitiful record was the result of the coaching staff's failure to put in place a proper "system" for the players. While Benoit later maintained that Lapointe had misunderstood him, the only word that mattered when it got out was "system." Lapointe did not cover the team regularly and never traveled with the Senators. For those who did, "system" had long ago become code for "Mel."

Only days earlier, Bowness had heard through the grapevine that Bridgman had told other general managers he should have taken on the coaching duties himself to put the "systems" in place. That's why the code word was so explosive when it caught up with the Senators. Bowness heard about it between planes in Detroit and called Bridgman. The exchange was curt and ended with the receiver being slammed down. In the following morning's *Citizen,* the headline SENATORS SQUABBLE – CLUB'S BLEAK FUTURE SPARKS INTERNAL BLOWUP – pushed Bill Clinton's presidential inauguration off page one.

That Bridgman and Randy Sexton worked so desperately to defuse the scuffle showed just how frail the team had become. A sense of dread had fallen over the players: were they indeed as bad as or worse than their 4–42–3 record suggested? The most recent four games had been even worse than usual, with stupid penalties, thoughtless play, players sniping at each other on the bench, and an 0–for–28 power play. In the CFRA pregame show that went back to Ottawa, color announcer Gord Wilson said out loud what everyone else was saying: "It's conceivable that this team might not win another game." The North Stars reinforced his comment with a 7–2 victory. "The effort was fine," Bowness told the press. "The reality is they deserved to win the hockey game."

A few days later the team landed in Washington to a story in the *Post* that detailed how Bruce Firestone – whose hopes for a 22-point season seemed to be slipping out of reach – had sought to arrange a lecture for the Senators on the psychological trauma of losing too often. Firestone hoped the talk would be delivered by Yvon Labre, the Capitals' director of community relations, who had been a member of the disastrous 1974–75 Capitals. According to the *Post*, Firestone wanted Labre to tell the Senators, "You wouldn't want to hear about that for the rest of your life." He would himself be living proof of how deep the scars would go. Labre had refused the request.

But the article alone had some effect. The Senators played their best road game in months and were beaten on a bizarre play. Ottawa's Doug Smail fired a weak shot from the corner that kept slipping toward the net, then turned on end and rolled along the goal line. The Senators on the ice thought it had gone in. Meanwhile, the Capitals swept the puck away, moved up the ice, and scored themselves. For several minutes it was total confusion. The video replay offered only one angle, and that view had been blocked by players.

Witnesses came out of the stands to support the Senators, but to no avail. The officials ruled no goal for Ottawa, goal for Washington. At the end of the game, Bowness sat on the bench, head in hands, staring blankly at the wall.

On to St. Louis, where the story was the surprise arrival of Rod Bryden, Randy Sexton, and John Ferguson. At a hastily called press conference in the Adams Mark, Bryden announced that he was becoming chief executive officer of the franchise. As the senior manager of the team, he said, he wished to state for the record that the Senators were expected to do their best for the remainder of this dismal season, even if it cost them the number-one draft pick. Bryden revealed that a despondent Bowness had come to him and asked aloud the question the team was whispering: "Are we even supposed to try?" Bryden understood that there was only one answer for the team – even if it made no sense to the franchise.

Bryden had just received the results of the internal audit he had ordered in December. As suspected, the Senators had lost control of spending. So many players were on two-year deals with one-way clauses that – on paper, anyway – the worst team of all time would continue unchanged into the 1993–94 season. When Bryden demanded answers, he was told that the coaching and scouting staffs had blown their budgets. The scouting staff, getting wind of this, met secretly to tally their accounts and discovered that they were, in fact, under budget. The coaches, it turned out, had never had a budget.

Mel Bridgman's days were counting down from the moment the audit came in. The original plan for the road trip had been for Bridgman to meet the press and deliver a midseason "State of the Union" address, but it was delayed until the team returned home. In Ottawa, flanked by Bowness and Ferguson, Bridgman stated, "It's hard for me to say there are any major weaknesses in this hockey club." Ferguson stared straight ahead, blinking slowly. Bowness kept his eyes fixed on the blank notepad in front of him.

BIG BOB BOWNESS HAD STOPPED IN ST. LOUIS ON HIS WAY DOWN TO winter in Florida. He and Thelma had also had stopped in Saint John, New Brunswick, to visit the widow of his old hockey friend, Gordie Drillon, who had starred for Toronto and Montreal in the 1930s and 1940s and been elected to the Hockey Hall of Fame in 1975. Drillon had died more than six years earlier, but it had still been an emotional visit. Bowness had left the Drillon home with his old friend's all-star ring as a memento of better times.

Big Bob sat in the stands slipping the ring on and off his finger. The ring with the tiny diamond and the inscription was proof that his great friend had once stood with the gods of this game. But Big Bob was not thinking about Drillon's all-star appearance. He was thinking, instead, about the stigma his dear friend had never been able to shed – the year that had haunted Gordie Drillon to the end.

It was the 1942 Stanley Cup playoffs. Drillon's Maple Leafs were playing the Red Wings and had fallen behind in the series three games to none. Drillon, then 27 years old and the star of the team, had been benched by coach Hap Day as a lesson to the other Leafs who were not performing. While the star sat watching, his teammates came back to win four games in a row, but Drillon – in shock from his treatment – never got back in a single game. The series would be remembered as the greatest comeback in the history of the Stanley Cup, and Drillon as the player Day had benched to start it. He would be remembered forever for this shame, not for the three all-star selections, or the 1937 Lady Byng he won, or the 1938 Art Ross Trophy, or for being the last Maple Leaf to win an NHL scoring title. All the honors that followed, all the years that passed, would never ease Drillon's pain.

Big Bob sat in the St. Louis Arena, twirling the ring that could not fix history, watching his son put the Senators through the drills that would not change the history they were now making. The 1992–93 Ottawa Senators were heading for the record books as surely as the 1941–42 Toronto Maple Leafs. His son had said that what really bothered him was not so much how it felt today, but how it would feel forever. How it had felt to Gordie Drillon.

Big Bob nodded as his son left the ice, the awning down. Then the elder Bowness forced a smile: "It won't do his chances of getting into the Hall of Fame much good." Father stared at son until the son finally looked up and smiled.

"I'll get you a pair of skates," Rick called. The father who never quite made it would at least get a skate in an NHL rink.

Big Bob pushed Drillon's ring hard onto his own finger and headed for the ice. His old friend's pain was close to him, but not nearly as close at that moment as his son's.

CHAPTER EIGHT

THE DAIGLE CUP

Daly City, California

HERE AT THE COW PALACE, ON THE ROAD BETWEEN SAN FRANCISCO and San Jose, Ronald Reagan seconded the nomination of Barry Goldwater as candidate for President of the United States. Here Elvis appeared, Evil Knievel landed, Joe Louis fought. And here, on a Tuesday night in March, the two worst teams in hockey – arguably the two worst in the history of hockey – met to fight it out for last place. To the loser would go the spoils.

Bowness and his players had left Ottawa at the beginning of March with a wildly unusual send-off: even their most loyal fans were praying for the worst. According to an unscientific telephone poll in *The Ottawa Citizen*, most people in Ottawa were saying that the Senators had better take a dive in San Jose if they hoped to salvage anything from the season. Of the 948 callers, 518 were advising their team to "tank it" – to lose deliberately, throw the game. CFRA, the Senators' broadcast station, had even recorded a highly professional spoof of an old Dionne Warwick hit and had been playing the song for a week: "Should We Blow the Game in San Jose?"

For the second time in the season, the Senators and the Sharks were to play "a four-pointer" – a victory by either team would result in a four-point shift in the standings. The phrase is usually reserved for teams battling for first place, not last; the first time the Sharks and Senators had met, in Ottawa in early January, calling the match "a four-pointer" had seemed a joke. By February the matter had become so serious that the NHL was considering altering the draft system to put an end to the embarrassing reality that tanking it had become the sensible thing to do.

At the time of their first meeting, the Sharks were barely visible on the horizon, having earned 14 points to Ottawa's nine. The dismal Senators had even fallen behind the pace set by the 1974–75 Washington Capitals. The Sharks, on the other hand, were thought to be slumping rather than innately horrible. In their first year they had finished with an admirable 39 points; soon, surely, they would pick up again, and last place would indisputably be Ottawa's.

By January the fans were coming to the same conclusion that Bowness had reached so painfully in November – that coming last fit the franchise's long-term plans. Ever since 1969, when the NHL switched to the last-place-picks-first system, coming last had had a silver lining – in some years gold. The right draft choice could make a franchise.

The first franchise player to come along after the changes to the draft rules was Guy Lafleur in 1971. He joined the Stanley Cup champion Canadiens only because Montreal had been able to manipulate the 1970–71 standings. Having already obtained the top draft choice of the Oakland Seals in an earlier deal, the Canadiens traded veteran center Ralph Backstrom to give a boost to the struggling Los Angeles Kings when it seemed the Kings might finish lower than the Seals. The ploy worked – Oakland finished last, Montreal drafted first, and Lafleur became the foundation of five more Montreal championships.

Few first picks have such impact. Denis Potvin went to the Islanders in 1973 and, within a decade, had led the team to four Stanley Cups. More often, however, the top choice turns out to be just another good journeyman, Mel Bridgman in 1975 being a prime example. Sometimes the top player is rarely heard of again: Washington's Greg Joly in 1974, Montreal's Doug Wickenheiser in 1980, Minnesota's Brian Lawton in 1983.

Two years stand out above all others, and it is these that torment any foundering team in a premium draft year. The first is 1984, the year Pittsburgh picked Mario Lemieux. Last place that season was in dispute until the final weeks. New Jersey looked as if it would finish last, thereby gaining the right to claim the best talent to come along since Gretzky (who was never drafted into the NHL, having jumped to the World Hockey Association when he was 17). But New Jersey was coached by Tom McVie, who had been with the Capitals in their dark years and been fired by the Winnipeg Jets in their year of record-setting disaster. McVie was so determined not to go down again in the record books that he drove his team into a flurry at season's end that lifted them out of last place – and handed Lemieux to Pittsburgh.

Max McNab was the Devils' general manager that year and is now their executive vice-president. He will concede that consideration was given to tanking it. "Some people in the organization thought it might be a good idea to lose," he said one evening when the Senators were in New Jersey. "But there was never any question in my mind. You play every game to win." New Jersey owner John McMullen backed McNab, and McVie was encouraged to fight to the end.

Today, it is generally conceded in NHL circles that by winning, the New Jersey franchise did the worst thing it could have done. McVie's stubbornness cost the Devils years of profit and progress and, probably, a chance at the Stanley Cup. McVie will not discuss the matter. McNab will admit that "every club that's ever won has done it through the draft," but he is adamant that the decision was the right one. "I can retire," he says, "with a clear conscience."

When Eric Lindros was being hailed as the next franchise player, Rick Curran, Lindros's agent at the time, became convinced that Quebec deliberately tanked it in 1991 to ensure last place. At one point he claimed that a member of the Nordiques' coaching staff had told him that the team deliberately started weak goaltenders to ensure losses; and that they also made four key player movements that involved replacing competent players with future draft picks, or with less gifted players who were immediately dispatched to the minors. Lindros himself believes that Quebec deliberately lost to gain his rights.

Lindros refused to play for Quebec, of course, but in the end the Nordiques wound up with four proven NHLers, the rights to Sweden's Peter Forsberg – who is also said to be a franchise player – and $15 million with which to pay for the new talent. In a single move, the Nordiques had become the most improved club in the NHL.

In the 1992–93 season, coming last was being viewed as essential to later success, for the 1993 draft was shaping up as an extraordinarily rich one. Alexandre Daigle had already emerged as the next phenomenon. He had the skills. He had demonstrated the meanness that so attracts NHL general managers. And even if he was not going to be the franchise player Lemieux had been, his trade value was as high as Lindros's. He had added value.

When Lafleur was in his prime, Ken Dryden recalls, the Canadiens had talked openly about getting away from rink ownership. The overhead and upkeep of the Montreal Forum was considered a financial burden by the team owner, Molson Breweries. In those days the dream of NHL owners was to have a municipality build and run the hockey rink and rent it out to the hockey team. Fans in the seats were the important income producer; the gravy, if any, came from television.

By the 1990s that theory had been turned on its ear. Total rink control – either by ownership or by lease arrangement – was now considered the route to profit. Fans in the seats were a given; the real money would come from other revenue streams such as concessions, parking, and souvenirs – and especially from corporate boxes and other premier seating. For owners, the new ideal scenario was for the taxpayers to build (or help build) a new facility and then vanish from the scene.

For sports owners, the perfect arrangement is the one the Blue Jays have at the SkyDome in Toronto. The deal struck by the corporate consortium that took over the SkyDome has cost Ontario taxpayers more than $200 million; it is so one-sided that *Financial World* has estimated that taxpayers will not be getting any of their investment back until at least the middle of the next century, by which time the SkyDome will be a memory. "Stop looking at the Skydome with rose-colored glasses," the American magazine warned Ontario taxpayers, "and start to understand just how much this deal has and will cost."

New facilities can also be built by athletes. Just as Yankee Stadium has long been known as "the House That Ruth Built," Quebec City's Colisée has always been regarded as the rink that Jean Beliveau built. In 1949, the year the original Colisée burned down and was replaced by a new structure, Beliveau was merely a prospect joining the Quebec Citadelles from the Junior-league Victoriaville Tigres; but his appeal was such that on December 8, 1949, when the new Colisée opened, he packed the place, even though workers had yet to install seats. Once the 10,000 seats were finally in, Beliveau sold them out and then some, in one game packing 16,806 fans into the new rink. If he did not play because of injury, the rink might be half-full.

Beliveau's reward – paid for out of fans' pockets – was a new Nash and what may have been the first vanity license plate: "9B", for his number and name. Apart from this perk and a small endorsement fee from a local dairy, Beliveau received nothing. His added value was not understood until a war broke out for his services between the Montreal Canadiens of the NHL and the Quebec Aces of the old Quebec Senior Hockey League. The Aces placed his worth at an extra 3,000 to 4,000 fans per home game – enough to make the small franchise hugely profitable for the team's owners, Anglo-Canadian Pulp and Paper. And this was only semiprofessional hockey.

Beliveau was the first franchise player of the modern era, though Cyclone Taylor and King Clancy in other decades had a similar impact. The Canadiens offered Beliveau a $53,000 package – $10,000 in the first year, $11,000 in the second, and $12,000 in the third, with a $20,000 signing bonus – but Beliveau stunned the NHL club by turning it down. The only player on the Canadiens making similar money was the long-established star, Maurice Richard. But Beliveau had a strong sense of his own worth, and in October 1953, he finally settled for a $110,000 contract over five years with Montreal. The Canadiens realized that his ability to bring in the Quebec fans was unequaled. Asked how he convinced Beliveau to sign, Frank Selke said, "It was really simple. All I did was open the Forum vault and say, 'Help yourself, Jean'."

FORTY YEARS LATER IT WAS TIME TO BUILD A NEW COLISÉE IN QUEBEC City. The owners of the Nordiques, led by Marcel Aubut, had grandiose plans for a new rink that would hold 20,000 fans and 100 corporate boxes. But Aubut would need a Beliveau, not only to fill it but also to finance it. The ordinary fans would be there, but the financing of a new $100 million-plus facility would depend largely on other factors: corporate boxes, lodge seating, television and advertising revenues, and the sale of Nordiques sweaters and caps.

Aubut had no francophone star to front the enterprise. He had an exciting team, but his stars were either unilingual anglophones like Joe Sakic, Owen Nolan, Mike Ricci, and Ron Hextall, or Europeans like Valeri Kamensky and Mats Sundin, the NHL's number-one draft choice in 1989. There was, however, a *new* Jean Beliveau coming along, a slim, slick center then starring for the same Victoriaville Tigres that had produced Beliveau more than four decades earlier.

The Nordiques would have no chance at claiming the rising superstar in the June 1993 draft, but that did not mean he was out of reach. They could simply continue the dealing that had started with the Lindros trade. They now had a surfeit of talent and money and even draft choices. More importantly, they had Forsberg. At the World Junior Tournament in Sweden at Christmas, the 19-year-old Forsberg had emerged as the dominant player, while Daigle spent much of the same tournament on the bench, his coach displeased with his performance. To Quebec, Forsberg could offer only tremendous ability; in Ottawa he could be a franchise player. In Aubut's opinion, Forsberg could not build the new Colisée; Daigle could.

In a carefully intentioned chat with the Quebec media, Aubut let it be known that to get Daigle, the Nordiques would be willing to give up not just Forsberg's rights but a number of high-quality players. The gossip had it that even Sakic, at 23 the team captain and scoring leader, might be available. The same for Owen Nolan, the NHL's first draft choice in 1990. Forsberg, Sakic, Nolan, a couple of other NHL players, and perhaps $10 million – all for the rights to Alexandre Daigle.

From that moment on, Daigle had a lock on being chosen first.

If the Senators had lost an entire year because of poor player acqui-
sition – which is what some were saying – they could do instant
repairs with such a deal. If the San Jose Sharks were going backwards, as the record was indicating, such a deal could reverse their
fortunes instantly. If Daigle was worth more to the Nordiques – or,
for that matter, to the Canadiens (who were also seeking a francophone superstar and planning a new rink) – than to the Senators
or the Sharks, those teams would be foolish not to strike a deal.

And there was another reason to chase last place and claim
Daigle. The backroom deals surrounding the expansion rules for the
new teams in Florida and Anaheim were coming to light. The league,
under Bruce McNall's control, was going to make sure that the new
franchises were dealt a better hand than San Jose, Ottawa, or Tampa
Bay. Disney and Blockbuster were guaranteed to draft first and second in 1994, however they placed in the 1993–94 standings, which
meant that the Sharks and the Senators would have only this one
chance to capitalize on their ineptitude. Coming dead last would pay
such high dividends only in 1993. This was no year to blow the
opportunity of the decade.

Which is why, in January, the media were calling the first
Ottawa-San Jose match between the two worst teams in hockey a
"four-pointer." Five points separated the teams. A San Jose win
would increase the spread to a probably insurmountable seven; an
Ottawa win would reduce the spread to three and leave last place up
for grabs. Reporters began referring to the competition as "the Daigle
Cup," which infuriated Sharks coach George Kingston, who called it
"an insult to the integrity of the game." No one would ever inten-
tionally lose, he suggested, no matter what the perceived stakes.
Kingston's team lost a poorly played game that featured a hat trick
by Ottawa's Bob Kudelski and a shoulder injury to the Sharks' best

player, Pat Falloon. Suddenly, with only three points separating the teams, and with Falloon out of action, the race for the Daigle Cup was on in earnest.

The Senators players knew what was being said in the press and were convinced that some senior people in the Ottawa franchise had been counting on another loss. The players were starting to think they were not only expected to lose, but required to lose. Players were losing faith in the coaches. The veterans were grumbling that the coaches were not teaching the younger players. The coaches themselves had lost faith in general manager Mel Bridgman and now knew that no real players – particularly scorers – would be brought in.

One January morning Bruce Firestone, Rod Bryden, and Randy Sexton (Bridgman was in California at the general managers' winter meetings) all came out in overcoats and suits to the Kanata practice facility to tell a room full of naked, toweling men that they were to "play to win." The stated goal was repeated – 22 points. Firestone added later to the gathering press, "Wherever we draft in June is where we draft." Two weeks later, in St. Louis, with the increasingly unhappy Senators about to lose their eighth in a row since their victory over San Jose, the message was repeated. And it was repeated again in Bridgman's "State of the Union" address the following week.

On January 28 the Senators won again, this time against lowly Hartford. It moved them to 13 points, a single point back of the Sharks. The victory heightened interest in the Daigle Cup and intensified the talk of tanking it. Some of the players were becoming so depressed that Bowness requested that a sports psychologist be brought in from Detroit to help them. The request was refused.

Bridgman and Sexton had quietly been working on a document titled *The Ottawa Senators: Building a Successful Hockey Club in the NHL.* The team still planned to challenge for the Stanley Cup within 7 to 12 years, but the document went into far more detail on how the franchise would get there. Under "Basic Strategy," they offered these as the franchise's guiding principles: "(i) Establish and maintain fan identification with the team by maintaining the continuity of both players and management; and (ii) Focus on the development of players from within the organization, primarily based on the annual NHL player drafts." Part (i) was self-serving, but part (ii) was critical, particularly when read beside a passage stressing the importance of maintaining "early draft positions." Specific mention was made of the need to spend massive amounts of capital to land a franchise player. The strategy was precisely the one the team had been following. The unexpected twist was San Jose's dismal performance.

That weekend Bryden arrived at what he thought was a graceful way to end all talk that either the Senators or the Sharks were tanking. It would preserve the integrity of the game while acknowledging the reality that Daigle would be going first in the June draft. On Monday afternoon he had Sexton fax the details of the proposal to Art Savage, president of the Sharks. The two teams, Bryden suggested, should formally agree that at the end of the year, they would swap draft picks. The effect would be to guarantee that the best pick would go to the team finishing second-last.

A similar fax was sent to NHL headquarters in New York. Commissioner Gary Bettman, who was brand-new to the job, called back immediately to ask, "Are you *sure* you want to do this?" Bryden assured Bettman he was. The NHL ruled that if Ottawa and San Jose wished to swap draft positions, they had the right to do so. The NHL would honor the agreement.

In a memorandum Bryden sent off to Bridgman, he said, "We believe that we should be rewarded for winning, not losing, and that this agreement would ensure that result. The agreement would certainly raise the value of winning and increase the pain of losing."

A few hours after the fax arrived in San Jose and New York, Ottawa managed to tie Winnipeg, which meant the Senators now stood even with San Jose at 14 points. The Sharks, however, were not responding to the fax. Two days later, the Senators defeated Edmonton, putting Ottawa up two points as the league broke for the all-star game. In Montreal that weekend, San Jose informed Ottawa that it would not agree to Bryden's proposal. Who could blame them? Ottawa was on a roll. On Monday the Senators beat Buffalo and were suddenly up by four points.

For that one week Ottawa was the hottest team in the NHL. What turned the Senators briefly into a powerhouse is hard to say. The players thought they had done it themselves. Certainly Daniel Berthiaume finally got hot enough to steal a close game. Bridgman liked to talk about the "intangibles" in hockey, those qualities that defy tabulation. In this case the intangibles were the goaltending of Berthiaume and then Sidorkiewicz, the frantic hustle of Darcy Loewen, the dressing room pumping and on-ice example of Brad Marsh, and – though several players grew to despise it – the fierce drive of Rick Bowness not to let his team die as everyone seemed to think it deserved to.

The veterans were the real key. The coaches had earlier given out short questionnaires to the players. One of the questions had been, "What would you do to change the way we are playing?" The veteran defensemen thought the team's forechecking had been ineffective and suggested that the team scrap its standard first-forward-goes-deep style. Other teams were getting too much time to organize, and the outlet pass was almost guaranteed success. The Ottawa defense found itself dealing with an endless stream of three-on-two breaks. This was causing panic, particularly among the younger defensemen, who feared above all being caught out of position. Better, they suggested, to send two forwards in not quite so deep and keep one back to help the defense. Two forecheckers might cause turnovers and create Ottawa chances. With a forward to back them up, defensemen like Norm Maciver would feel free to jump into the attack. During the hot streak they had tried it and it had worked.

There was also the matter of the veterans' pride. Any NHLer will have spent nearly 20 years as a winner before reaching this level. The NHL is the place where all great players want to play. It is a seductive life of high pay, first-class accommodation, continent-wide travel, and easy fame and adulation. Once a player arrives, he rarely if ever leaves of his own accord. He not only fights to stay, he believes till the bitter end that he belongs. He may be 26, he may be 35 – at any age he believes that he has earned his right to be in the NHL and that no one has the right to take his place away.

It had been said from the beginning that the Ottawa veterans were merely stopgaps, there to hold the line until the younger players were ready. After that, barring further NHL expansion, they were probably through. The Senators' veterans deeply resented this notion. They were the first to note that the young players – Brady, Hull, Rumble, Murphy, Luongo, Loach – were not working out as predicted, and they saw an opportunity to prove that they still belonged in the NHL.

The flurry had been impressive – three wins, a tie, and a disputable loss in five games – but it could not last. In Philadelphia, Eric Lindros personally pounded the smaller Senators into submission, and so began another Ottawa losing streak. And as the Senators returned to losing, veterans' pride also began to take hold in San Jose. The Sharks had tied the NHL record for consecutive road losses at 17 and were expected to set it in Winnipeg in mid-February, but two goals by 33-year-old Kelly Kisio (including the winner) produced a win for them. When they beat Winnipeg again four days later, they were suddenly tied with Ottawa again in the race for the Daigle Cup.

The Senators had one flurry left. February ended with two games at home against two of the league's best teams, the Penguins and the Nordiques. Playing vintage Bowness strategy – lull them to sleep, dump the puck in and run for the bench, interfere whenever possible, slow things down – the Senators won both matches. Those four points put them four up on the Sharks again – but also gave them a total of 22, one more than the 1974–75 Capitals. They would not go down as the worst team of all time. The players and coaches broke open champagne in the dressing room.

THE MARCH GAME IN SAN JOSE HAD AN AIR OF IMPORTANCE USU-ally reserved for playoff hockey. The game was a sellout. A one-hour pregame special, with phone-in lines, was broadcast back to Ottawa, where fans fought to stay awake through the three-hour time difference. The callers all wanted to talk about whether it made sense to tank the game. No one was sure how it might be done. Missed passes and missed shots by either team would be nothing out of the norm. Goaltenders could hardly leap out of the way. Everyone in Daly City, and everyone listening in Ottawa, knew that this game would have an impact far greater than any other game either team would play all year. With both teams long ago eliminated from the playoffs, last place was all that was left.

Those watching the Senators were concentrating on the upcoming trading deadline. If the Senators moved Maciver or Lamb or Peluso – the three players most coveted by playoff-bound teams – it would be a sure signal that the franchise was actively seeking last place. Those watching the Sharks pointed to Pat Falloon, already out two months with a separated shoulder, and hinted that he would not return to the lineup that season. Falloon found the suggestion that a team might deliberately underachieve "humiliating" to consider. Besides, he was not the only Shark out – defenseman Doug Wilson was also injured, as was the superb young Russian defenseman Sandis Ozolnich. Skeptics pointed out that the Sharks had traded scorer Brian Mullen and bought out three contracts belonging to veterans. "You bite a bullet when you go with younger players," said coach George Kingston. He talked again about "the integrity of the game" – on the same day Bettman, McNall, and Michael Eisner lifted duck calls to their mouths to herald the Mighty Ducks of Anaheim.

The game itself was flat. Little Darcy Loewen tried to fire up his teammates by going knee-to-toe with the Sharks' Robin Bawa, who had five inches and 50 pounds on him. Ottawa led 1–0 after the first period; the third period ended 2–2. In overtime no player on either team seemed interested in taking a shot until finally, with only seconds left, the Sharks' Johan Garpenlov scored a goal that the Senators said was kicked in. A furious Bowness protested the game, but the ruling and the victory stood. Back in Ottawa, some in the Senators' organization were saying, "We dodged another one."

The Sharks won their next game as well, which put the two teams dead even after 67 games, with 22 points each. The Senators, meanwhile, had set off on a 14-game losing streak that took them into April. The only exposure they got on the sports highlights came the night Andrew McBain got kicked out of a game in Chicago, left in a snit, and fell all the way down the steps leading to the dressing room. It was worth wondering whether they would ever win again. They had their 22 points – Bruce Firestone's stated goal – and they were virtually guaranteed of finishing last. They were still tied with

San Jose, but the NHL would look first to games won when breaking a tie in the standings. Ottawa had nine victories (and four ties) against San Jose's ten wins (and two ties). The Senators had 22 points and they had Daigle: the season was a success.

Except that the Senators had picked up a new nickname – "Road Kill." And they found, as the losses added up, that they hated it even more than they had despised the Yelnats Puc or the Daigle Cup. The NHL record for longest road losing streak was 37 games, again established by the 1974–75 Capitals. After losses in Los Angeles and Chicago, the Senators were 0–35–0 on the road.

Senators officials contacted the league and petitioned for a favor, which was granted. The Senators had lost two neutral-site games – one to Toronto in Hamilton, the other to Winnipeg in Saskatoon. These games had been part of the "neutral sites" package the players and owners had agreed to at the end of the 1992 strike. In the official NHL schedule Ottawa was listed as the visiting team against Toronto and as the home team against Winnipeg. Even the league's daily standings had accepted this.

But now the NHL, at the Senators' prodding, declared that neither game would count for the record book as a road loss. This became known as "the Asterisk Affair" and it deeply embarrassed the players and coaches. If we must get into asterisks, reporters suggested, then perhaps it should be admitted that 22 points in 1992–93 was *not* better than 21 points in 1974–75. The Capitals' record had been set over an 80-game season, that is, at a pace of .2625 points per game. Over 84 games 22 points amounted to .2619 points per game. At 22 points, then, the Senators were technically still worse than the 1974–75 Capitals. Just when it seemed that the ridicule was behind them, it had picked up again. The players were furious with management for drawing such attention to their ineptitude.

Rick Bowness was beside himself over all the distractions. Andrew McBain and Darcy Loewen had had their contracts renegotiated by Bridgman under threat of being sent to the minors. Bowness had his own problems with management, and now his players as a group had lost trust in their employer. Bowness also knew that the trading deadline was fast approaching and that, almost certainly, nothing was going to happen – the Senators were not actively working on any deals. The opportunities for help were now all past.

In Boston, a traffic jam forced the Senators to board the subway for the ride in from the airport. They stood, two dozen young men wearing expensive suits and carrying fine luggage, while the common folk of Boston looked them up and down. Finally, one rider could take it no longer.

"Where you guys from?" he asked in a loud, Boston accent.

"Ottawa."

"*Ottawa!* Great capital, *lousy* team!" An awkward silence followed, then the passenger caught on: "This *is* the team?"

A nod, another silence.

"A *hockey* team riding da subway – no wonda you guys stink!"

They stunk and the whole world seemed to know it. Newspapers everywhere began tracking the Senators' Road Kill trek to the record. "It's like a snowball," Peter Sidorkiewicz said, "and that snowball keeps getting bigger. Time is running out." Bowness had become obsessed with getting a win on the road, and was so consumed by his team's predicament that his own family had trouble reaching him. On one road trip he almost broke down when he reached into his pocket for the small plastic ice surface he carried for scribbling down plays and discovered another thought already written: "I love you, Dad."

Bowness may have been the only NHL coach whose briefcase

held an article from the *Harvard Business Journal*. It was an interview with the legendary football coach Bill Walsh in which Walsh called playing on the road a "crippling disadvantage" in football. One of the ways Walsh had worked around this was to "feed on the emotions of the situation without being intimidated by the other teams or their fans." Bowness once moved the Senators to a smaller, more compact ice surface for a practice and tried to get them to "feel" that they were in Boston Garden, but it hadn't worked. He was discovering that George Allen, the onetime coach of the Washington Redskins, had more to say to him than the erudite Walsh. "Winning is living," Allen once said. "Every time you win, you're reborn, when you lose you die a little." Bowness was beginning to feel as if they were digging him up and killing him all over again. When a Boston reporter asked him how he could take it so well, Bowness replied, "You don't see my insides."

The players were faring no better. They felt abandoned, as if they were expected to lose. Some players believed other players were keen to lose just to get it over with, to give management what it wanted. They hated the laughter. They hurt. At one March practice, they stayed out on the ice in a circle, quietly talking about their predicament. "They've given up on us," captain Laurie Boschman told his teammates. The rest agreed. They decided that, if they could, they would do it themselves for, as Norm Maciver put it, "professional pride."

The next day they bussed to Montreal for their 36th road game of the season – 35th with an asterisk. They had always played well against the Canadiens. A large contingent of Ottawa fans made the trip, including Ryan Bowness's Novice hockey team. Judy Bowness was convinced that this one night would save the year. Her husband had a plan. Pat Burns was having success in Toronto, his fellow coaches were saying, because his players were terrified of him. Bowness intended to use shame. Everyone was feeling it; perhaps it could be turned to advantage.

The plan was to bench someone no one would expect to be benched. He had a player in mind, Jamie Baker, who had not been playing well on the road. Yet Baker was one of the team's few skilled players, as well as its second-leading scorer. Bowness would nail Baker, and the others would react. It was the same trick Hap Day had used 50 years earlier on Gordie Drillon. But Bowness, unlike Day, would only resort to it once. He waited until the pregame skate was over, then closed the folding metal doors leading into the visitors' dressing room at the Forum. He entered the room, caught their attention, and ripped into them as never before. He screamed at them for floating, for not caring, for playing out the string. He let them know their jobs were on the line over the remaining games and that they had better play well or they'd be history. Some of them, he said, deserved to be history.

"*You!*" he shouted at Bob Kudelski. "You've been floating and not helping your teammates one fucking bit the last little while."

The quiet Kudelski recoiled in shock.

"You're sitting in the press box tonight!" Bowness shouted.

He had chosen Kudelski by chance. He had caught Kudelski's eye, and it felt right, so he'd chosen Kudelski over Baker.

"And *you!*" he shouted, now pointing to Baker. "You're next!"

He pointed to Turgeon: "And you're next!"

It is difficult to say whether it was Boschman's speech at center ice or Bowness's rant in the dressing room, but something worked. Kudelski sat up in the rafters in utter disbelief while his teammates played the game of their year. Berthiaume had been saying he would steal another one, and this night it seemed he would.

Marsh tied up every Canadien who dared enter his side of the ice. Loewen kept slamming into unsuspecting defensemen after they had gotten rid of the puck. Boschman himself scored to put the Senators up 2–0. Going into the third period, the Senators were up 3–2. When Montreal's Eric Desjardins took a five-minute major penalty halfway through the third period, a Montreal comeback seemed out of reach.

Some in the press box were already filing their ROAD KILL NO MORE stories when the Canadiens pulled goaltender Patrick Roy and, with only 1:19 left in regulation, Vincent Damphousse scored for Montreal to send the game into overtime. In extra time, unbelievably, Montreal scored again when a blind dump from the corner by little Oleg Petrov bounced in off Jamie Baker's skate. God Himself was joining in the ridicule.

Bowness stood, arms folded, chin in hand, staring at the clock. Jacques Demers, the Montreal coach, left his bench and came over and hugged Bowness for several seconds, whispering in his ear that it would get better, one day they would get him some players. Demers hugged Alain Vigneault, who was too stunned to speak. Vigneault remained behind the bench for several seconds with his face in his hands. Then he walked slowly across the ice trailing E.J. McGuire, who had his head down as if he would never look up again. In the dressing room some of the players were crying. Brad Shaw sat like an accident victim on the side of a road. Jody Hull could not speak. Outside the dressing room Judy Bowness had a Kleenex clenched in one fist. "Are we *ever* going to get a point?" she wondered. It no longer seemed so.

Late that night, on the charter flight to Buffalo, Bowness brought the players who had been on the ice in the final minutes up to sit with him, one at a time. The one who seemed in the worst shape was young Darren Rumble, who had lost the puck on one of the Montreal goals. Bowness tried to make him see that these things happen, that it wasn't his fault. "Don't let it destroy you," he said. But it was destroying them all.

They lost in Buffalo and they lost in Pittsburgh. In Hartford the Whalers scored on their first shot, their second, their third, their fourth. Even with the asterisk, the Senators had now lost 38 straight. They were unquestionably the worst team ever on the road. Like the 1974–75 Capitals, they would live forever.

Three days after the Senators set the all-time record for road futility, a score came in from the West Coast: the Sharks had beaten the sinking Oilers. The standings were now Sharks 24 points, Senators 22. Last place was in the bank for Ottawa. But then, in the second-last game of the year, the Senators went into Long Island. The team got off to a typically bad start: Darcy Loewen took a penalty and, to make matters worse, Islanders coach Al Arbour called Bowness out on a mistake in the Senators' starting lineup. Two men short, the Senators were instantly down 1–0. But then the unexpected: Sidorkiewicz knocking sure goals away with his toe, the Islanders hitting posts, Sylvain Turgeon tying it on a lucky bounce off the boards, the Islanders hitting a crossbar, little Darcy Loewen battling big Mick Vukota to a draw, Mike Peluso taking on two Islanders at once, Norm Maciver racing into the net to stop a point-blank shot by Ray Ferraro that would have put the Islanders ahead, Laurie Boschman – who had scored only five goals all season – scoring a hat trick to give the Senators, finally, a win on the road.

If the Senators had caught the Islanders by surprise, it was nothing compared with the shock felt by the team's senior management. The race for last place was once again a tie. In Ottawa they stayed up past midnight to catch the late score from California, hearts palpitating as the Sharks game against the Kings went into overtime, hearts sinking as the Kings scored. The Sharks had only one game remaining, a road game against Calgary that they could not possibly win. The Senators, on the other hand, had three games left – two on the road (in Boston and Quebec) and their season finale back in Ottawa against the Bruins. Three chances to win or tie, and a single point would be one point too many.

THE SENATORS LOST IN BOSTON AND LOST IN QUEBEC. THEY RETURNED to Ottawa for the season's finish, the players relieved it was almost over, the senior management in a panic that it was not yet settled. A call was put in to the Boston ownership with an unusual request: would the Bruins *please* bring their best players to Ottawa? The Bruins' playoff position was already settled, and the Senators were desperate for them to take the game seriously – as the league bylaws require – and not rest their best players. The Bruins assured Ottawa they would do what they could: tough winger Cam Neely would come, but star defenseman Raymond Bourque was injured and would not. The Ottawa brass winced at the news.

Privately, the players wanted to deny their employers the satisfaction of coming last. They wanted to protect their own jobs and knew that a postdraft trade with Quebec would bring in some superior players who might well bump them from the team. And Bowness, of course, wanted nothing more than to beat the team that had fired him.

The players were aware of the importance of coming last to management. Many took the arrival of Radek Hamr from New Haven for the final four games of the season as a key signal. Officially it was said that the Senators wanted to get a look at the young prospect. Hamr was 19 years old and claimed to weigh 167 pounds. He would play a regular shift, including penalty-killing duty. To some of the other players, sending out the diminutive Hamr was the same as inviting the other teams to charge the Ottawa net.

The crucial game was decided, in part, by the crowd. By the midway point, Boston was ahead 4–0 and the game seemed out of reach. But then the Senators started to come to life. Dave Archibald scored before the second period ended. Before the last period began, the players vowed to do everything possible to come back. They wanted to stick it to those who were praying for a loss.

While the players sat in the dressing room firing each other up, senior management unwisely called a press conference to talk about the state of the Palladium project – the new arena they hoped to build. The gathering ran overtime and the reporters were getting anxious to return to the game and their deadlines. The roar of the crowd kept penetrating the room where the press conference was being held. When, five minutes into the third period, Boschman scored to make it 4–2, Bruce Firestone, sitting at the press table beside Rod Bryden, visibly flinched.

The crowd loved that goal, but it was not the goal they wanted. They began to call, ever louder, for *The Goal* – Brad Marsh's goal. With the final game now in the final period, everyone in the building knew that the year of innocence was coming to an end. Hockey in Ottawa would never again be the same as this – so simple, so forgiving. And never again, everyone thought, would there be Brad Marsh to cheer. They wanted the goal they'd been screaming for ever since he emerged as the crowd darling. In 1,086 NHL games, Marsh had scored 23 goals. Except at the all-star game, he had not scored all year. But the crowd wanted *this* goal, and Bowness, hearing their wishes, decided to give Marsh every opportunity to score one. He played the 35-year-old throughout the period – after a shift on defense he would play on a forward line for better scoring chances. Marsh brought the crowd to its feet every time he touched the puck and played like a man possessed – rushing up the ice, throwing himself into the opposition net, doing whatever it might take to get the one goal the crowd wanted as desperately as he himself did.

Marsh's ice time, of course, cut sharply into the ice time of others who might have scored. But Bowness could see – as everyone saw – that Marsh's continued presence on the ice was firing up the other players as well as the crowd. It would turn out to be a futile effort, but no one would ever be able to say there had been no effort when the inevitable arrived.

The score remained 4–2 for Boston, but as the final seconds ticked away, the mood in the Ottawa Civic Centre was joyous. In total defeat was ultimate victory: the Senators would be picking first in the 1993 draft. They joked in the press box that if a Senator ever got a breakaway, a rifle was going to suddenly appear at the Senators' box to put an end to it.

Marsh was on the ice for the final minutes. He rushed, he gambled, he lost. People in the crowd broke into tears watching his effort – watching the hope and then the desperation spread across his face. The puck squirted one final time to his stick, but he couldn't get off a shot. When the buzzer went to end the season and the fans rose to their feet, Marsh bent down and picked up the puck – the last time he would ever touch a puck as an NHL player.

An odd thought flashed through Marsh's mind and made him smile. This moment would make a great commercial – he could turn now with the puck, face the camera, and shout, "I'm going to Disneyland!" But he was not a star, going somewhere. He was just Brad Marsh, and he was more likely at the end.

They named him second star of the game. While the crowd was still on its feet, he raced to center ice and stopped, one last time, in a huge spray of snow and ice. They cheered even louder. Marsh stood for a moment, then raised his stick like a sword and saluted, tears dripping down his face.

In the dressing room, Rick Bowness was telling reporters, "It was the worst season we'll ever have." He looked forward to going back to his family. Firestone was running around shaking his players' hands and calling this "an unbelievable fairy tale story." He talked about reaching the 22 points. He talked about the road win. And he mentioned the entry draft, which was now certain as destiny itself. He then proclaimed, "There are two NHL teams that will have achieved their goal this year: the Stanley Cup champion, and us."

ALEXANDRE DAIGLE WAS THE CONSOLATION FOR THIS TERRIBLE YEAR, but he also raised difficult questions. How intentional was Ottawa's last-place finish? Did, in fact, the Ottawa Senators do what so many said they should do, and what the league practically guaranteed teams would do in 1971, 1984, 1991 and now 1993 when it put in place a system that placed such a high reward on finishing last? From January on, the Ottawa fans had debated whether the Senators should tank it. Now they were asking how deliberate, or fortunate, the final happy result actually was.

There's a difference between letting it happen and making it happen. On one level there can be no argument that the Senators let it happen. The Senators called the Bruins to ask that they send a legitimate team to Ottawa for the final game. The team was not improved upon when improvements such as hiring goal scorer Dan Quinn would have been a simple matter. Few trades were made or attempted. Radek Hamr was too small. On the other hand, given the talent he was competing against for a defensive position, Hamr did not look all that out of place. And the way goal-less Brad Marsh played that final period, he probably had as much chance to score as any other Senator.

"We tried our best every night," John Ferguson told the *Sun's* Bruce Garrioch at the end of the season. "It got to the point where we knew we couldn't improve the club a great deal if we wanted that first-round draft pick. It was difficult because you have to have integrity, but we couldn't afford to improve by one or two points and blow that first pick. If we finish with 35 points, then we're drafting second overall. That hurts our future."

Making it happen would be another matter altogether. It would harm the integrity not only of the players and the franchise, but of the league itself. Professional hockey had been through a difficult year. The Ziegler years were being held in disgrace. Alan Eagleson had been under investigation by the FBI and the RCMP and the media. There were questions about Bruce McNall's $25 million "indemnification" fee and about the propriety of Gil Stein entering the Hockey Hall of Fame. The NHL could ill afford a scandal over a team deliberately taking a dive.

It had taken baseball decades to recover from the Black Sox Scandal of 1919, when Shoeless Joe Jackson and seven other players on the Chicago White Sox were banned forever from baseball for throwing the World Series. The scandal rocked the sport and led directly to the naming of baseball's first commissioner, Judge Kenesaw Mountain Landis. Hockey hardly needed such a scandal in the year of its first commissioner, Gary Bettman.

And yet, toward the end of August, the sports pages of North America began to fill with questions about whether there had been a "Senators Scandal" in 1992–93. On August 17, Firestone resigned as governor of the Ottawa Senators and sold his remaining shares of the team to Bryden, who assumed full ownership and the title of governor. Firestone – an ideas man who hated managing – had long been casting about for other projects, particularly in the area of specialty television channels. Financially and personally he was not against moving on, and when it began to look as if the difficult job of financing the team's new arena might go more smoothly if the team had a single owner, the obvious solution was to have Bryden assume full control.

Over the next two days, newspapers gave heavy coverage to a conversation Firestone had had with five reporters on June 26 at the Club Sportif in Quebec City. According to the account that appeared in *The Ottawa Citizen*, Firestone had revealed that the Senators had a back-up plan for the final game of the year in the event that it began to look as if Ottawa might somehow beat Boston. A tie or a win by the Senators would have moved them out of last place and denied them first pick in the June draft, which was being celebrated that night at the Club Sportif. If necessary, he had told the reporters, the team would have removed its goaltender and played the remainder of the game with the net empty.

He further stated that the franchise's biggest problem of the final two months of the season had been "keeping the restraints on Rick Bowness." Bowness, it seemed, wanted to win too badly for the liking of some in the franchise. Finally, Firestone added that sometime after the team reached its stated goal of 22 points on February 28, four Senators players had met with him to discuss the team's goals from then on. He had indicated to them that the goal had been reached and that the team was content. He said they then talked about the next goal – being able to draft first in June – and he had further indicated that this was what the franchise wanted. "It is no coincidence," he added, "that all four players are back with the team" for the upcoming season. Firestone would not say who the four players were.

His comments seemed too incendiary to report without first checking. At least two of the reporters present did limited investigations. *The Ottawa Citizen* was able to determine that the story of the four players had been repeated within the Senators organization enough that a list of players had been assembled by concerned senior staff. The franchise also held strategy meetings to discuss how the matter would be handled once the story became public, as they knew it had to, and as it did during the week of Firestone's resignation.

Rick Bowness's reaction to the idea of pulling the goaltender was one of indignation and fury. He knew of no such plan, he said, and would have refused to carry it out. In interviews, no other senior manager acknowledged knowing of such plans or meetings. Two players on the list compiled by senior management had precisely the same reaction as Bowness, saying no such meeting had ever taken place. While no one believed anything untoward had actually happened, all were concerned that the innuendo would be extremely harmful. Some within the organization wanted the comments aired so that they could be dealt with quickly and buried forever.

Firestone's initial response to the published reports only served to muddy the waters further. He told *The Globe and Mail* that the team did indeed have a "contingency plan to match rosters" if either Quebec or Boston iced inferior teams for the final two games of the regular season. He said there had been a meeting with four players during which he told them picking first in the draft would help the team and "the long-term good of the organization." In an 18-point rebuttal to the published stories, Firestone talked about the Senators' concern that either Quebec or Boston might ice a "B" team "to prevent the No. 1 pick from ending up in their division." He also said that management had been concerned about the possibility of a tie in the final two games and that a decision had been made that if, in the third period, the teams were tied, "the standard NHL tactic of pulling the goalie would be used in an effort to win the games." With the success rate for pulling the goaltender and scoring running, coaches say, at 10 or 15 percent, such a plan would far more likely lead to a loss. The debate heated up, with editorials across Canada calling for a full league investigation.

Bettman reacted swiftly. He reconvened the special two-man inquiry that had looked into (and overturned) Gil Stein's appointment to the Hockey Hall of Fame and sent Yves Fortier and Arnold Burns to Ottawa to interview Firestone, the journalists, and various players, coaches, and managers with the Senators, as well as representatives of the Boston Bruins. In all, 50 people were interviewed. Within two weeks, Fortier and Burns reported to Bettman that there was no foundation to the conspiracy theory – that no players or coaches had been involved in any secret plan to lose in order to guarantee the first draft pick.

Had Bruce Firestone not been an NHL governor when he spoke to the reporters, that might well have been the end of it. But the comments had profound repercussions for the integrity of the game and for the reputations of all the Ottawa Senators players. The inquiry was never able to determine Firestone's precise wording, but the comments were confirmed and deemed "clearly improper." Bettman found, and Firestone acknowledged, "that certain intemperate and inappropriate comments were made concerning the club's performance last season." And while the inquiry also concluded that there was no basis in fact to those comments – as the *Citizen* had also concluded in its limited investigation – Bettman ruled that the "statements created an unfortunate situation" and such talk "cannot be tolerated."

On September 2, Bettman levied a fine of $100,000 against the

Senators for Firestone's comments and for the team's failure to noti-
fy the league of the allegations, which the team had known of since
late June. Firestone had already declined to continue on as an alternate governor for the team. "This incident," added Bettman, "should
not reflect adversely on his reputation as a man of integrity."

It was a difficult time for Bruce Firestone, but in the end his
"intemperate" remarks may have served the NHL well. After the
incident, it was widely presumed that the league's ridiculous draft
rules would be altered.

CHAPTER NINE

THE FRANCHISE

Quebec City, Quebec

ON SATURDAY, JUNE 26, 1993 – A DAY WHEN MORNING RIPPLED OVER Quebec City like air over a hot stove – Alexandre Daigle woke early in his hotel room. He had slept well but was nervous the moment he remembered that this was the day of the 1993 NHL entry draft. For two years he had been dreaming about and praying for the moment that was now at hand. It did not matter to him whether the Ottawa Senators took him and kept him, took him and traded him, or traded their right to pick first so that another team could take him – just so long as he was Number One. As he would shortly say into a thicket of microphones, "No one remembers who came second."

An hour later Daigle was at the Ménage militaire, once home to the Old City's equestrian guard. On this day nine wooden tables had been placed strategically about its vast floor. On the left sat Guy Lafleur, who had filled Quebec City's Colisée when he played for the Junior-league Remparts and filled the imagination of an entire country when he played for the Canadiens. At separate tables to his left sat nine more Hall-of-Famers: Glenn Hall, Bobby Hull, Henri Richard, Billy Smith, Denis Potvin, Gordie Howe, Maurice Richard, Ted Lindsay, and, at the final table, Jean Beliveau, the hockey immortal who had built the Colisée. At the same table, to Beliveau's left, sat Daigle.

A thousand, perhaps two thousand people had been expected at this early-morning autographing session; by closing time people were still being turned away at the doors. If hockey is the true religion of Canada, in Quebec it is a cult. High on the wall of the Canadiens' dressing room are inscribed Colonel John McCrae's words, "To you from failing hands we throw the Torch; be yours to hold it high," and in this room were three men who had held that torch: Richard, Beliveau, and Lafleur. Only Lafleur had had no one to pass it to: Denis Savard had gone to Chicago in 1980; Mario Lemieux had gone to Pittsburgh in 1984; the stars of Quebec's other team, the Nordiques, were from elsewhere. Had the people thronging the Ménage militaire been able to play God on this day, they would have made sure the torch of Quebec hockey pride was passed into the hand of the dark young man in the blue suit sitting beside Jean Beliveau.

All week long Quebec City had been consumed with Daigle: he was on the front page of *Le Soleil* and *Le Journal de Québec* and on the cover of *The Hockey News*. He was the subject of a feature in *Sports Illustrated* and of a full documentary, *The Franchise Kid*, on The Sports Network. On Thursday he had held a press conference to announce his choice of trading-card companies. It had been standing room only – even reporters had lined up for autographs.

On Friday, Daigle and the other top prospects had been taken to a suburban shopping mall and put on display in a setting even Fellini would never have dared: the 21 young men had skated onto an ice surface while a carousel circled lazily nearby and a roller coaster rose and plummeted slowly in the background. Of the 21, as many as six – Canadian Junior players Daigle, Chris Pronger, Chris Gratton, and Rob Niedermayer, American college star Paul Kariya, and Russian Viktor Kozlov – were being spoken of as franchise players. This was an exaggeration yet at the same time proof that

1993 was a special draft year. And no one was more special than Alexandre Daigle.

Marcel Aubut, president of the Nordiques, had seen what was happening and could feel Daigle slipping away. This week's draft would overlap with the festivities in honor of Saint-Jean-Baptiste, Quebec's patron saint, and as one of the week's hosts, Aubut wanted nothing more than to bring Daigle home where he belonged. With Daigle, he could build the new Colisée; the newest francophone superstar would attract the investors and lease the corporate boxes and fill the seats. Aubut now knew this for certain: he had been to the Ménage militaire and seen the lineups. The throng in front of Beliveau and Daigle had been even bigger than Lafleur's. The one they all wanted to wave to, to smile at, to touch, was Daigle. Even Beliveau was amazed.

Daigle was young enough to be Beliveau's grandson, too young to have seen Lafleur play. He had never seen anything like this. Youths were bringing their girlfriends for photographs. "Il sera la future vedette," a mother explained to a child too young to comprehend why he was being placed on Daigle's lap for a photograph. He is the coming star. At the end of the session Daigle needed a phalanx of security guards to get out of the building while Beliveau, Lafleur, Richard, Howe, and Hull all walked out unaccompanied. People had brought babies for him to touch – *babies*, as if his hands were those of an eighteenth-century bishop rather than an 18-year-old hockey player.

Outside the Ménage militaire, Aubut had broken into a sweat. Partly it was the mugginess, the dark, threatening clouds, but mostly it was the clock. Time was running out. The Hall-of-Famers and the draft choices were being loaded into *calèches* for a horse-drawn procession through the Old City to the Colisée. Beliveau and Daigle were already in the first carriage, the sky divers were in the air, the ribbon had been cut, and the 105-mm cannon had sounded. Then they were off, with Aubut fluttering like a huge hen beside the lead carriage as Beliveau and Daigle waved to the cheering crowds. "Listen to him!" Aubut shouted to Daigle. "Il est le mâitre." Beliveau was the master: he would talk sense to the young man. Perhaps Beliveau would deliver him yet.

But it was already too late. Daigle's agent, Pierre Lacroix, had passed word along that the deal with Ottawa was settled. Daigle would go first and the Senators would keep him. The contract was for $12.25 million. He was 18 years old and had never played an NHL game, but he was already the new superstar. In the streets of the Old City, all he had to do was raise a hand and thousands recognized him and cheered.

MORE THAN A YEAR HAD PASSED SINCE JOHN ZIEGLER HAD APPEARED ON television with color-coded charts and argued that the players' greed would bring certain doom. He had claimed then that the owners would lose more than $150 million over the coming two seasons, and that a players' strike timed to the Stanley Cup playoffs would hurt the fans more than the owners because the playoffs accounted for only 11 percent of revenues – roughly $8.8 million. It was a ludicrous claim, but these few figures were as far as the NHL would go in disclosing its finances. The true health of the hockey business was unknown.

If owning a team was such a bad investment, why had Disney bought in? Why had Blockbuster? Why were those groups who'd been denied a new franchise howling in outrage? If owning a team was such a bad investment, why was the NHL refusing to open its books to the Players' Association? Some teams, like the Oilers and the North Stars, were even refusing to show their books to Edmonton and Minneapolis–Saint Paul, the cities that – by refusing to agree to better leasing arrangements or to build new facilities – were supposedly denying them profitability. The fans in those cities, who had poured their money, energy, and faith into their teams, were being told they weren't good enough "partners" – that fans elsewhere would pay more for the privilege of supporting an NHL franchise. But nowhere was there proof of the owners' claims.

At the end of each NHL season a confidential document called the Unified Report of Operations is delivered by the league to the team owners. The figures are in "mixed" dollars, meaning that Canadian teams report in Canadian currency and American teams in American. According to the 1991–92 report on the 22 clubs then in operation, revenues from the regular season amounted to about $467 million in mixed dollars and operating expenses came to about $505 million. In other words, the teams suffered a total net loss from the regular season of roughly $38 million. (See Appendix I for the exact figures.) In the season before that, 1990–91, total revenues were about $417 million and total operating expenses about $400 million, for a regular-season profit of about $17 million.

The NHL documents list playoff figures separately. And it is during the playoffs that, whatever Ziegler's claims, the great profits are reaped. The Unified Report shows that 1991–92 playoff revenues reached about $49 million against expenses of roughly $25 million, for a profit of $24 million. When the playoff profits are combined with the regular-season losses, the overall net loss is said to have been about $13 million. The season before that, playoff profits reached about $29 million, for an overall 1990–91 net profit of $46 million.

This means that in one year, according to the league's own confidential information, the NHL went from profits of $46 million to losses of $14 million. That's a financial downturn of $60 million.

The report suggests that the average club made a profit of about $2.2 million in 1990–91 and suffered a loss in 1991–92 of $605,000. The NHL further claims that the most profitable clubs showed a profit of only about $3.3 million in 1991–92, while the bottom third lost an average of $4.2 million.

What, then, can possibly make a franchise worth $50 million? And why would Edmonton's Peter Pocklington – presumably in the bottom third of the league – turn down an offer of $65 million for his franchise in the spring of 1993?

All of the above presumes that the NHL's own figures are accurate. They seem not to be. Even in the internal financial reports of the league (also confidential), expenses are reported more thoroughly than revenues. Only 19 of the 22 teams reported revenue from radio-broadcast rights. Which three teams could not sell those rights? Under the "special games" category, how is it that 20 of the teams claimed expenses but only 19 appeared to have put on special games? Under concessions, why did more than half the teams report nothing? Under parking, how is it that only five teams showed any income from this highly lucrative revenue stream?

The bookkeeping is even spottier during the playoffs. Only nine teams claimed to have taken in novelty sales during this time – a total of $138,000. Yet fans watching on national television during the Montreal–Los Angeles series were told that the novelty boutiques at the Great Western Forum did $125,000 worth of business in two hours one evening. And the idea that only one NHL team, out of the 22 existing that year, was savvy enough to charge extra for "signage" during the playoffs strains belief. As does the column showing that only nine of the 16 clubs that reached the playoffs had playoff programs for sale. And why would ten clubs have claimed expenses on programs when only nine admitted that they published programs?

Where might revenue be hidden by individual clubs? One need only look at the Unified Report's final notes: "(3) Luxury Suite revenues are reported with gate receipts to the extent of the ticket value of the seats only; (4) In Arena revenues are limited to the extent that those types of revenues are reported by the team. Such revenues reported on the books of an affiliate (such as the Arena) are not included." Nor is mention made anywhere in that report of the increased equity value of individual franchises.

To realize that the NHL does not mention the real money-makers in its own documents is to begin to understand what owning a sports franchise is all about in the 1990s, and what a player like Alexandre Daigle can mean to a team like the Ottawa Senators. *Financial World* says that the most valuable sports franchise in the United States is the Dallas Cowboys of the National Football League. The owner, Jerry Jones, was ridiculed when he purchased the Cowboys in 1989 for $135 million. Today the value of the franchise is $165 million and rising, because of the use Jones makes of Texas Stadium. The latest plan is for 70 new corporate boxes and for 4,000 seats in the end zone to be designated as "club seating," which will feature a small personal television set for each high-paying fan. As the magazine put it, "Jones knows where the action is. And it's not on the playing field ... it is increasingly the stadiums that will determine which franchises are the most valuable."

This is why *Financial World* declared hockey's Detroit Red Wings the most profitable team in professional sports. The Red Wings' operating margin is 50.7 percent, largely because of the lease arrangement owner Mike Ilitch has with the city on the 19,275-seat Joe Louis Arena. Using similar criteria, the magazine determined that the Vancouver Canucks are rising in value more quickly than any other hockey franchise —35.4 percent in the past year. The

Canucks are now worth $61 million. The new arena they are build-
ing will increase their value even more. The next three fastest-grow-
ing hockey franchises are the St. Louis Blues (up 34.6 percent to $52
million), the Pittsburgh Penguins (up 30 percent to $53 million), and
the Red Wings (up 24.7 percent to $87 million).

A team's financial success is determined mainly by who owns
the arena, or runs it. Most rinks are community-owned, but some –
most notably the Spectrum in Philadelphia, the Forum in Montreal,
Madison Square Garden in New York, Chicago Stadium, Maple
Leaf Gardens in Toronto, and the Great Western Forum in Los
Angeles – are owned by individuals or corporations that generally
also own the hockey club. "Owning an arena," David Cruise and
Alison Griffiths wrote in *Net Worth*, "in addition to being immense-
ly profitable in its own right, provides many opportunities to make
the resident hockey team appear to lose money. The simplest method
is to have the arena charge the club exorbitant rent for the facilities.
Another equally effective technique is for ancillary revenues from
beer sales, souvenirs and other concessions to end up in the arena's
books, or in a separate branch of the parent corporation. Suddenly,
the team that sells out every game chronically loses money or breaks
even at best."

It is the same story throughout professional sport. Paul Bees-
ton, president of the Toronto Blue Jays, once told *The Wall Street
Journal*, "Under generally accepted accounting principles, I can turn
a four-million-dollar profit into a two-million-dollar loss, and I can
get every national accounting firm to agree with me."

Whatever means the teams have at their disposal to conceal
their real financial condition, the simplest measure of financial success or failure – gate receipts – suggests that the NHL is very healthy
indeed. Other confidential league documents indicate that only three

teams in the entire league saw their gate receipts fall during the 1992–93 season. The 984 regular-season games (i.e., not including the two "alternate venue" games each team played) brought in a league total of about $364 million – almost 25 percent more than the previous season's $292 million (see Appendix II). More than $50 million in playoff money can be added to that.

These numbers – the NHL's own, remember – tell a fascinating story. This extraordinary increase came during the worst North American recession since the 1930s. (Even if the two new teams, Ottawa and Tampa Bay, are subtracted from the total, the increase is still more than 16 percent.) Ticket prices also went up significantly – an average of $3.31 – and have gone up again for 1993–94. Curiously, the North Stars abandoned the Twin Cities area, which they described as a "poor NHL market," despite enjoying a 34 percent increase in gate revenues in 1992–93.

Anyone questioning whether marquee players pay off need only look to Vancouver (gate-receipt increase, 34 percent); Quebec (29 percent); Toronto (27 percent); Detroit (27 percent); Philadelphia (25 percent); Pittsburgh (19 percent); and Buffalo (17 percent). In those cities' respective uniforms are found Pavel Bure; Mats Sundin and Joe Sakic; Doug Gilmour; Steve Yzerman and Sergei Fedorov; Eric Lindros; Mario Lemieux; and Pat LaFontaine and Alexander Mogilny.

How does a team pay for a marquee player? An obvious way is by increasing ticket prices. The Vancouver Canucks raised their average ticket price from $24.05 to $33.84 and easily got away with it. (The Hartford Whalers, without a superstar, raised their average price only 23 cents, to $26.61, and lost fans.) The other obvious route is television, when that's possible. The Unified Report on Operations put the NHL's television revenues at slightly more than $35 million. Local and cable television added another $55 million or so. Even if such revenues were shared, they would not in a given year amount to as much as what each team gets when a new franchise is sold. With prospects for an American network deal dim at best – NHL playoff hockey could not outdraw a seniors' golf tournament in the spring of 1993 – regular television is not enough.

Pay-per-view television remains the great fantasy. PPV has now been approved by the federal regulatory agencies in both Canada and the United States, but the prospects are not as grand as Bruce McNall once painted them. American college football has not worked on pay-per-view. A tennis match between Jimmy Connors and Martina Navratilova flopped. The PPV Olympic package from Barcelona lost $50 million for NBC. Early experiments in the Canadian Football League have shown little promise. The North Stars did have some success with it during their surprising run to the NHL finals in 1991. And the Penguins, with the most stars to sell, have created PenVision, which has successfully packaged games not shown on free or cable television.

A number of NHL teams are now considering the advantages of in-house broadcasting; the team does not sell broadcast rights but instead produces its own broadcasts and sells its own advertising. The Portland Trail Blazers of the National Basketball Association have done this since 1980 and claim to have netted twice what they would have through the direct sale of rights. Other NBA teams have gone this route, as have a few baseball teams and the Buffalo Sabres.

Beyond the reality of seat sales and the fantasy of pay-per-view are "linkages." The most intriguing linkage of all is the sale of corporate boxes, which exist so that – as one advertising executive put it – men in suits at a leisure event can "financially moon the common folk below." The revenue generated by these boxes is astonishing. An executive box at the SkyDome in Toronto can lease for $250,000 a year. In

Detroit's new baseball stadium the Tigers hope to generate $10 million a year from boxes alone. The leasing costs are sky-high, the food and bar costs astronomical, the sight lines often the worst in the building; yet, so long as well-heeled executives can write off most of the costs of taking friends, families, and clients to sports events, corporate boxes will be worshipped by owners. For those facilities without boxes, or with too few, the solution is simple: build. Better yet, have the taxpayers build a new facility for you, then have the city hand it over.

Another increasingly important linkage is rink advertising, both on the dasher boards and throughout the facility. The NHL's Unified Report shows 17 teams reporting dasher-board sales of about $11.5 million, with signage adding another $4.5 million. A confidential study made by the Walt Disney Company makes clear that the potential for such advertising is enormous. In March 1993, Disney hired the National Sports and Entertainment division of Ernst & Young to prepare an analysis of arena advertising. In its confidential report, E&Y identified more than 4,000 corporations that spend more than $1.5 billion a year forging links with professional sports teams. By allowing such companies to become their "marketing partners," teams with the right image were able to increase their revenue flow substantially. According to the same report, a pair of signs (entrance and exit) is worth $25,000 a season; a marquee ad on the main arena sign, $200,000; ads on an electronic message board, $30,000 each; panels in the concourse, $6,000; panels in the food areas, up to $19,000; a full-color ad in the program, $10,500; a scoreboard ad, $32,500; and an ad on the Zamboni, $50,000 to $65,000. One NHL team was charging $110,000 for nothing more than a top-skirt placement on the main scoreboard.

The same report shows plainly why teams are so determined to control their facilities. A single dasher board now goes for about

$75,000 a panel, since a typical dasher-board ad is seen 216 times during a telecast – that is, for more than nine-and-a-half minutes. In other words, the Coke ad gets more ice time than the average NHL player. The NHL is now also moving toward "in-ice" ads, which are painted on to the ice surface. Such ads are relatively new and still restricted; even so, E&Y found one team charging $200,000 for them. Another team was getting $40,000 a season for the space on the back of its ticket stubs. Some teams were putting together full promotional packages for corporate partners, guaranteeing them their own "player" for personal appearances and tying together various sorts of advertising, at anywhere from $150,000 to $350,000 a package. And finally, E&Y suggested, the name of the rink might be sold to a corporate sponsor for anywhere from $550,000 to $1.2 million a year.

During the 1992–93 season new luxury rinks were being either built or planned by no fewer than 13 of the 24 NHL franchises: Boston, Buffalo, Chicago, Montreal, Ottawa, Philadelphia, Quebec, St. Louis, San Jose, Tampa Bay, Toronto, Vancouver, and Winnipeg. The new Florida Panthers would also be building a rink, and the New York Rangers would be refurbishing Madison Square Garden. Detroit owner Mike Ilitch, who already has the best lease deal in hockey, was talking about a 25,000-seat facility. That is 16 of 26 sites. And not one of those new sites would feature the larger ice surface used in international hockey, which many fans regard as superior for displays of speed and skill; a bigger ice surface would mean fewer seats.

To GAIN BETTER FACILITIES, OR MORE CONTROL OF THEM, A NUMBER OF NHL owners have turned to history's most effective tool of diplomacy: threat. No owner was as successful as Seymour Knox III of

Buffalo, who said he would move his Sabres unless the franchise got a brand-new arena. That threat worked, and not just on the city of Buffalo; it also got New York governor Mario Cuomo's signature on a bill that will provide $25 million of taxpayers' money for the project. Hartford's Richard Gordon suggested he could no longer sustain losses of $6 million a year; Connecticut governor Lowell P. Weicker Jr. came through with a two-year, $4 million loan and a $10 million guarantee on bank loans up to $25 million, and promised to redo Gordon's "stinky" lease agreement, which allowed the Whalers no revenues on concession sales or parking. Not enough, said Gordon – he might still move. Never was it mentioned that the Whalers were, after the expansion teams, the worst show in the NHL. But professional sports is unlike any other business. Only in sports can a mediocre to terrible product demand profitability or else.

Peter Pocklington, another owner of a bad team, said he would have to take his Oilers out of Edmonton if the city that had made him rich could not give him a more favorable lease on Northlands Coliseum. Pocklington had been trying to get his lease rewritten since 1990 – one year after he signed it. He also wanted a new arena built, with favorable arrangements on concessions and parking. Pocklington painted his team as a bottomless money pit into which he had dropped a fortune. At one point he sought a deal whereby he would receive virtually all income derived from the building, including from non-hockey events – all the perks of total ownership with none of the burdens. Either that, he said, or his team was off to Hamilton, the NHL's eternal bridesmaid.

But Pocklington has at other times – for example, when chasing a possible partner – portrayed the team as a money machine. The true picture is indecipherable, for again, the books are closed. It is known, however, that the team is worth $65 million to someone, for this amount was offered at one point by the group controlling the Edmonton arena. Pocklington turned the offer down and suggested $105 million would be more like it. Pocklington paid $6,503,000 for the Oilers in 1979. By 1983 he was valuing his team at $20 to $25 million; now he was portraying the Oilers as a financial disaster. (Pocklington actually does know something about financial disasters – his Patrician Land Corp. and Fidelity Trust lost $200 million in the 1980s and went bankrupt.)

Pocklington named Hamilton's Copps Coliseum as his alternative and added that Toronto's neighbor was prepared to give him guaranteed concession and parking revenues. That city, he said, was prepared to build him 110 sky suites that would generate $9.6 million a year. He calculated that moving the team would automatically put another $19 million a year in his pocket. Such brinksmanship had Edmonton fans panicking until Hamilton politicians denied they had made him any such offer. Unfazed, Pocklington conceded that the deal was the one he understood Hamilton had been willing to strike with Ron Joyce, the donut king, during the city's 1990 franchise bid. Surely, he suggested, the Hamilton fans – his partners in negotiation – would insist on the same deal for the Hamilton Oilers.

"He is not coming here," Hamilton alderman Henry Merling told the press. "He is just using us shamelessly and we are stupid enough to fall for it."

It was more important that Edmonton be made to fall for it. As Pocklington had hoped, the city began negotiating to redraft his 10-year lease. At the same time, however, serious questions were being raised about Pocklington's pleas of poverty. He claimed to have lost $1.5 million in 1992–93, but he had neglected to add in the more than $3 million in expansion money from the Disney and Blockbuster franchises. He claimed a player payroll of $13 million, but the

Edmonton Journal calculated the figure as $10.5 million – and this before Pocklington dumped two of the team's more expensive players, Esa Tikkanen ($900,000 a year) and Bernie Nicholls ($522,000).

For those who openly doubt the claims of NHL owners, it was a fascinating duel between assertion and reality. Pocklington held a press conference, where he tried to prove that his lease was unfair compared with those of the Red Wings, North Stars, and Penguins, all of whom – he claimed – received 100 percent of revenues from parking, concessions, rink advertising, and corporate boxes. The *Journal* again took him to task: Pittsburgh was receiving 41 percent of concessions and only a small percentage of parking. Pocklington was saying that the Winnipeg Jets received 100 percent of dasher-board advertising – the true figure turned out to be 50 percent.

Pocklington's lease was indeed tough when compared with the sweetheart deals enjoyed by many other owners. He paid $3 million a year in rent and received none of the profits from parking or concessions. Nor did he share in the advertising revenues, or profit from non-hockey events. But remember – his critics were saying – that Pocklington had drained more than $50 million from this once-wonderful franchise to finance other operations and in the process had devalued his own product. For instance, the $15 million that he received from Bruce McNall in the 1988 Gretzky trade had gone into his own pocket, not back into the team. In 1993 he had stripped his team of its high-salaried players and it had missed the playoffs. The days of Gretzky, Kurri, Messier, Anderson, and Coffey were now a distant memory.

In 1983 Pocklington campaigned to become leader of the Progressive Conservative Party and, possibly, Prime Minister of Canada. The way to run a country, he once said, was to put an end to government handouts. Although he was already in debt to the

Alberta provincial government on his other businesses, he now wanted the taxpayers of Edmonton to subsidize him. He proposed that his lease be reduced to one dollar a year and that he receive all benefits from the venue – that way he would accumulate enough money to build his own arena, which he would own outright, and leave the taxpayers stuck with an obsolete and NHL-less Coliseum. The suggestion did not fly, but in the closed world of the NHL almost anything is possible.

Most threats to move a franchise are never carried out. But in 1993 Norm Green made his North Stars the exception. According to NHL sources, his team was a fairly healthy, profitable, and promising operation. Gate receipts had gone from $8.4 million in 1991–92 to $11.2 million in 1992–93. Revenues from corporate sponsorships had doubled from $1.5 million to $3 million. According to *Financial World*, the franchise was worth $42 million – an $8 million increase in a single year.

In June 1990, when he arrived from Calgary to take over the North Stars, Green had been regarded as a guardian angel. Fans felt they finally had an owner who would never let them down, the way the Gund brothers had. "Can you imagine saying, 'Buy tickets or we're going to move the team'?" Green said in a local interview soon after taking over. "That's the worst possible approach you could have. You can't blackmail people." Minnesotans fell in love with him for such talk. They cheered him like a star player during the team's 1991 playoff drive, which took them to the cup final.

Less than two years later, Green had to avoid home games for fear of physical violence. He had in fact said, "Buy tickets or we're going to move the team." Apparently North Stars fans still weren't buying enough. Not enough fans, not enough corporate boxes, not enough linkages. For Green, blackmail was not an alternative – he already had one of the best lease deals in the NHL. He was able to claim the profits on the facility in return for a percentage of gross income. (In 1991–92 he paid $244,000.). He profited from all events, hockey and non-hockey, held at the Met Center. He paid no property tax and was responsible for no debt service on the building. He had only to pay for maintenance and capital improvements. But all of this was not enough – not when other cities were offering even better deals so that they, too, could be major-league.

Green claimed various losses – at one point saying the team had cost him $24 million. Though local politicians and the media disputed his calculations, he was adamant: he was going broke. The *New York Times* requested permission to look at his books. "No," he told the paper. "It's a private company."

Green announced that he was moving the franchise to Dallas for the 1993–94 season. The fans who had supported the North Stars for 26 seasons had no say in the matter. Toward the season's end Minnesotans were coming by the thousands to the Met Center to chant "Norm sucks!" while their team sank like a stone and missed the playoffs.

"The move is something that shouldn't have happened," Bob Gainey, the North Stars' general manager and coach, told *Sports Illustrated*, "something that should have been avoided. You have a place with a grass-roots interest and suddenly ... I was thinking about the historical precedents. Hockey started in western Canada, you know. All the little towns had teams. Then there was a team in New York, in the big cities in the U.S. The players from the little towns went to New York, and suddenly there were no teams in western Canada. Same thing in France. I played over there. Hockey started in the Alps. Then a guy in Paris started a team, and all the players went, and there was no hockey in the Alps. It all winds up where the money is."

For Green, the money was in Dallas. Before the NHL winter meetings in West Palm Beach in December 1992 he had been shopping around for a potential site and had settled on Anaheim, only to be told that the NHL had other plans for the city. In return for accepting that he was locked out of Southern California, he was allowed to move to Dallas without penalty. Had he succeeded in getting his team into Anaheim, Joe Lapointe of the *New York Times* would later note, "McNall wouldn't have pocketed those $25 million Disney dollars. In exchange for getting Green to avoid Anaheim, the owners gave [Green] permission to abandon Minnesota. It all happened while McNall was announcing expansion to Anaheim and Miami while introducing Bettman. Somehow McNall forgot to mention the deal with Green."

Meanwhile, the loyal fans of Minnesota had not been forgotten. The NHL thoughtfully scheduled six "neutral site" games for the Met Center in 1993–94. The first would feature the last-place Ottawa Senators against the new Dallas Stars.

"THERE ARE TWO NHL TEAMS THAT WILL ACHIEVE THEIR GOALS THIS year," Bruce Firestone had said after his Senators' 84th game, and 70th loss. "The Stanley Cup champions, and us." The Senators had indeed achieved goals in 1992–93: they had scored more than 21 points (24); they had sold out every night; and, most importantly, they had finished last. The NHL devised the system; the Senators were in a position to take advantage of it. Ottawa had tried to save the league from embarrassment by attempting to strike a deal with San Jose that would have rewarded winning rather than losing. The Senators were covered.

The celebrations were still going on in the dressing room when co-owner and alternate governor Rod Bryden walked up to general manager Mel Bridgman and said, "Let's do breakfast."

At 8 a.m. the following morning, Bridgman was fired. A few hours later, casually dressed in a burgundy golf shirt and jeans, Bridgman stepped out of his office with his Wharton diploma under one arm and a memento of his glory days with the Flyers under the other. He had no comment. The deal struck with Bryden was well worth the silence – the remaining three years of his contract would be honored at full value, $225,000 a year – but Bridgman couldn't hide his pain or his bitterness.

An hour earlier, Randy Sexton, whom everyone thought had hired Bridgman, had taken over Bridgman's job. Sexton, of course, had even less experience than Bridgman.

On the surface it looked like more corporate ineptitude by the league leaders in bungling. But it was not that simple. No one had bothered to scribble out a pro-and-con list for Bridgman's year, but the pro side was fairly slim – a couple of fair trades, a couple of good hirings. The con side was familiar to all: the Loewen and McBain contracts; the players lost on waivers; the inability to get along with the coaches in both Ottawa and New Haven; the poor draft performance in 1992. Even the franchise's senior executives would concede privately that the first year had been a lost year, a disaster redeemed only by a fluke of the draft rules.

It had been Bryden's decision rather than Sexton's to fire Mel Bridgman. A failed season will often cost a job – the San Jose Sharks were about to fire their coach, George Kingston, though they would not say whether it was for doing so badly or for not doing badly enough. The difference here was that Bridgman had been fired less for what had happened during the season than for what was likely to happen the following weekend.

On Sunday, April 18, Bryden met with the team's executive

and scouting staff, and here the plan for the Quebec draft was set down. Ottawa would pretend to be interested in Peterborough Petes defenseman Chris Pronger, as well as in Alexandre Daigle – but only for the purposes of negotiation. (They would not even bother meeting with Pronger until they arrived in Quebec City, and then only out of courtesy, for ten minutes.) Pronger would be a name to float to keep Daigle off guard. The Senators were certain, and for good reason, that Daigle's obsession with being chosen first in the draft would help them.

At this point there was a possibility that the Senators would trade the rights to Daigle to Quebec. Any such trade, however, would hinge on the Nordiques' ability to deliver Swedish sensation Peter Forsberg. The Nordiques would have to sign Forsberg before Ottawa would consider trading the rights to Daigle, and there was now considerable doubt that the Swede would sign. For their part, in order to trade Daigle the Senators would probably have to sign him before the draft was held. In Bryden's opinion, Mel Bridgman was not up to handling such a complicated deal.

The Senators confirmed that Daigle would be their choice when Randy Sexton and coach Rick Bowness slipped out of Ottawa and drove to Daigle's home in Laval, outside Montreal. There they met with the young man and his parents and received the answer they wanted: if drafted, Daigle would not rebuff the Senators as Lindros had Quebec and Lemieux nearly had Pittsburgh. What mattered most to Daigle was that he be chosen first.

At that point Daigle had been taking English lessons for less than three months, yet he was already capable of witticisms in English. He was a warm, friendly kid with movie-star looks and a love of the limelight. Unlike Lemieux, he seemed to crave recognition. Unlike Lindros, he was certain to be cooperative with the team that took his rights. Unlike Gretzky, he was only 18 years old.

Sexton and Bowness reported all this to Bryden, who by now had something more important on his mind than the future of an 18-year-old kid. The Palladium, the team's long-heralded new facility, was in deep trouble. Soon it would be a year since the Senators had unwisely held their sod-turning ceremony in the empty cornfield west of Kanata. The huge shovel used at the original sod-turning ceremony had sat idle ever since, waiting for the financing to come together. The symbolic hole had been blown full of field dirt; the sign had fallen down.

A half-dozen times the project had been on the verge of going ahead, only to stumble at the final moment. Canadian financing had been lined up, then had fallen apart when the provincial government demanded that Terrace Investments, the Senators' holding company, build a $34 million highway interchange. Terrace was unable to finance it at reasonable rates. It sought a loan guarantee from the Ontario government to get a lower-interest deal, but the province had failed to come through. Terrace would later turn the highway project over to the region, meaning the interchange would have no value and Terrace would have no equity in it. In June 1993, just before the draft, the whole fragile $190 million investment package collapsed.

Bryden had, by this time, sketchy details of the 1992 study the Quebec Nordiques had commissioned on Eric Lindros's impact on a hockey franchise. Bryden began speculating on what Daigle might do for the Senators. If Lindros meant far more to Philadelphia than fans – if he could conceivably affect everything from corporate-box sales to television penetration to the building of a brand-new facility – what might Daigle's added value be in Ottawa? Might it be enough to get the Palladium built?

At the same moment that Bryden began tracking down a copy of the New York consultant's report – he never did obtain one – the man who had ordered the report, Aubut, was certain he had landed Daigle. There were three weeks to go before the draft and he thought he had put together the package of players Ottawa wanted. The signals he was picking up from Ottawa suggested the deal was on – that Daigle was his. It was only when he learned that the Palladium financing had fallen through that Aubut understood what had happened to his own plan to build the new Colisée around Daigle. "Such is life," Aubut said. "We will have to find another way."

When Aubut wistfully suggested that the Senators had suddenly "just decided to go for it," he was quite correct. The Senators had liked Daigle very much as a hockey player, as did everyone, but they were not mesmerized by him. There was, in fact, some internal debate about whether Pronger might not be the better player. At the time, the Senators expected a deal with Quebec to happen. This expectation, however, was based on hockey considerations. In June, when the other factors had to be looked at, Daigle became the only choice. As Bryden put it in Quebec City, "If he comes, they will build it."

In all the past year's talk about Daigle, his charisma had been overlooked – at least in English North America. By the time the NHL gathered in Quebec City for the draft, however, his charisma was blindingly obvious and his English surprisingly good. He had star quality: green eyes, a lopsided, infectious grin, and devilish good looks of the sort made popular by the television series "Beverly Hills 90210." The press adored him. When asked what made him different from Lindros, Daigle didn't miss a beat: "I *drink* my beer."

The hockey world debated his skills. Daigle, it is said, can change speed as abruptly as Bobby Orr; it is also said that he has never shown he can win. It is said that he is one of the best playmakers ever to come out of Junior; it is also said that he is oblivious to team defense. At the time he was drafted, however, the issue was celebrity, not ability, and Daigle, in the mysterious process by which these things happen, had become an instant celebrity in a sport that was desperate for North American heroes.

DAIGLE'S BACKGROUND IS A FAMILIAR ENOUGH CANADIAN STORY. HE was born on February 7, 1975, in Montreal, and raised in suburban Laval. His parents, Jean-Yves and Francine Daigle, were not athletes, nor was his older brother, Sebastian, though his sister, Veronique, now 19, would develop into a fine softball player. The Daigles stopped flooding their backyard rink when Sebastian lost interest. His father laughed at Alexandre's clumsy first attempts to play the game that matters most in Quebec. He scored 150 goals as a Pee Wee, starred as a Midget, and impressed in his rookie year of Junior, but it was only in the fall of 1992 that people began to notice his unusual glow. Francine Daigle says it took her son a long, long time to learn the game; those who were taught only in June how to pronounce his name would say that he arrived like lightning.

The Daigle Cup may have started as a joke, but it was not ending as one. Rod Bryden, on the verge of announcing that the Palladium's financing had fallen through, began discussions with Hill and Knowlton, the huge North American public-relations firm, to see what Daigle might mean to the Senators. Without the Palladium the Senators would never be able to afford Daigle, whose agent was already talking about a contract as lucrative as the one Lindros had signed with Philadelphia. No Palladium would also mean no more Ottawa Senators. Like Norm Green's North Stars, they would move to a better deal.

The trade with Quebec was quickly falling apart. Trading for four or five excellent players made little sense if the Senators had to stay in the Civic Centre, where seat sales are limited. It would probably produce instantly the best team Ottawa would ice for a decade, but that team would already be fading by the time the Palladium was ready – if it was ever to be ready. Keeping Daigle seemed the only sensible course. If the Senators had to move, what better way than with the next superstar to sell to another city's fans?

But what if they *could* stay? What if Daigle's promise attracted new investors to the Palladium? And if his promise were fulfilled, the possibilities would be endless. If pay-per-view took off in Canada, the fans would want to see the teams with the top players; in that case Daigle might lead the Senators to untold riches. He would help sell corporate boxes. He would gain the team more national television coverage. More television would allow the Senators to charge more for signage and for dasher boards and for in-ice advertising and for the advertising vehicles to come, such as a Coke logo on Daigle's jersey arm or a Chrysler logo on his back. When Bryden had his consultants run the image of Chris Pronger across the screen, it did not sparkle like Daigle's. For the dream to come true, the Senators were going to need the young center from Victoriaville. The Senators would take him and keep him.

At the Colisée, Daigle sat at the front of section 9 with his mother and father, his sister and brother, none of them able to see the floor clearly for the cameras and microphones waiting to collect the moment. When NHL commissioner Gary Bettman announced that Ottawa would make the first selection, Daigle swallowed hard. He turned to look at his agent for one final confirmation that he was indeed Number One. Pierre Lacroix, two seats back, stuck out his tongue and winked.

"Alex-andre *Daaa-igle!*" Randy Sexton shouted into the

microphone. The Colisée exploded with every emotion but surprise.

While his parents and sister wept, Daigle, now property of the worst team in the NHL, happily made his way to the podium, tugged on a Senators sweater and cap, and pumped his fist in the air.

When rumors of Daigle's contract hit the floor of the Colisée – could it really be $12.25 million over five years? – many hockey people reacted with outrage. Phil Esposito could not believe it and promised to eat his hat if it turned out to be true. "He's fortunate that we didn't have the first pick," growled Boston's Harry Sinden, "because he's about 11.5 million dollars richer than he would be." Edmonton's Glen Sather conceded that Daigle had great promise, "but can he command two million a year? I don't think it's right. He may be the best thing since sliced bread, but he hasn't proven it yet."

Days later, Sather was still fuming. "The rationalization for the salaries that are being paid has gone so far in one direction," he told Scott Taylor of the *Winnipeg Free Press*, "that many NHL clubs will be forced out of business. This is absurd. There is absolutely no sanity to it. Is this kid good enough to command the types of salaries that Wayne Gretzky, Mario Lemieux and Brett Hull have earned over a number of years in the league? It's sick. The guy who offered this deal should be thrown out of hockey."

The guy in question was Bryden. In fact, $12.25 million was merely a figure everyone had agreed to throw around freely. It brought attention to Daigle and the Senators, and it allowed Lacroix to bill himself as the hottest agent in the land.

The deal was actually two separate contracts, one for hockey, one for marketing. The signing bonus was $2 million, but payable at $500,000 a year for four years. Daigle's base salary in the first year would be $550,000, meaning the contract could also have been described as $1.05 million in year one, rising to $2.65 million by the final year. But those aren't the sort of numbers that make headlines.

Daigle's marketing contract is a variation on the deal that Pittsburgh put together for Mario Lemieux and relates to about one-third — $4 million — of the total package. One requirement is for the Senators to establish a marketing plan through Hill and Knowlton that will ensure for Daigle — presuming he pans out — the sort of corporate linkages that basketball's stars have long enjoyed. Daigle will never flog cars for a local dealer, never pitch for a local merchant. The aim is to market his image at the level Wayne Gretzky reached late in his career and ultimately to move beyond that into the orbit kept by McDonald's, Nike, and General Motors.

The $4 million, then, is really more an advance against future income than a salary. The Senators have guaranteed that sum to Daigle over five years, but they expect to make it back and far more. Daigle will receive 25 percent of the first $10 million, the Senators 75 percent. Any marketing earnings beyond $10 million, they will split. This means that at the $13 million mark, Daigle will have earned back his advance. The Senators will have made $9 million on his image and all but covered the cost of his contract. At $19.5 million, the Senators will have made $12.25 million back on their $12.25 million deal with Daigle. Given that Disney may be the ticket to North American acceptance of hockey, and keeping in mind that Michael Jordan pulls in $25 million a year from endorsements, it is not beyond the realm of possibility that a young, good-looking North American hockey superstar could bring in $19.5 million over the next five years.

Still, Glen Sather has predicted that Daigle's contract "will be the beginning of the end for small-market teams unless the league eventually finds its sanity and creates a salary cap. Will this kid be an impact player? I doubt it, but he'd better be."

SATHER IS RUNNING LATE ON THAT ONE. IN THE NEW WORLD OF PROFESsional sports, Daigle's impact has already been felt. Marketing plan in hand, Bryden passed through New York City en route to Quebec City and there began discussions with American investors, including Ogden Corporation, which runs or owns arenas in several NHL markets. Ogden liked his pitch, and liked Daigle, and liked the Palladium – and jumped in for $20 million as well as a guarantee of certain revenues.

The New York firm of Goldman Sachs began putting together a new financial package. If the Ontario provincial government would guarantee the loan for the interchange, American investors would provide the $105 million still required to build the Palladium.

So, too, did the public like Daigle. The media feeding frenzy in Quebec and the $12 million-plus contract had made him an instant celebrity and, once he'd arrived in Ottawa, a bigger star than Kim Campbell. When the brand-new NHL star and the brand-new prime minister ran into each other during the Canada Day celebrations on July 1, Campbell graciously moved aside as the cheering crowd rushed Daigle.

Two weeks later, Gary Bettman and Bruce McNall traveled to Cambridge, Massachusetts, to address the first World Hockey Summit on the state of the sport and its prospects for the next century. They talked about the possibilities for further expansion, particularly into Sweden, Finland, and Russia. They said that the league's top priority was to do a better job of marketing the game's superstars. They mentioned Wayne Gretzky, of course, but everyone knew it was too late for Gretzky. They mentioned Mario Lemieux, and everyone listening hoped it was not too late for Lemieux.

Somewhere, some day soon, another superstar will emerge. Brett Hull has come close. Eric Lindros may be the one. Or it may be Alexandre Daigle, even though the hockey world still describes him as an unknown quantity.

Unknown, but not without added value. By August, Goldman Sachs had oversubscribed the new offering on the Palladium. Word that new money was attaching itself to the Palladium rekindled political interest in Canada. With a federal election looming, and with the Palladium sited in one of the few government-held ridings in the capital, the federal Treasury Board voted in early August to give a $6 million grant to jump-start the project. This, at a time when governments everywhere were preaching, and largely practicing, restraint. The federal government was assuming the provincial government would join in with the loan guarantee to build the highway interchange. And if it didn't all work out finally in Ottawa, there was always Phoenix, or Cleveland, or Houston ...

Eighteen years old, never having so much as laced up skates for an NHL training camp, Alexandre Daigle was already the franchise.

APPENDIX I
UNIFIED REPORT OF OPERATIONS
(all figures in 000's)

REVENUES: 1991-92 REGULAR SEASON

GATE RECEIPTS	# reporting		
Gross revenue	22		$313,081
Admission tax	17		(20,447)
	22		$292,634

BROADCAST			
NHL TV revenue	22		$35,835
Local TV revenue–net	17		31,267
Cable TV revenue–net	14		23,438
Local radio revenue–net	19		8,880
	22		$99,420

IN ARENA REVENUES			
Luxury suites–net	13		$7,247
Dasher boards	17		11,560
Signage	11		4,553
Publications			
Program revenue	21	$9,667	
Program expenses	18	(4,654)	
	21		5,013
Novelty, net			
Arena	17	$2,065	
Non-arena	17	1,491	
	19		3,556
Concessions, net	10		6,843
Parking	5		742
	22		$39,514

SPECIAL GAMES			
Revenue	19		$5,885
Expenses	20		(3,185)
	20		$2,700

PRESEASON AND TRAINING CAMP

Revenue	22	$20,624
Expenses	21	(10,533)
	22	$10,091

OTHER HOCKEY REVENUES 22 $22,429

TOTAL REVENUES 22 $466,788

EXPENSES: 1991–92 REGULAR SEASON
Team expenses

NHL PLAYERS	# reporting	
Salaries		
Base contract	22	$186,967
Signing bonuses	22	17,782
Performance bonuses		
Individual	22	7,706
Team	17	2,823
Deferred compensation		
earned in year	16	7,948
Buyouts	15	7,011
Amortization of player		
acquisition costs	12	3,172
	22	$233,409
Benefits		
Pension	22	$4,526
Other	22	15,189
	22	$19,715
TOTAL NHL PLAYERS	22	$253,124
DEVELOPMENT		
Minor-league salaries		
One-way	17	$4,735
Two-way	22	19,011
Other, net	22	1,676
	22	$25,422
Scouting		
Salaries and fees	22	$9,718
Travel and other	22	8,741
	22	18,459
Draft fees	21	4,084
TOTAL DEVELOPMENT	22	$47,965

OTHER

Salaries

General manager and assistants	20	$9,700
Coaches and assistants	21	10,481
Trainers	22	3,252
Pension and other benefits	22	3,268
Travel	22	21,109
Other insurance	17	2,930
NHL assessments	22	14,809
Medical costs	22	2,982
Uniforms, supplies, and equipment	22	4,458
Practice ice	20	707
Other	22	8,221
TOTAL OTHER	22	**$81,917**
TOTAL TEAM EXPENSES	22	**$383,006**

Game expenses

Arena rent	21	$25,541
Other arena costs	18	13,008
Other game expenses	18	2,442
	22	**$40,991**

General and administrative expenses

Salaries	22	$13,737
Payroll taxes and employee benefits	22	3,656
Insurance	21	3,422
Legal, acting, and professional fees	21	6,320
Office supplies and expenses	22	5,892

Telephone and telegraph	22	2,302
Travel and entertainment	22	3,929
Other general		
and administrative expenses	22	9,127
	22	$48,385

Marketing, public-relations, and ticket office expenses

Salaries and related costs	22	$14,303
Publicity and promotion	22	8,330
Ticket and box office expenses	21	3,810
Travel and entertainment	21	1,607
Other costs	16	4,088
	22	32,138

REVENUES: 1992 PLAYOFFS

GATE RECEIPTS

Gross revenue	16	$45,474
Admission tax	13	(3,025)
	16	$42,449

BROADCAST

Local TV revenue–net	7	$1,968
Cable TV revenue–net	9	2,076
Local radio revenue–net	8	475
	11	$4,519

IN ARENA REVENUE

Luxury suites net	3		$201
Dasher boards	4		180
Signage	1		90
Publications			
Program revenue	9	241	
Program expenses	10	(239)	
	10		2
Novelty			
Revenue	9	138	
Expenses	2	91	
	9		229
Concessions, net	5		855
Parking	2		89
	15		$1,646

OTHER HOCKEY REVENUES 7   784

TOTAL REVENUES, PLAYOFFS 16 $49,398

EXPENSES: 1992 PLAYOFFS
Team expenses

NHL PLAYERS

Salaries

Base contract	1	$9	
Performance bonus			
Individual	4	1,575	
Team	9	1,812	
	11		$3,396
Benefits	3		66
	11		$3,462

DEVELOPMENT

Scouting

Salaries and fees	11	433
Travel and other	4	154
	11	$587

OTHER

Salaries

General manager and assistants	10	$553
Coaches and assistants	12	675
Trainers	8	186
Pension and other benefits	2	8
Travel	15	2,249
Other insurance	1	150
NHL Assessments	16	9,867
Medical costs	8	73
Uniforms, supplies, equipment	9	173
Practice ice	5	52
Other	13	584
	16	$14,570

TOTAL TEAM EXPENSES, PLAYOFFS	16	$18,619

Game expenses

Arena rent	14	$4,045
Other arena costs	12	1,038
Other game expenses	11	320
	16	$5,403

Marketing, public-relations, and ticket
office expenses

Salaries and related costs	1	$5
Publicity and promotion	9	231
Ticket and box office expenses	14	552
Travel and entertainment	6	62
Other costs	4	58
	14	$908

TEAM	RECEIPTS			AVE. PRICE PER TICKET	
	1992-93	1991-92	CHANGE	1991-92	1992-93
Chicago Blackhawks	$21,445,389	$17,691,090	21.22%	$31.16	$26.68
New York Rangers	20,753,151	17,607,458	17.87%	31.07	29.06
Vancouver Canucks	20,659,981	14,766,287	39.91%	33.84	24.05
Detroit Red Wings	19,746,813	15,564,667	26.87%	25.94	21.05
Toronto Maple Leafs	18,808,244	14,768,489	27.35%	29.40	23.77
Los Angeles Kings	18,538,881	17,289,766	7.22%	31.21	29.38
Montreal Canadiens	17,996,223	15,218,080	18.26%	26.29	22.88
Boston Bruins	17,930,891	15,885,892	12.87%	31.95	29.46
Pittsburgh Penguins	17,370,131	14,274,375	21.69%	26.91	22.90
Calgary Flames	16,844,108	16,333,627	3.13%	21.62	21.21
Philadelphia Flyers	16,196,423	12,993,025	24.65%	23.47	19.90
St. Louis Blues	15,274,579	13,942,325	9.56%	23.96	21.39
Ottawa Senators	14,833,730	n/a	n/a	36.05	n/a
Quebec Nordiques	13,641,647	10,610,054	28.57%	22.24	18.98
Edmonton Oilers	13,419,725	13,658,955	(1.75%)	23.50	22.46
New Jersey Devils	13,407,055	11,951,440	12.18%	23.91	22.74
Buffalo Sabres	12,188,445	10,376,541	17.46%	21.32	17.80
San Jose Sharks	12,038,473	10,745,720	12.03%	28.12	26.03
Minnesota North Stars	11,285,549	8,424,017	33.97%	21.39	16.90
Winnipeg Jets	11,281,177	10,083,780	11.87%	21.52	20.46
Hartford Whalers	10,748,960	11,006,932	(2.34%)	26.61	26.38
Washington Capitals	10,328,132	10,129,328	1.96%	19.94	18.35
Tampa Bay Lightning	9,905,304	n/a	n/a	27.34	n/a
New York Islanders	9,632,273	8,573,947	12.34%	20.71	22.23
LEAGUE TOTAL	$364,275,324	$291,895,795	24.80%	$26.17	$22.86

(from)
PLAYOFFS AND STANLEY CUP CHAMPIONSHIP
ECONOMIC IMPACT ESTIMATE FACT SHEET
PITTSBURGH, PENNSYLVANIA
APRIL 1992

LOCAL SPENDING
Spending by attendees not requiring hotel rooms

1. DIVISION SEMIFINALS & FINALS

   Number of people 15,500
   Ticket $38
   Parking $5
   Souvenirs, food $15
   Misc. $5
   Daily expenditure $63/person*

   Division semifinals (min. 2 games, max. 4) .... $1,953,000 to $3,906,000

   Division finals (min. 2 games, max. 4) .... $1,953,000 to $3,906,000

Division semifinals and finals subtotal $3,906,000 to $7,812,000
(1) SUBTOTAL $3,906,000 to $7,812,000

2. CONFERENCE FINALS

   Number of people 15,500
   Ticket $38
   Parking $5
   Souvenirs, food $25
   Misc. $5
   Daily expenditure $73*

Conference finals subtotal $2,263,000 to $3,394,500 (min. 2 games, max. 3)
(1 + 2) SUBTOTAL $6,169,000 to $11,206,500

3. STANLEY CUP CHAMPIONSHIP

Number of people 15,500

Ticket $38

Parking $5

Souvenirs, food $25

Misc. $5

Daily expenditure $73*

Stanley Cup SUBTOTAL $2,263,000 to $3,394,500 (min. 2 games, max. 3)
(1 + 2 + 3) TOTAL $8,432,000 to $14,601,000

NOTE:
Figures do not include sponsor-hosted parties and private events.

* Souvenirs, food estimates are not exclusive to the Civic Arena. They reflect spending throughout the community at a variety of retailers, restaurants, etc. The economic impact figures in this report are estimates.

Prepared by the Greater Pittsburgh Convention & Visitors Bureau.

APPENDIX IV

THE 1992–93 OTTAWA SENATORS

	GP	G	A	PTS	=/-	PIM

SKATERS

15 — Dave Archibald — C/L
6'1", 190 lbs. Shoots left. Born Chilliwack, B.C.,
April 14, 1969. Obtained from Rangers
for a 5th-round pick in 1993 entry draft.

	GP	G	A	PTS	=/-	PIM
4th NHL season.	44	9	6	15	16–	32

27 — Blair Atcheynum — R
6'2", 190 lbs. Shoots right. Born Estevan, Sask.,
April 20, 1969. Claimed from Hartford in 1992

	GP	G	A	PTS	=/-	PIM
expansion draft. Rookie.	4	0	1	1	3–	0

13 — Jamie Baker — C
6'0", 190 lbs. Shoots left. Born Ottawa, Ont.,
August 31, 1966. Signed as free agent, Sepember

	GP	G	A	PTS	=/-	PIM
1992. Fourth NHL season.	76	19	29	48	20–	54

16 — Laurie Boschman — C
6'0", 185 lbs. Shoots left. Born Major, Sask.,
June 4, 1960. Claimed from New Jersey in 1992

	GP	G	A	PTS	=/-	PIM
expansion draft. 14th NHL season.	70	9	7	16	26–	101

12 — Neil Brady — C
6'2", 200 lbs. Shoots left. Born Montreal, Que.,
April 12, 1968. Obtained from New Jersey for
future considerations, September 1992.

	GP	G	A	PTS	=/-	PIM
4th NHL season.	55	7	17	24	25–	57

33 — Tony Cimellaro — C

	GP	G	A	PTS	=/-	PIM
5'11", 179 lbs. Signed as free agent, July 1992.	2	0	0	0	2–	0

6 — Gord Dineen — D

6'0", 195 lbs. Shoots right. Born Quebec City, Que., September 21, 1962. Signed as free agent, August 1992. 11th NHL season.

32	2	4	6	19–	30

11 — Mark Freer — C

5'10", 180 lbs. Shoots left. Born Peterborough, Ont., July 14, 1968. Claimed from Philadelphia in 1992 expansion draft. 6th NHL season.

63	10	14	24	35–	39

5 — Ken Hammond — D

6'1", 190 lbs. Shoots left. Born Port Credit, Ont., August 22, 1963. Claimed from Vancouver in 1992 expansion draft. 8th NHL season.

62	4	4	8	42–	104

2 — Radek Hamr — D

5'11", 167 lbs. Shoots left. Born Usti-Nad-Labem, Czech., June 15, 1974. Chosen 4th (73rd overall) by Ottawa in 1992 entry draft.

4	0	0	0	4–	0

17 — Jody Hull — R

6'2", 200 lbs. Shoots right. Born Cambridge, Ont., February 2, 1969. Traded from Rangers for future considerations, July 1992. 5th NHL season.

69	13	21	34	24–	14

25 — Tomas Jelinek — R

5'9", 189 lbs. Shoots left. Born Prague, Czech., April 29, 1962. Chosen 11th by Ottawa in 1992 entry draft. First NHL season.

49	7	6	13	21–	52

26 — Bob Kudelski — R

6'1", 200 lbs. Shoots right. Born Springfield, MA, March 3, 1964. Traded from Kings for J. Thomson and M. Fortier, December 1992. 6th NHL season.

48	21	14	35	22–	22

2 — Jim Kyte — D

6'5", 210 lbs. Shoots left. Born Ottawa, Ont., March 21, 1964. Signed as free agent, September 1992. 11th NHL season.

4	0	1	1	0	4

7 — Mark Lamb — C
5'9", 180 lbs. Shoots left. Born Ponteix, Sask.,
August 3, 1964. Claimed from Edmonton in
1992 expansion draft. 8th NHL season.   71   7   19   26   40–   64

28 — Jeff Lazaro — L
5'10", 180 lbs. Shoots left. Born Waltham, MA,
March 21, 1968. Claimed from Boston in 1992
expansion draft. 3rd NHL season.   26   6   4   10   8–   16

10 — Darcy Loewen — L
5'10", 185 lbs. Shoots left. Born Calgary, Alta.,
February 26, 1969. Claimed from Buffalo
in 1992 expansion draft. Rookie.   79   4   5   9   26–   145

23 — Chris Luongo — D
6'0", 180 lbs. Shoots right. Born Detroit, MI,
March 17, 1967. Signed as free agent,
September 1992. Rookie.   76   3   9   12   47–   68

22 — Norm Maciver — D
5'11", 180 lbs. Shoots left. Born Thunder Bay,
Ont., September 8, 1964. Acquired from Edmonton
in 1992 waiver draft. 7th NHL season.   80   17   46   63   46–   84

14 — Brad Marsh — D
6'3", 220 lbs. Shoots left. Born London, Ont.,
March 31, 1958. Traded from Toronto for future
considerations, July 1992. 15th NHL season.   59   0   3   3   29–   30

20 — Andrew McBain — R
6'1", 205 lbs. Shoots right. Born Scarborough,
Ont., January 18, 1965. Signed as free agent,
July 1992. 10th NHL season.   59   7   16   23   37–   43

55 — Brad Miller — D
6'4", 220 lbs. Shoots left. Born Edmonton,
Alta., July 23, 1969. Claimed from Buffalo in
1992 expansion draft. 5th NHL season.   11   0   0   0   5–   42

18 — Rob Murphy — C/L

6'3", 205 lbs. Shoots left. Born Hull, Que.,
April 7, 1969. Claimed from Vancouver in 1992
expansion draft. 6th NHL season.

44	3	7	10	23–	30

3 — Kent Paynter — D

6'0", 183 lbs. Shoots left. Born Summerside,
P.E.I., April 17, 1965. Claimed from Winnipeg
in 1992 expansion draft. 6th NHL season.

6	0	0	0	7–	20

44 — Mike Peluso — L/D

6'4", 200 lbs. Shoots left. Born Pengilly, MN,
November 8, 1965. Claimed from Chicago in
1992 expansion draft. 4th NHL season.

81	15	10	25	35–	318

34 — Darren Rumble — D

6'1", 200 lbs. Shoots left. Born Barrie, Ont.,
January 23, 1969. Claimed from Philadelphia in
1992 expansion draft. Rookie.

69	3	13	16	24–	61

21 — Martin St.-Amour — L

6'3", 194 lbs. Shoots left. Born Montreal,
Que., January 30, 1970. Signed as free agent,
July 1992. Rookie.

1	0	0	0	0	2

4 — Brad Shaw — D

6'0", 190 lbs. Shoots right. Born Cambridge, Ont.,
April 28, 1964. Claimed from Hartford in
1992 expansion draft. 8th NHL season.

81	7	34	41	47–	34

9 — Doug Smail — L

5'9", 175 lbs. Shoots left. Born Moose Jaw, Sask.,
Sept 2, 1957. Signed as free agent, August 1992.
13th NHL season.

51	4	10	14	34–	51

61 — Sylvain Turgeon — L

6'0", 200 lbs. Shoots left. Born Noranda, Que.,
January 17, 1965. Claimed from Montreal in 1992
expansion draft. 10th NHL season.

72	25	18	43	29–	104

GOALTENDERS

	GP	MIN	AVG	W-L-T	EN	GA	SV%

32 — Daniel Berthiaume
5'9", 150 lbs. Catches left. Born Longueuil,
Que., January 26, 1966. Signed as free agent,
December 1992. 8th NHL season.

	25	1326	4.30	2-17-1	3	95	.871

30 — Darrin Madeley
5'11", 165 lbs. Catches left. Born Holland
Landing, Ont., February 25, 1968. Signed
as free agent, June 1992. Rookie.

	2	90	6.67	0-2-0	0	10	.773

31 — Peter Sidorkiewicz
5'9", 180 lbs. Catches left. Born Dabrowa
Bialostocka, Poland, June 29, 1963. Claimed
from Hartford in 1992 expansion draft.
6th NHL season.

	64	3388	4.43	8-46-3	7	250	.856

1 — Steve Weeks
5'11", 170 lbs. Catches left. Born Scarborough,
Ont., June 30, 1958. Traded from Washington
for future considerations, August 1992. 13th
NHL season.

	7	249	7.23	0-5-0	0	30	.792

APPENDIX V

SUPERSTARS – 1992–93

	GP	G	A	Pts.	PIM
93 — DOUG GILMOUR					
Toronto Maple Leafs					
Center. 5'11", 165 lbs. Shoots right.					
Born Kingston, Ont., June 25, 1963.					
10th NHL season.					
REG. SEASON	83	32	95	127	100
PLAYOFFS	21	10	25	35	30
99 — WAYNE GRETZKY					
Los Angeles Kings					
Center. 6'0", 170 lbs. Shoots left.					
Born Brantford, Ont., January 26, 1961.					
14th NHL season.					
REG. SEASON	45	16	49	65	6
PLAYOFFS	24	15	25	40	4
16 — BRETT HULL					
St. Louis Blues					
Right wing. 5'10", 201 lbs. Shoots right.					
Born Belleville, Ont., August 9, 1964.					
8th NHL season.					
REG. SEASON	80	54	47	101	41
PLAYOFFS	11	8	5	13	2
66 — MARIO LEMIEUX					
Pittsburgh Penguins					
Center. 6'4", 210 lbs. Shoots right.					
Bon Montreal, Que., October 5, 1965.					
9th NHL season.					
REG. SEASON	60	69	91	160	38
PLAYOFFS	11	8	10	18	10

88 — ERIC LINDROS
Philadelphia Flyers
Center. 6'4", 225 lbs. Shoots right.
Born London, Ont., February 28, 1973.
Rookie.

REG. SEASON	61	41	34	75	147
PLAYOFFS [team missed playoffs]					

11 — MARK MESSIER
New York Rangers
Center. 6'1", 210 lbs. Shoots left.
Born Edmonton, Alta., January 18, 1961.
14th NHL season.

REG. SEASON	75	25	66	91	72
PLAYOFFS [team missed playoffs]					

APPENDIX VI

EUROPEANS

	GP	G	A	Pts.	PIM
16 — NIKOLAI BORSCHEVSKY					
Toronto Maple Leafs					
Right wing. 5'9", 180. Shoots left.					
Born Tomsk, USSR, January 12, 1965.					
Toronto's 3rd choice, 1992 entry draft.					
Rookie.					
REG. SEASON	78	34	40	74	28
PLAYOFFS	16	2	7	9	0
10 — PAVEL BURE					
Vancouver Canucks					
Right wing. 5'9", 180 lbs. Shoots left.					
Born Moscow, USSR, March 31, 1971.					
Vancouver's 4th choice, 1989 entry draft.					
2nd NHL season.					
REG. SEASON	83	60	50	110	69
PLAYOFFS	12	5	7	12	8
91 — SERGEI FEDOROV					
Detroit Red Wings					
Center. 6'1", 191 lbs. Shoots left.					
Born Pskov, USSR, December 13, 1969.					
Detroit's 4th choice, 1989 entry draft.					
3rd NHL season.					
REG. SEASON	73	34	53	87	72
PLAYOFFS	7	3	6	9	23
17 — VALERI KAMENSKY					
Quebec Nordiques					
Left wing. 6'2", 198 lbs. Shoots right.					
Born Voskresensk, USSR, April 18, 1966.					
Quebec's 8th choice, 1988 entry draft.					
2nd NHL season.					
REG. SEASON	32	15	22	37	14
PLAYOFFS	6	0	1	1	6

89 — ALEXANDER MOGILNY

Buffalo Sabres
Right wing. 5'11", 187 lbs. Shoots left.
Born Khabarovsk, USSR, February 18, 1969.
Buffalo's 4th choice, 1988 entry draft.
4th NHL season.

REG. SEASON	77	76	51	127	40
PLAYOFFS	7	7	3	10	6

68 — JAROMIR JAGR

Pittsburgh Penguins
Right wing. 6'2", 208 lbs. Shoots left.
Born Kladno, Czech., February 15, 1972.
Pittsburgh's 1st choice, 1990 entry draft.
3rd NHL season.

REG. SEASON	81	34	60	94	61
PLAYOFFS	12	5	4	9	23

13 — TEEMU SELANNE

Winnipeg Jets
Right wing. 6'0", 181 lbs. Shoots right.
Born Helsinki, Finland, July 3, 1970.
Winnipeg's 1st choice, 1988 entry draft.
Rookie.

REG. SEASON	84	76	56	132	45
PLAYOFFS	6	4	2	6	2

13 — MATS SUNDIN

Quebec Nordiques
Center/right wing. 6'2", 190 lbs. Shoots right.
Born Bromma, Sweden, February 13, 1971.
Quebec's 1st choice (1st choice overall) in 1989 entry draft.
3rd NHL season.

REG. SEASON	80	47	67	114	96
PLAYOFFS	6	3	1	4	6

TOP DRAFT CHOICES — 1992–93 ENTRY DRAFT

	GP	G	A	Pts.	PIM

1. ALEXANDRE DAIGLE
Ottawa Senators
Center. 6'0", 170 lbs. Shoots left.
Born Laval, Que., February 7, 1975.

1992–93 with VICTORIAVILLE TIGRES, QMJHL	53	45	92	137	85

2. CHRIS PRONGER
Hartford Whalers
Defense. 6'6", 192 lbs. Shoots left.
Born Dryden, Ont., October 10, 1974.

1992–93 with PETERBOROUGH PETES, OHL	61	15	62	77	108

3. CHRIS GRATTON
Tampa Bay Lightning
Center. 6'3", 202 lbs. Shoots left.
Born Brantford, Ont., July 5, 1975.

1992–93 with KINGSTON FRONTENACS, OHL	58	55	54	109	16

4. ROB NIEDERMAYER
Florida Panthers
Center. 6'2", 200 lbs. Shoots left.
Born Cranbrook, B.C., December 28, 1974.

1992–93 with MEDICINE HAT TIGERS, WHL	52	43	34	77	67

5. PAUL KARIYA
Anaheim Mighty Ducks
Left wing. 5'10", 157 lbs. Shoots left.
Born North Vancouver, B.C., October 16, 1974.

1992–93 with MAINE BLACK BEARS, HE	39	25	75	100	12

6. VIKTOR KOZLOV
San Jose Sharks
Right wing. 6'5", 219 lbs. Shoots right.
Born Togliatti, Russia, February 14, 1975.

1992–93 with MOSCOW DYNAMO	32	7	4	11	10

(San Jose traded draft positions
with Hartford, June 26, 1993.)

APPENDIX VIII

1992-93 NHL FINAL STANDINGS

Wales Conference

Adams Division

	W	L	T	Pts	F	A	Home	Away
Boston	51	26	7	109	332	268	29-10-3	22-16-4
Quebec	47	27	10	104	351	300	23-17-2	24-10-8
Montreal	48	30	6	102	326	280	27-13-2	21-17-4
Buffalo	38	36	10	86	335	297	25-15-2	13-21-8
Hartford	26	52	6	58	284	369	12-25-5	14-27-1
Ottawa	10	70	4	24	202	395	9-29-4	1-41-0

Patrick Division

	W	L	T	Pts	F	A	Home	Away
Pittsburgh	56	21	7	119	367	268	32-6-4	24-15-3
Washington	43	34	7	93	325	286	21-15-6	22-19-1
NY Islanders	40	37	7	87	335	297	20-19-3	20-18-4
New Jersey	40	37	7	87	308	299	24-14-4	16-23-3
Philadelphia	36	37	11	83	319	319	23-14-5	13-23-6
NY Rangers	34	39	11	79	308	308	20-17-5	14-22-6

Campbell Conference

Norris Division

	W	L	T	Pts	F	A	Home	Away
Chicago	47	25	12	106	279	230	25-11-6	22-14-6
Detroit	47	28	9	103	369	280	25-14-3	22-14-6
Toronto	44	29	11	99	288	241	25-11-6	19-18-5
St. Louis	37	36	11	85	282	278	22-13-7	15-23-4
Minnesota	36	38	10	82	272	293	18-17-7	18-21-3
Tampa Bay	23	54	7	53	245	332	12-27-3	11-27-4

Smythe Division

	W	L	T	Pts	F	A	Home	Away
Vancouver	46	29	9	101	346	278	27-11-4	19-18-5
Calgary	43	30	11	97	322	281	23-14-5	20-16-6
Los Angeles	39	35	10	88	338	340	22-15-5	17-20-5
Winnipeg	40	37	7	87	322	320	23-16-3	17-21-4
Edmonton	26	50	8	60	242	337	16-21-5	10-29-3
San Jose	11	71	2	24	218	414	8-33-1	3-38-1

APPENDIX IX

OTTAWA AND SAN JOSE
GAME-BY-GAME RESULTS
1992–93

	OTTAWA		SAN JOSE
Oct. 8	**Montreal 3 at 5**	2–2	**Winnipeg 3 at 4**
Oct. 10	2 at Quebec City 9	2–2	Detroit 6 at 3
Oct. 12	3 at Boston 6	2–2	1 at Los Angeles 2
Oct. 14	1 at Hartford 4	2–2	
Oct. 15		2–2	Boston 6 at 2
Oct. 16	1 at Washington 5	2–2	
Oct. 17		2–2	Calgary 6 at 2
Oct. 20	3 at Toronto 5 (NS)	2–2	
Oct. 21		2–2	4 at Montreal 8
Oct. 22	Hartford 5 at 1	2–2	
Oct. 23		2–2	4 at Buffalo 5
Oct. 24	Rangers 3 at 2 (OT)	2–2	1 at Toronto 5
Oct. 26		2–2	1 at St. Louis 4
Oct. 27	Pittsburgh 7 at 2	2–2	
Oct. 28		2–2	3 at Detroit 4
Oct. 30	3 at Buffalo 12	2–4	**2 at Tampa Bay 1**
Oct. 31	**Buffalo 2 at 2**	3–4	
Nov 1		3–5	**4 at Chicago 4**
Nov. 3	2 at Edmonton 5	3–5	
Nov. 5	4 at Calgary 8	3–7	**Buffalo 5 at 7**
Nov. 6	1 at Vancouver 4	3–7	
Nov. 7		3–7	New Jersey 6 at 1
Nov. 8		3–7	Los Angeles 11 at 4
Nov. 9	Toronto 3 at 1	3–7	
Nov. 10		3–7	2 at Vancouver 6
Nov. 11	Quebec City 7 at 3	3–7	
Nov. 12		3–7	Edmonton 4 at 3
Nov. 13	0 at Tampa Bay 1	3–7	
Nov. 14		3–7	Vancouver 5 at 2
Nov. 15	2 at Philadelphia 7	3–7	

Nov. 17	3 at Montreal 5	3–9	**Los Angeles 0 at 8**
Nov. 19	Hartford 4 at 2	3–9	Toronto 2 at 0
Nov. 21	1 at Montreal 3	3–9	Chicago 2 at 1
Nov. 23	Boston 3 at 1	3–9	
Nov. 25	**New Jersey 1 at 3**	5–11	**4 at Calgary 3**
Nov. 27	1 at Buffalo 4	5–11	2 at Winnipeg 3 (OT)
Nov. 28		5–11	3 at Minnesota 10
Nov. 29	Buffalo 5 at 2	5–11	
Dec. 1	Minnesota 3 at 1	5–11	Edmonton 3 at 1
Dec. 3	**New Jersey 3 at 3**	6–11	Hartford 7 at 5
Dec. 5	**Philadelphia 2 at 3**	8–11	Pittsburgh 9 at 4
Dec. 7	Washington 6 at 5	8–11	
Dec. 9	2 at Hartford 6	8–11	3 at Vancouver 8
Dec. 10	2 at Boston 4	8–11	St. Louis 3 at 2
Dec. 12	**Calgary 1 at 1**	9–11	Quebec City 8 at 7 (OT)
Dec. 15	Detroit 3 at 2 (OT)	9–11	
Dec. 16		9–11	Tampa Bay 5 at 4 (OT)
Dec. 17	3 at Islanders 9	9–11	
Dec. 18		9–11	1 at Vancouver 8
Dec. 19	1 at Toronto 5	9–11	Vancouver 6 at 3
Dec. 21	Washington 4 at 3	9–11	4 at Winnipeg 5
Dec. 23	Chicago 4 at 2	9–11	2 at Edmonton 4
Dec. 26	2 at Quebec City 4	9–13	**Los Angeles 2 at 7**
Dec. 27	Quebec City 6 at 1	9–13	
Dec. 29		9–13	5 at Vancouver 7
Dec. 30		9–13	Philadelphia 6 at 2
Dec. 31	4 at Detroit 5 (OT)	9–13	
Jan. 2	Buffalo 7 at 2	9–14	**Vancouver 2 at 2**
Jan. 4		9–14	Montreal 4 at 1 (NS)
Jan. 5		9–14	Montreal 2 at 1
Jan. 6	2 at Rangers 6	9–14	
Jan. 8	4 at New Jersey 6	9–14	1 at Toronto 5
Jan. 10	(H) DEFEATS SAN JOSE 3–2	11–14	
Jan. 12	Los Angeles 3 at 2	11–14	1 at Winnipeg 4
Jan. 14	St. Louis 4 at 1	11–14	
Jan. 15		11–14	3 at Detroit 6
Jan. 16	1 at Pittsburgh 6	11–14	1 at Quebec City 4
Jan. 17	Islanders 7 at 2	11–14	
Jan. 18		11–14	3 at Boston 4

Date		Record	
Jan. 19	Quebec City 5 at 2	11–14	
Jan. 21	2 at Minnesota 7	11–14	2 at Hartford 4
Jan. 23	4 at Washington 6	11–14	1 at Tampa Bay 5
Jan. 26	1 at St. Louis 5	11–14	1 at Los Angeles 7
Jan. 28	**Hartford 2 at 5**	13–14	
Jan. 29		13–14	Chicago 4 at 2
Jan. 30	3 at Montreal 5	13–14	Calgary 5 at 4
Feb. 1	**4 at Winnipeg 4**	14–14	Tampa Bay 5 at 4
Feb. 3	**Edmonton 2 at 3**	16–14	Minnesota 7 at 3
Feb. 8	**Buffalo 2 at 4**	18–14	
Feb. 9	1 at Philadelphia 8	18–14	
Feb. 10		18–14	1 at Calgary 13
Feb. 12		18–14	0 at Edmonton 6
Feb. 13	Montreal 4 at 1	18–14	
Feb. 14		18–16	**3 at Winnipeg 2**
Feb. 16		18–16	Washington 4 at 3
Feb. 17	4 at Quebec City 6	18–16	
Feb. 18		18–18	**Winnipeg 3 at 5**
Feb. 20	4 at Montreal 5	18–18	Rangers 6 at 4
Feb. 22	3 at Winnipeg 6	18–18	Rangers 4 at 0 (NS)
Feb. 23	Winnipeg 8 at 2 (NS)	18–18	Calgary 6 at 3
Feb. 25	**Pittsburgh 1 at 2**	20–18	Toronto 5 at 0
Feb. 27	2 at New Jersey 5	20–18	4 at Calgary 5
Feb. 28	**6 at Quebec City 4**	22–18	1 at Edmonton 4
Mar. 2		22–20	**(H) DEFEATS OTTAWA 3–2 (OT)**
Mar. 4	6 at Los Angeles 8	22–20	
Mar. 7	2 at Chicago 4	22–22	**Edmonton 3 at 6**
Mar. 9		22–22	2 at Minnesota 4
Mar. 11		22–22	2 at St. Louis 5
Mar. 13	3 at Boston 6	22–22	
Mar. 14		22–22	Detroit 4 at 1
Mar. 16		22–22	Islanders 6 at 0
Mar. 18	Boston 4 at 1	22–22	
Mar 19		22–22	1 at Rangers 8
Mar. 21		22–22	3 at Washington 5
Mar. 22	Rangers 5 at 4	22–22	
Mar. 23		22–22	2 at Pittsburgh 7
Mar. 25	Tampa Bay 3 at 2 (OT)	22–22	2 at Philadelphia 5
Mar. 27	3 at Montreal 4	22–22	3 at Islanders 7

Mar. 28	3 at Buffalo 1	22–22	
Mar. 29		22–22	0 at New Jersey 5
Mar. 30	6 at Pittsburgh 4	22–22	
Apr. 1	Quebec City 4 at 2	22–22	Winnipeg 9 at 5
Apr. 3	3 at Hartford 7	22–22	Calgary 3 at 2 (OT)
Apr. 4	Vancouver 3 at 0	22–22	Calgary 4 at 3 (OT)
Apr. 6		22–24	**Edmonton 2 at 5**
Apr. 7	Hartford 6 at 1	22–24	
Apr. 8		22–24	1 at Los Angeles 2
Apr. 10	**5 at Islanders 3**	24–24	Los Angeles 3 at 2 (OT)
Apr. 11	2 at Boston 4	24–24	
Apr. 13	2 at Quebec City 6	24–24	
Apr. 14	Boston 4 at 2	24–24	
Apr. 15		**24–24**	3 at Calgary 7

OTTAWA 10–70–4   SAN JOSE 11–71–2

OTTAWA FINISHES LAST IN LEAGUE
BY VIRTUE OF FEWER WINS

(NS) = neutral site
(OT) = overtime
(H) = home

APPENDIX X

JOHN KORDIC
1965 – 1992

6'2", 210 pounds. Right wing, shoots left.
Born Edmonton, Alberta, March 22, 1965.
Montreal's 6th choice (78th overall) in 1983 entry draft.

Season	Club	Regular season					Playoffs				
		GP	G	A	TP	PIM	GP	G	A	TP	PIM
1982–83	Portland	7	3	22	25	235	14	1	6	7	30
1983–84	Portland	67	9	50	59	232	14	0	13	13	56
1984–85	Seattle	46	17	36	53	154	—	—	—	—	—
	Portland	25	6	22	28	73					
	Sherbrooke	4	0	0	0	4	4	0	0	0	11
[WHL Second All-Star Team, West Division]											
1985–86	Montreal	5	0	1	1	12	18	0	0	0	53
	Sherbrooke	68	3	14	17	238	—	—	—	—	—
1986–87	Montreal	44	5	3	8	151	11	2	0	2	19
	Sherbrooke	10	4	4	8	49	—	—	—	—	—
1987–88	Montreal	60	2	6	8	159	7	2	2	4	26
1988–89	Montreal	6	0	0	0	13	—	—	—	—	—
	Toronto	46	1	2	3	185	—	—	—	—	—
1989–90	Toronto	55	9	4	13	252	5	0	1	1	33
1990–91	Toronto	3	0	0	0	9	—	—	—	—	—
	Newmarket	8	1	1	2	79	—	—	—	—	—
	Washington	7	0	0	0	101	—	—	—	—	—
1991–92	Quebec City	18	0	2	2	115	—	—	—	—	—
	Cape Breton	12	2	1	3	141	5	0	1	1	53

Traded to Toronto by Montreal with Montreal's 6th round choice (Michael Doers)
in 1989 entry draft for Russ Courtnall, November 7, 1988. Traded to Washington
by Toronto with Paul Fenton for Washington's 5th round choice (Alexei Kudashov)
in 1991 entry draft, January 24, 1991. Signed as a free agent by Quebec, October 4, 1991.

Died August 8, 1992.

INDEX

INDEX

This book was designed by Peter Enneson under the creative direction of James Ireland and set into type by Peter Enneson for James Ireland Design Inc., Toronto, Ontario.

Text, heads folios and captions are set in Sabon. Sabon was designed by Jan Tscichold and originally issued in 1964. Intended as a general-purpose book face, Sabon is based on the work of Claude Garamond and his pupil Jacques Sabon. It was issued in digitized form by Monotype and Adobe. This version is by Monotype.